As writing and specialist studies on Christian mission have proliferated, there has been a growing need for a single volume overview of developments in the century. This book gives historical focus and perspective to mission by concentrating on the leading figures of each decade, beginning with that leading up to the Edinburgh Conference of 1910 and including treatment of the other great missionary conferences. German mission theory between the wars (1918–39) is addressed, as are the writings of Roland Allen and D. J. Fleming. In Part II (1940–90) the responses to the religious pluralism of the modern world, Hindu, Buddhist, Jew, and Muslim, which emerged from the conferences before 1939, are pursued through the writings of figures like Stephen Neill and Kenneth Cragg, the documents of Vatican II, and the Lausanne Conference of 1974, concluding with the varied responses of writers as diverse as John Hick and Lesslie Newbigin.

CHRISTIAN MISSION IN THE
TWENTIETH CENTURY

CHRISTIAN MISSION IN THE TWENTIETH CENTURY

TIMOTHY YATES

CAMBRIDGE
UNIVERSITY PRESS

Published by the Press Syndicate of the University of Cambridge
The Pitt Building, Trumpington Street, Cambridge CB2 1RP
40 West 20th Street, New York NY 10011-4211, USA
10 Stamford Road, Oakleigh, Melbourne 3166, Australia

First published 1994
First paperback edition 1996

Printed in Great Britain at Athenæum Press Ltd, Gateshead

A catalogue record for this book is available from the British Library

Library of Congress cataloguing in publication data

Yates, Timothy, 1935–
Christian mission in the twentieth century / Timothy Yates.
p.   cm.
Includes bibliographical references and index.
ISBN 0 521 43493 9
1. Missions – Theory – History of doctrines – 20th century.
I. Title.
BV2063.Y37   1994
266'.009'04 – dc20   93 – 24330   CIP

ISBN 0 521 43493 9 hardback
ISBN 0 521 56507 3 paperback

Stephen Charles Neill
Max Alexander Cunningham Warren
Scholars of Cambridge, missionary statesmen, servants of Christ
in grateful recognition

Contents

Preface   *page* xi
Acknowledgements   xiii
List of abbreviations   xv

PART I 1900–1940   1

Introduction   3

1   Mission as expansion 1900–1910   7
2   Mission as the church of a people (*Volkskirche*)
    1910–1920   34
3   Mission appraised (1): 1920–1940   57
4   Mission appraised (2): 1920–1940   94

PART II 1940–1990   125

Preface to part II   127

5   Mission as presence and dialogue 1950–1960   133
6   Mission as proclamation, dialogue and liberation
    1960–1970   163
7   Mission as proclamation and church growth
    1970–1980   193
8   Pluralism and enlightenment 1980–1990   224

Appendix   Missionary conferences of the twentieth
           century: a guide   252

Select bibliography   253
Index   262

Contents

Preface

Anyone who undertakes a broad overview of a subject and period such as the title of this book assumes is likely to be keenly aware of its inadequacies and limitations. Partly this is occasioned by the inability of one person to read and digest all that is necessary in order to do justice to such a large body of material. So much must, of necessity, remain unexamined, if the book is to be of reasonable size, while the field for original research in many of the areas touched on remains formidable. Despite these provisos, I believe that it is better that such an undertaking should be made rather than left unattempted at this juncture of the church's life and mission.

The genesis of this book may be said to go back to 1967, when, prompted by the then Principal of St John's College, Durham (J. P. Hickinbotham) the head of the department of theology in the University of Durham (H. E. W. Turner) invited me to give a course of lectures entitled 'Mission and Ecumenism'. My growing awareness of the field of study represented by the theory and practice of Christian mission led, with Professor Turner's encouragement, to research into the nineteenth-century figure, Henry Venn. Venn is known missiologically for his advocacy of the '*euthanasia* of the mission', whereby the missionary scaffolding was to be removed so that the indigenous church might stand free of missionary dominance. Venn was a man before his time, a combination of visionary and practical administrator which is rare. Study of Venn brought me in touch with the academic department of mission in the University of Uppsala, where I received much help and advice from Emeritus Professor Bishop Bengt Sundkler and his successor Professor Carl-Fredrik Hallencreutz. Ultimately, Uppsala did me the honour of both awarding me a doctorate in 1978 and, later, appointing me an honorary 'docent' in the 'science of missions' in 1985, which I record here with grateful appreciation.

It was while working on the Venn originals that I came to know and admire Max Warren, Venn's successor in office as secretary of the Church Missionary Society; and, through him, to be introduced to Bishop Stephen Neill. For this I was particularly grateful, not only because the latter read and commented on my Venn material but because, by then, I had owed so much of my adult understanding of Christian theology, faith and life to him as a writer. For me, Warren and Neill represent a strand of tradition of great importance, which requires recognition. I must hope that, in a book so open to criticism as this must be, my dedication of it to their contribution to missionary life and thought may still be held to be a proper act of appreciation.

TIMOTHY YATES
Great Longstone
Derbyshire

Acknowledgements

A writer incurs many debts. First and foremost of mine, as relating specifically to this book, is to The Queen's College, Birmingham, who awarded me a research fellowship for the academic year 1991–2. It is a simple statement of fact that, without this help, the circumstances of my life would not have permitted the book to be written. In the college community, Sheila Russell, librarian of the college, was ever patient and helpful and the staff and students befriended my wife and myself. Birmingham, with its missionary library at Selly Oak, whose staff have consistently helped me, and its resident experts in the department of mission, not least the present holder of the chair of mission, Professor Werner Ustorf, its surrounding colleges and their staffs, has been a valued resource. At an early stage Bishop Lesslie Newbigin arranged for me to have access to David Bosch's *Transforming Mission* in manuscript, a timely intervention: it has been a source of great sorrow that Professor Bosch has been killed in a car accident before this book has been completed. His loss is grievous to missiology as a field of study. I have benefited from two visits to Yale and the opportunity to avail myself of the resources of the Day Missions Library of the Yale Divinity School. I must thank the head librarian of the time, John Bollier, the staff and archivist of the John Mott archive, Martha Smalley, for their kindness and help. Dr G. H. Anderson, Director of the Overseas Ministries Study Centre and editor of the *International Bulletin of Missionary Research*, has read my manuscript and saved me from more than one serious error. I am indebted to the Principal of The Queen's College, Dr James Walker, and

xiii

the Principal of Crowther Hall, Colin Chapman, who have also read the manuscript in part or whole, and to Christine Lyall Grant for her copyeditorial work to improve the text. None of these can be held responsible for mistakes of fact or interpretation. The editors of the journal *Anvil* have allowed me to use material which first appeared in its pages. I have to thank my diocesan bishop, the Right Reverend Peter Dawes, Anglican Bishop of Derby, and his suffragan, the Right Reverend Henry Richmond, the first for giving me nine months' study leave as his director of ordinands and the second for being willing to take on additional duties to allow this to happen. Bishops who believe in and enable the writing of theology are surely important to the church. The local congregations of Great Longstone and Ashford have given generous support in friendship to my wife and myself. Mrs Penny Robinson has typed with great attention to detail and accuracy. Like many modern authors, I must pay tribute to my family, my daughter Catherine, who typed some of the manuscript before her own theological studies intervened, my son Mark, who has shown steady interest in the project, and particularly my wife, who has borne the brunt of changes in her life and setting brought on by the project with cheerful adaptability and unfailing support. Finally, I must mention with great appreciation the religious editor of the Cambridge University Press, Alex Wright, who first persuaded me to address these themes in the form of a book rather than disconnected papers; and whose steady encouragement during an arduous project has supplied me with the confidence necessary for completion.

Abbreviations

AACC	All-Africa Conference of Churches
AG	*Ad Gentes* (Decree on the Church's Missionary Activity of the Second Vatican Council)
AMZ	*Allgemeine Missions-Zeitschrift*
CDCWM	*Concise Dictionary of the Christian World Mission*
CIM	China Inland Mission
CMS	Church Missionary Society
COWE	Congress on World Evangelization of the Lausanne Committee
CSI	Church of South India
CWME	Commission on World Mission and Evangelism of the World Council of Churches
EACC	East Asia Christian Conference
EFMA	Evangelical Foreign Missions Association
EJCSK	L'Église de Jésus-Christ sur la terre de la prophète Simon Kimbangu
EMM	*Evangelische Missions Magazin*
EMQ	*Evangelical Missions Quarterly*
EMZ	*Evangelische Missions-Zeitschrift*
EN	*Evangelii Nuntiandi* (Apostolic Exhortation of Pope Paul VI)
ER	*Ecumenical Review*
IBMR	*International Bulletin of Missionary Research*
IFMA	Interdenominational Foreign Mission Association
IMC	International Missionary Council
IRM	*International Review of Mission(s)*
IVCF	Inter-Varsity Christian Fellowship

LFMI	Laymen's Foreign Missions Inquiry
NA	*Nostra Aetate* (Declaration on the relation of the Church to non-Christian Religions of the Second Vatican Council)
NCC	National Christian Council
NTM	New Tribes Mission
RGG	*Religion in Geschichte und Gegenwart*
SCM	Student Christian Movement
SIL	Summer Institute of Linguistics
SPCK	Society for Promoting Christian Knowledge
SPG	Society for the Propagation of the Gospel
SVM	Student Volunteer Movement
UMCA	Universities' Mission to Central Africa
WBT	Wycliffe Bible Translators
WCC	World Council of Churches
WMC	World Missionary Conference
WSCF	World Student Christian Federation
YDS	Yale Divinity School
YMCA	Young Men's Christian Association
YWCA	Young Women's Christian Association

PART ONE

1900–1940

Introduction

This book is an attempt to provide some historical perspective on the development of the Christian mission in the period since 1900 as the Christian church approaches its third millennium. The chapters roughly coincide with the eight decades of the century, the first being the decade which led up to the World Missionary Conference at Edinburgh in 1910. Such an attempt has to be highly selective and I am well aware that different minds would make very different selections. To give only one example, up to and after the Edinburgh Conference of 1910 there were flourishing Roman Catholic missions, not to mention the remarkable work of Archbishop Nicolai of the Russian Orthodox church in Japan. The method adopted here of taking large issues in each period and concentrating on them, largely to the exclusion of sideways glances elsewhere, may assist in helping the eye to focus but undoubtedly limits the possibility of demonstrating the kaleidoscopic variety of Christian missionary endeavour in the period.

In addition to providing some perspective and overview of the century, the book also attempts to provide material towards a twentieth-century missiology. As far as the English theological scene is concerned, missiology, or the study of the theory and practice of the Christian mission, has been sadly neglected in the faculties and seminaries. Certainly it is a relatively new arrival on the theological stage. In an important sense, however, it is as old as the New Testament. The writings of Paul and Luke, to mention only the most immediately obvious of the New Testament writers, are clearly missiological in intent, providing a rationale for Christian mission in both

cases and, in the case of Luke, an account of the conduct of it in
the *Acts of the Apostles*. Modern missiology, however, is usually
seen to date from the pioneering studies of Gustav Warneck
(1834–1910) at Halle in Germany and his Roman Catholic
counterpart, Josef Schmidlin of Münster (1876–1944), who
paid generous tribute to Warneck by modelling much of his
own work on that of his Protestant fellow worker, while not
failing to point out sharp divergences of view.[1] These pioneers
have given rise to schools of missiology in the universities of
Germany, Holland, Scandinavia, North America and South
Africa, a development still, sadly, not reflected in Britain by
any widespread attention to this important branch of Christian
theology, 'the science of missions' or *Missionswissenschaft*.

Because it is the study of the practice of Christian mission,
missiology must take history seriously. As Stephen Neill
pointed out in his *History of Christian Missions*, Luke seems to
have been the first to be aware that 'the new Israel, like the old,
would have its history and recognised that sacred history must
be related to the history of the world (Luke 3:1–2)'.[2] Luke's
historical method is very different from that of a modern
historian; but the inter-relation between, in his case, the historical environment of the ancient world (in Luke 3) of Tiber-
ius Caesar, Herod and Pilate's period of office in Judaea and
the religious movements associated with John the Baptist and
Jesus gives an example of the kind of interplay between historical environment and religious movement with which missiology is concerned. The preaching of the Baptist did not take
place in a vacuum. He belonged to an identifiable historical
period and his ideas, strongly eschatological as they were, had
historical effects, which included his own execution. While he
may have been the first witness to the Christ who ended his

[1] Schmidlin based his *Katholische Missionslehre im Grundriss* on Warneck's *Evangelische
Missionslehre*, 5 vols (1897–1903). The latter has never appeared in English, although
Schmidlin's book was translated as *Catholic Mission Theory* (Techny, 1931). Warneck's fine book *Abriss einer Geschichte der protestantischen Missionen von der Reformation bis
auf die Gegenwart* (Leipzig, 1882) was translated as *Outline of a History of Protestant
Missions from the Reformation to the Present Day* (London, 1906).
[2] S. C. Neill, *A History of Christian Missions* (London, 1964), p. 22 and note 1.

career in imprisonment and death, he was the first of a great number.

At its best, then, the study of the theory and practice of the Christian mission will attend with care to the historical setting and much of the interest will lie in the interplay, or dynamic relationship, between the setting and the message or messenger in a given society. Again, missiology will provide the kind of graphic pen-portraits of individuals which Luke gives us in the Baptist or the more recognisably missionary figure of Paul: but this will be done in a wider setting, so that the Christian mission is seen in historical context. In the view of the writer, missiology is at its best when history and theology are held in tension and there is a continuing oscillation between historical context and Christian input, so that the analysis of the form in which the gospel is expressed, the theory of the mission, is related firmly to the setting. In the twentieth century, for example, the 'theology of crisis', associated with Karl Barth, did not arise in a historical vacuum but was one man's response to the post-1914–18 situation in the Western world: and Barth's expression of Christian faith and life continued to interact with a world dominated by the rise of the dictators in the 1930s, issuing in the Barmen Declaration of 1934 and the witness of the Confessing Church in Germany. In the world of mission, figures like the German director of mission, Karl Hartenstein, and the Dutch theologian, Hendrik Kraemer, used Barthian forms to address the needs of the church's mission in the same period. Indeed, an inescapable reality in the twentieth century remains the relationship of the Christian gospel to relativism, how to balance the great danger of absolutes, with their oppressive and suffocating effect when improperly deployed, with a prevailing relativism. The 1930s provided a climate in which Fascists and Marxists supplied false absolutes and new tribalisms, to fill the void and longing for certainty which the human heart continues to crave. As this book is written, contemporary examples of the same malaise appear, embraced in the term 'fundamentalism', Christian, Islamic and Hindu.

Both Karl Barth and John the Baptist (to whom Barth often

appealed as the definitive portrait of the Christian witness, who points away from himself to the Christ) provide examples of those who operate *within* a given cultural tradition, trying to alert their contemporaries, in their different ways, to the judgement of God on prevailing thought and life. Missiology has traditionally been concerned with the *cross-cultural*; in the nineteenth century, for example, primarily studying Westerners crossing cultural boundaries into African, Asian and Oceanic societies. If mission is to do fundamentally with sending and the missionary is one who is understood as being sent by God to a given setting, fulfilling the Church's apostolic role, there will always be an element of crossing boundaries in Christian mission. However, in a world of increasingly one culture, the boundaries may be as much within a given society as beyond; and, as a further differentiation from nineteenth-century experience, the presence of mature Christian communities throughout the world will mean that the inter-territorial mission will be pluriform. An example observed recently has been of a Christian from Pakistan, supported by a Finnish Lutheran missionary society, working among the Asian community in the English northern town of Preston in Lancashire.

One set of boundaries which will recur in what follows is that between Christian faith and the faiths of Jews, Muslims, Hindus, Buddhists and others, what in the early years of the century were referred to as the non-Christian religions. Missiology has to address the questions raised by other religions and should reflect in particular on the interaction between the Christian message and these other faith commitments. From early in the century a book like J. N. Farquhar's *Crown of Hinduism* (1913) or the series of articles in the early issues of the *International Review of Missions* entitled the 'Vital Forces of Islam, Buddhism. . . .', and still earlier the study carried out by D. S. Cairns through questionnaires to missionaries in the field in 1908 towards Commission IV of the Edinburgh Conference of 1910, through the century to present-day debates raised by writers like Wilfred Cantwell Smith and John Hick, this has remained a necessary preoccupation. What is the relationship to be between Christian faith and other faiths?

CHAPTER I

Mission as expansion 1900–1910

For Luke, writing the first history of the Christian mission, mission involved, among other things, geographical extension. The risen Christ, commissioning his chosen witnesses, directed them to begin at Jerusalem but then to move outwards into Judaea, Samaria and to the ends of the earth (Acts 1:8). Here is a programmatic scheme, which Luke works out in the rest of Acts. So, Philip the deacon preaches successfully in Samaria (for any Jew, a major frontier to cross), Peter crosses the immense barrier of the Jew–Gentile divide, Paul pursues the Gentile mission into what we would call Europe until, at the end of the book, he can be shown to have proceeded from Jerusalem to Rome. For Paul himself Spain may have seemed the ultimate geographical boundary of the world he knew (Rom.15:24, 28) but for Luke's programme it may have been enough (and symbolically more important) to emphasise the presence of the gospel and its leading emissary in the city which stood as capital of the wider world, whether or not Paul reached Spain and Luke knew of it.

In the period up to and after Edinburgh 1910, mission as expansion was a dominant understanding, not least in the Anglo-Saxon world. Before too easily condemning a vision which, in its less acceptable forms, became identified with world conquest and cultural and spiritual imperialism, it is important to notice that this understanding of mission has been present from the beginning. It had been reinforced at certain historical periods. In the age of the explorers, as the Portuguese felt their way down the coast of Africa, directed and inspired by Henry the Navigator (1394–1460) and the Pope was moved to divide the world between the two great maritime powers of Portugal and Spain in the bull *Ceteris Partibus* (1493), the Portuguese extended their empire and religious influence to West and East Africa, Goa in the Indian continent and Brazil; while Spain was to acquire great territories, especially in Latin America through the activities of Cortés and Pizarro and to sponsor an accompanying Christian mission through the religious orders of the Roman Catholic church. Then, again, for the Protestants of the great missionary awakening of the eighteenth and nineteenth centuries, mission was also seen in terms of geographical extension: brave Moravian Christians, from Count Zinzendorf's (1700–60) pietist centre at Herrnhut, went literally to the ends of the earth, as Luke's missionaries did not, and were to be found in Greenland among Eskimos, in Tibet, among North American Indians and Negro slaves in the West Indies. Again, William Carey and his friends in India, and sundry other nineteenth-century missionaries to far-flung parts of the world like the 'South Seas', Madagascar and New Zealand, spoke to the Christian churches in Europe in the same language of expansion. The twentieth century may well be viewed by historians as the American century, as much as the nineteenth has been considered to be the British century: it should occasion little surprise that expansion and extension, so much a part of the American experience as the frontier moved steadily Westwards, should have become the staple vision of the Christian mission for men like J. R. Mott, who will be discussed later in this chapter.

THE AMERICAN BACKGROUND

In view of the dominance of North American culture and life in this century, there may have been a certain appropriateness that the century opened with the most massive demonstration of missionary confidence seen to that date in the New York Ecumenical Missionary Conference of 1900. This was attended in all by some 200,000 people, addressed by the then President of the United States, President McKinley, by one of his predecessors (President Harrison) and by the then Governor of

New York, Theodore Roosevelt. There had been large missionary conferences before this, in New York itself in 1854 (when Alexander Duff, the great Scottish educational missionary in India, had been the central figure), in Liverpool in 1860, in London in 1878 and 1888, but nothing of this size and immediate impact. As compared with the later conference at Edinburgh in 1910 it was aimed rather to demonstrate and inspire than to plan and reflect; and its title 'ecumenical' was intended to show the world-wide nature of the Christian mission. Edinburgh, more aware of the meaning of the term in church history as denoting the unity of the Christian church, disavowed it in favour of 'World Missionary Conference'.

Before examining some of the features and persons present at New York 1900, with their importance for the future, some of the background of mission in North America deserves notice. North American Christianity had deep roots in New England Puritanism. These hardy pioneers developed an understanding of their presence in the New World in terms of God's 'manifest destiny'. Their 'errand in the wilderness' was also a divine calling to subdue it and civilise it. From being small communities of the godly, often set down in a vast sea of forest, where hostile indigenous Indians were a threat to life and to their embryonic Christian societies, under the sovereignty of God their destiny was to build, extend and expand into this untamed environment and reduce it for Christ and civilisation. Theologically, they were equally deeply rooted in classical Calvinism. As far as historical development was treated by some Calvinists, there were to be three stages in the Christian church's life before the return of Christ in glory: first was the period of the apostles, when the gospel was offered to the world; secondly, a period of the anti-Christ; finally, there would be a great expansion of the church, during which the anti-Christ would be defeated.

In this scheme the Puritans of the seventeenth century saw themselves also as living in the second epoch, but towards its very end. Their position was therefore an interesting blend of pessimism over present obstacles but optimism in view of the new age which was about to dawn. In the light of later debates

about mission, the overwhelming emphasis in Puritan theology
on the sovereignty of God is of importance. In later developments, this was equally present in what became known as
pre-millennialism and post-millennialism. In the first, Puritan
theologians thought of the cataclysm of the end, including the
return of Christ, as preceding the golden age of the thousand-
year reign of the saints. In the second, the golden age comes
before the return of Christ: it is tied to the church's mission and
its civilising activity but, even so, it is still God who brings in
his kingdom. Nevertheless, in the hands of the greatest of the
New England Puritan theologians, Jonathan Edwards, this
emphasis on gradualism, the steady expansion of the church's
influence towards the great *dénouement* at the end of history in
this form of millennialism, could link later with a view of the
kingdom of God coming in terms of social progress and a stress
on man and activist programmes. This shifted the theological
centre of gravity sharply. Successors of Edwards in the nineteenth century, like Samuel Harris, could write books on the
Kingdom of God on Earth (1870) stressing this social element,
while a Samuel Hopkins could give Calvinists a theoretical
basis for such an outworking of the gospel in his ideals of
'disinterested benevolence'.[1] In course of time this could lead,
in the words of one great American theologian, to 'the kingdom
of the Anglo-Saxon ... to bring light to the Gentiles by means
of lamps manufactured in America'.[2]

Whatever the ultimate directions of their theology, the Puritans of North America can be seen as pioneers of the Protestant
missionary movement; perhaps more so, as has been suggested,
than William Carey and the missionary awakening of the
1790s. The early missions of John Eliot (1604–90) among the
Indians of Massachusetts and of the short but influential life of
David Brainerd (1718–47), made widely known by Jonathan
Edwards's work on his life and journal, were signs of a Protestantism which, in contrast to the post-Reformation period

---

[1] H. Richard Niebuhr, *The Kingdom of God in America* (New York, 1959), pp. 142–61.
For Hopkins' influence see V. H. Rabe in J. K. Fairbank (ed.), *The Missionary
Enterprise in China and America* (Cambridge, Mass., 1974), p. 57.

[2] Niebuhr, *Kingdom*, p. 179.

elsewhere, accepted responsibility for mission. Although stigmatised by one historian as a 'sanctimonious masquerade', the Puritan mission of Eliot, Brainerd and Jonathan Edwards, who himself worked among the Indians of New England for seven years, are reminders that a century and a half of American missionary activity preceded the more conventionally accepted 'beginning' of the Protestant missionary movement.[3] In the nineteenth century, Americans had their missionary hero in Adoniram Judson, influenced by William Carey's example, who sailed for Burma in 1812. He and his party were the precursors of North American Protestant Christians serving as missionaries in China, Japan, the Middle East (where they gained a formidable reputation as educators) Africa and Latin America and, just prior to New York 1900, in the Philippines in 1899, a territory which became the nearest thing to an American essay in nineteenth-century imperialism.

Apart, then, from origins in the New Testament, Americans had cultural and historical reasons for viewing mission in terms of extension and expansion, whether as pioneers in an essentially hostile environment to be subdued, or as inheritors of strands of Calvinism which thought in terms of progressive development towards the kingdom of God or as sharers in the general territorial expansionism of Christendom of the nineteenth century. It was no wonder that the leaders of the SVM (Student Volunteer Movement), the YMCA, the WSCF (World Student Christian Federation), who were also to be the leaders of the Protestant missionary movement in the early twentieth century, had expansion as their chief category: 'the thrust towards extension, expansion and encompassment belongs to the substantive meaning of nineteenth and twentieth century American Protestantism'[4] is a fair judgement. Linked to nineteenth-century ideas of progress, a progress which could be easily demonstrated in the development of the United States itself, despite the terrible experiences of the Civil War in the mid-century (which many saw in terms of

---

[3] W. R. Hutchison, *Errand to the World* (Chicago, 1987), pp. 24–41.
[4] Catherine Albanese in R. P. Beaver (ed.), *American Missions in Bicentennial Perspective* (Pasadena, 1977), p. 67.

a victory for the kingdom of God in the realm of slavery and its
defeat in any case), the opening years of the twentieth century
provided much potential for heady optimism.

NEW YORK CONFERENCE 1900: SOME LEADING FIGURES

It had been pointed out that, as a prelude to the Edinburgh
Conference of 1910, New York 1900 was less significant in
certain respects than, for example, the missionary conference
at Madras in the same year.[5] Madras, like Edinburgh, was
thoroughly prepared as a working conference not, like New
York, primarily as a demonstration. The word 'demonstration'
was used at New York by a number of speakers. To Wardlaw
Thompson of the London Missionary Society the conference
was a 'demonstration' of Christian unity, even if he declared
himself distrustful of mere numbers;[6] for Dr Schreiber of the
German delegation it was a demonstration 'especially in the
face of Rome' of the unity of Protestant Christendom,[7]
although at least one speaker, Seth Low, President of Columbia University, looked to the day when all of Christendom 'the
Eastern Church and Roman Catholic brethren and Protestants
alike . . . by fusing their different coloured rays' would reflect in
the world 'that great white light' which enlightens all.[8] The
size and enthusiasm of the demonstration was especially
evident after the President of the United States addressed the
conference, when, between his speech and that of Theodore
Roosevelt, the audience burst into 'My country 'tis of thee'.
Such fervour is more easily understood against a background of
outstanding growth in missionary commitment by Americans,
not least through the Student Volunteer Movement and its
leaders. This crystallised in the missionary slogan or famous
watchword 'the evangelisation of the world in this generation'.

A. T. Pierson (1837–1911), editor of the *Missionary Review of*

---

[5] W. R. Hogg, *Ecumenical Foundations* (New York, 1952), p. 107. Although the Madras
Conference of 1902 is referred to here, Hogg has shown (pp. 21–3, 49, 97) that
the Madras Conference of 1900 set the model for this conference.

[6] *Ecumenical Missionary Conference, New York, 1900*, 2 vols. (New York, 1900), hereafter
EMC 1900 i, pp. 31–2.

[7] *Ibid.*, p. 34.   [8] *Ibid.*, pp. 14–15.

the World from 1888 until his death, and a leading figure in the North American missionary movement, who was present at the New York Conference, has been credited with the origin of the watchword.[9] Whether this was so or not, Pierson's friendship with the American evangelist D. L. Moody and his missionary enthusiasm had much to do with the bringing to birth of the SVM.[10] Pierson was a fluent, gifted and prolific writer, whose books include *The Crisis of Missions* (1886) and *The Divine Enterprise of Missions* (1891), which were widely read. He was also an able speaker: an example of his rhetoric came in his speech at New York, when he claimed that 'through thirty years ... of all the evidences of Christianity ... the study of missions has transcended all other subjects'.[11] Pierson found that Moody had regular meetings for college students. In 1886, at Northfield, Massachusetts, Pierson gave a rousing address which included the words 'all should go and go to all'. One of the Christian students present, R. P. Wilder, son of the founder of the *Missionary Review*, Royal Wilder, persuaded Moody to permit ten students to speak briefly (three minutes only were permitted to each) on missionary themes. Wilder, who had himself been deeply moved by the visit of British missionary volunteers in the shape of the 'Cambridge Seven' to Princeton in the 1880s, a group which included C. T. Studd and all of whom had offered to serve in China following Moody's mission in Cambridge of 1882, seized the opportunity at Northfield. Given the chance to respond to what they had heard, some 100 students signed the SVM pledge, a declaration of willingness to serve in the mission field. Among them, after spending a whole night in prayer after hearing the ten short addresses, was the signature of John R. Mott.[12] Although Mott was then a

---

[9] W. R. Hutchison, *Errand*, p. 99 and note 11, corrects this. Royal Wilder, not Pierson, was the originator of the watchword.

[10] *Dictionary of American Biography*, vol. XIV, p. 590 (hereafter *DAB*).

[11] *EMC 1900*, II, p. 325.

[12] For Mott, see R. P. Wilder, *The Great Commission* (London, 1936), p. 22; for D. L. Moody's influence, C. H. Hopkins, *John R. Mott: a Biography* (Geneva, 1979), p. 28 and *DAB Supplement 5*, pp. 506–8; for R. P. Wilder's part, his *The Great Commission*, pp. 20–3, and for his Princeton experience, p. 13. For D. L. Moody's missions in Cambridge, England and the Cambridge Seven see J. C. Pollock, *A Cambridge*

student of Cornell, the document became known as the Princeton Declaration and stated that the signatories were 'willing
and desirous, God permitting' to serve overseas. Largely
through the influence of the SVM, an American missionary
force of 350 in 1890 became 4,000 strong by 1915.

Of those who attended the Northfield conferences John
Mott (1865–1955), R. E. Speer (1867–1947) and G. Sherwood
Eddy (1871–1963), of Cornell, Princeton and Yale
respectively, were all to be very significant figures in the
development of the international missionary movement, as was
a Swedish student, Nathan Söderblom, who attended in 1890,
and became friends with Mott at that time.[13] Sherwood Eddy,
like Mott, worked for the YMCA and for the SVM: for him,
this included some years of service in India. Like Mott again,
he was in demand as an evangelist among students internationally. He conducted missions all over the world. Eddy has been
described as 'the socialist spell-binder', although he disclaimed
any formal political attachment to socialism.[14] His primary
commitment was certainly to the work of evangelism and his
experience of work with the YMCA in New York as a young
graduate apparently 'revolutionised his plan for life'.[15] Robert
Speer, son of a senator in the US Congress, will appear again in
this record. He became secretary of the Board of Foreign
Missions of the Presbyterian Church of the USA, a post which
he held for nearly fifty years from 1891. Like Mott and Eddy,
Speer worked for the SVM, in his case for only one year
(1889–90); like them also, although giving a life-time to Christian service, he was never ordained. His numerous writings
were weighty and well substantiated, based on wide and well-

Movement (London, 1953), pp. 54–89, and for the effect of the Cambridge Seven on
Mott see W. R. Hogg, *Ecumenical Foundations*, p. 85. Also W. R. Moody, *D. L.
Moody*, for the Northfield conferences at Mount Hermon and Moody's hesitation
over the SVM pledge (pp. 376–84).

[13] Hopkins, *Mott*, p. 389. Söderblom became Archbishop of Uppsala and a great
ecumenical pioneer; see B. G. M. Sundkler, *Nathan Söderblom: His Life and Work*
(London, 1968).

[14] W. R. Hutchison, *Errand*, p. 147, for the 'socialist spell-binder': but Eddy denied
that he had ever been 'a socialist or anything approaching it' in a letter to Mott of 7
April 1941: Mott Archive, Yale Divinity School, Box 25/473.

[15] J. K. Fairbank, *Missionary Enterprise*, p. 80.

digested reading, and he was also much in demand as a speaker to student audiences. His address to the SVM of 1903, published as *What Constitutes a Missionary Call*, was very influential and was reprinted several times during the first half of the century.[16] It was a sober and compelling tract of thirty-two pages, which set aside dramatic callings and Damascus-road experiences as prerequisites with humour and logic. Many who claimed to have had no call on this basis were enjoying a comfortable existence making money at home in the US. The more insistent question was not whether one had a sufficiently dramatic call but whether one had a sufficiently cogent reason to be exempt from what, when the respective needs of home and overseas were compared, constituted a presumptive duty. Many were affected by Speer's advocacy. He and his close colleague, Arthur Judson Brown, who wrote the influential book *The Foreign Missionary* (1907) (and lived to the age of 107), were a powerful partnership in the missionary cause.[17]

Of all these figures, John Mott acquired the greatest stature as an international statesman for Christian mission. He had been led into Christian faith during a visit to Cornell by J. E. K. Studd, brother of the member of the Cambridge Seven. After his missionary commitment at Northfield in 1886, he worked for the YMCA among colleges internationally and in the 1890s brought the YMCA and the SVM into an integrated programme. He was largely responsible for the formation of the World Student Christian Federation in 1895. The development and expansion of the WSCF was his 'consuming interest' for thirty years.[18] It was a remarkable achievement in itself; but it was also to have wide repercussions in the field of both developing ecumenism and in mission. It was to have much to do with the platform for success at Edinburgh 1910 through its

---

[16] See N. A. Horner in *International Bulletin of Missionary Research* (hereafter *IBMR*), 14, no. 1 (January 1990), p. 35; the writer was one of those who was influenced by Speer's tract (p. 36).

[17] This book gives support to those who hold that the missionary recruits from the US were an élite corps educationally. See A. J. Brown, *The Foreign Missionary* (New York, 1907), pp. 163–4; for the élite view see J. K. Fairbank, *Missionary Enterprise*, pp. 74–5.

[18] *DAB, Supplement 5*, p. 507.

development of international trust and relationships in the previous fifteen years. Mott was a leading evangelist among students across the world, missions which included those in Russia before the Revolution, where he won the approval of the Holy Synod of the Orthodox Church,[19] in China and in Japan. His books gained wide circulation. In one, *The Evangelisation of the World in this Generation* (1901), written in the context of New York 1900, he defended the famous watchword of the SVM against its critics. Above all, he became the master chairman, in demand for the Continuation Committee and its successor, the International Missionary Council, after his outstanding chairmanship at Edinburgh; and at the two succeeding conferences at Jerusalem in 1928 and Tambaram, Madras, in 1938. It was his abilities as an executive chairman of disparate, inter-denominational bodies which became largely responsible for the birth of National Christian Councils in India, China and Japan in the 1920s. Commanding in height and aspect, direct, clear and challenging in speech, decisive in execution, indefatigable in travel, Mott was a formidable figure; but to his intimates he was also one who inspired affection and respect. Men of the personal stature of the British leader and thinker, J. H. Oldham, and R. E. Speer, his friend from Northfield days, gave him ungrudging respect, admiration and loyalty. It was a recognition of worth also accorded by the US government, whether shown in appointments declined (as an ambassador to China) or in those accepted (as member of a war-time delegation to Russia in 1916). His influence among students of the time was legendary. A glimpse of it appears in this reminiscence by a young law student working on Wall Street:

one day I happened to be in the old New York Pennsylvania railroad station coffee shop, when across the way I saw an aged gentleman. I thought to myself 'That is Dr John R. Mott.' I walked over, introduced myself and then was treated to a remarkable few minutes I shall never forget. Dr Mott never took another bite of whatever he was eating. Until he had to hasten to catch his train he steadily

19 Hopkins, *Mott*, pp. 33–5.

quizzed me about my faith, my purposes in life, my plans for the future, my basic commitments. I mercifully cannot recall my answers but what I knew intensely was that at a very deep level I was being challenged in the name of Jesus Christ about who I was, who I might be and who God wanted me to be. It was an encounter never to be forgotten.[20]

The writer was himself to become a missionary in Latin America and a notable missionary statesman in WCC circles in the 1980s. As Mott is on record as travelling 7,000 miles by railway in one month and frequently 40,000 miles in a year,[21] such encounters must have been the staple fare of a life which, at one stage, was calculated to be the most widely travelled of any to that date in human history.

THE STUDENT VOLUNTEER MOVEMENT AND THE WATCHWORD

Strictly, the SVM dated from 1883, but the Northfield Conference of 1886 was a significant advance. In twenty-five years, chiefly through the influence of the SVM, the American missionary force was to increase more than tenfold: as we have seen, 350 in 1890 was to become 4,000 in 1915.[22] There is no doubt that the watchword, spoken into a context of increasing optimism and belief in the values of a North American culture and its potential for export, caught the imagination of young

---

[20] Eugene Stockwell in *IBMR*, 14, no. 2 (April 1990), p. 66; Roger Lloyd, *The Church of England 1900–1965* (London, 1966), pp. 201–4; cf. S. C. Neill, *Men of Unity* (London, 1960), pp. 13–25. See also W. A. Visser't Hooft, *Memoirs* (London, 1973), pp. 15, 18, 21, 35, 71, 102, 208, 348 for Mott's influence on the future general secretary of the WCC.

[21] *DAB, Supplement 5*, p. 506; B. Matthews, *John R. Mott, World Citizen* (London, 1934), p. 78, estimated Mott travelled 1·7 million miles.

[22] W. R. Hutchison in R. P. Beaver, *American Missions in Bicentennial Perspective*, pp. 376, 384. Roman Catholics were also influenced by this missionary phenomenon of the SVM. So, Mary Rogers, then a student at Smith College, experienced SVM at first hand and began her own Catholic Mission Study Club. She was to be a founding figure in the Roman Catholic order, the Catholic Foreign Mission Society, now known as Maryknoll; see A. Dries, 'The Foreign Mission Imperative of the American Catholic Church 1893–1925', *IBMR*, 15, no. 2 (April 1991): 'the group having the greatest impact on the development of an American Catholic foreign mission impulse was the Protestant Student Volunteer Movement (SVM)' (p. 64).

students. That very optimism and the apparently activist and human-centred view of mission which went with it, attracted criticism which people like Mott, Speer and Wilder were anxious to rebut. The Continental-European delegates arrived at New York with Gustav Warneck's warnings about Americans and their inadequately grounded missiology in their hands, though he himself was not present.[23] There had, indeed, been much debate among the Germans as to whether they should attend at all: in the event, it was decided that some sober German words would act as a necessary corrective to Anglo-Saxon tendencies.[24]

Warneck himself had given vent before 1900 to a well-sustained and argued protest at the watchword and concomitant Anglo-Saxon trends. He offered criticism of the student leaders, including Pierson and Wilder, in a 'brotherly spirit'. It was not enough to present mission in terms only of proclamation, like Pierson, or in the forms adopted by the great missionary leader in China, Hudson Taylor, much as Warneck admired him: 'such a spiritually minded man'. Mission involves discipling the nations and the apostles did not rush from place to place, but organised churches and established and visited them. Nor were ideas of 'hastening the Parousia', by jettisoning tried missionary methods, to be accepted: certainly, in both New Testament times and today, there was and is an incentive in looking towards the return of Christ; but a whole eschatological programme had to be fulfilled before the fulness of the Gentiles is gathered in. Warneck was clearly worried by the accounts of Mott's travelogues (144 colleges and universities have been visited etc.) and the whole activist tendency, which, he feared, would lead to a reaction against all mission. Rhetoric, watchwords, slogans (*Schlagworte*) could dangerously mislead and distort.[25] His deliverance to the New York Conference has to be seen against this background where his message included the words:

[23] *EMC 1900*, I, p. 34.
[24] W. R. Hogg, *Ecumenical Foundations*, p. 66 and note 116.
[25] G. Warneck, 'Die moderne Weltevangelismus-theorie', *AMZ*, 24 (1897), pp. 305–25. Warneck founded and edited the *Allgemeine Missions-Zeitschrift* from 1874.

very energetically are the watchwords promulgated nowadays ...
'expansion', 'diffusion', 'evangelisation of the world in this generation' ... such mottoes are entitled to consideration and so far as this
is the case I would not want to weaken their force. But ... I consider
them dangerous. The command ... bids us 'go' ... not 'fly'. *Festina
lente* applies also to missionary undertakings. The kingdom of heaven
is like a field ... not like a hot-house ... the non-Christian world is not
to be taken by assault. Mission history should also teach us not to
specify a time when the evangelisation of the world is to be completed. It is not for us to determine the times and seasons ... There is
a great danger of confounding the spread of European and American
culture ... the missionary command does not say 'go ye and teach
English to every nation'. Not more but less English ... should be the
watchword of the twentieth century in this respect.[26]

Mott and Wilder had been sufficiently worried by Warneck's earlier criticisms to seek out the learned missiologist in
person at Halle. In Wilder's account of the meeting, Warneck
had expressed some surprise when Wilder pointed to an
account of the Shanghai missionary conference of 1877 as the
source for the slogan: sober missionaries of many years experience in the field rather than young, hot-headed students and
their leaders were responsible. The careful professor, omnivo-
rous reader of missionary literature, had, on Wilder's account,
to admit that he had overlooked this.[27] Despite this interview,
his warnings stood in contrast to the defence of the watchword
put up by Anglo-American speakers at New York: both Mott
and Speer expounded it in speeches and the able Englishman,
Eugene Stock, historian and secretary of the Church Missionary Society, said 'there is nothing like a special formula to
touch hearts'.[28] Certainly, in the hands of men like Mott,
Wilder, Speer and the Scotsman Donald Fraser, who was
brought into the SVM field of work after hearing Wilder speak
at the English Keswick Convention, an opportunity arranged
through Stock, the watchword was an effective tool in the
colleges until the 1914–18 war cut swathes through both optimism and potential recruits, and the SVM declined in the

[26] *EMC 1900*, I, pp. 290–1.   [27] Wilder, *The Great Commission*, pp. 89–90.
[28] *EMC 1900*, I, p. 112; for Mott's speech p. 95; for Speer's, p. 59.

1920s. In whatever hands, however, 'the widely flaunted watchword, no matter how variously interpreted, served to epitomise the optimistic self-confidence of a rapidly expanding Anglo-Saxon empire'.[29] Both the optimism, amounting to utopianism, and the Anglo-Saxon constituent were equally unwelcome to thoughtful Continentals like Warneck.

Before leaving the New York Conference for the more influential conference at Edinburgh, two final aspects deserve notice: first, in contrast to Edinburgh, there was a very prominent participation by women. Here, New York was more representative of a remarkable development in missionary circles than Edinburgh was to be. Of the many women speakers, one, Lilavati Singh, made a deep enough impression on ex-President Harrison for him to say 'If I had given a million dollars to foreign missions I should count it wisely invested if it could lead only to the conversion of that one woman':[30] but the overseas input of such a speaker was less significant overall than the prominence of women who were speaking on behalf of the home supporting agencies. These demonstrated the new strength of women as supporters of overseas missions and the new status in leadership which the missionary movement was to give to women on the world stage.[31]

The second aspect of note was the presence, especially in the person of Hudson Taylor, of the so-called 'faith missions'. Hudson Taylor, founder of the China Inland Mission, spoke on more than one occasion at New York. His most powerful speech was composed toward the twin themes of millions of Chinese dying without the hope in God which the gospel could bring, alongside the experience of the CIM of offers of service and money in response to prayer; and this last despite CIM's settled policy of not making public appeals.[32] Not only in their

[29] W. R. Hutchison and T. Christensen, *Missionary Ideologies in the Imperialist Era* (Aarhus, 1982), p. 136. See also Denton Lotz, *The Evangelisation of the World in this Generation* (Hamburg, 1970).

[30] *EMC* 1900, I, p. 47; W. R. Hogg, *Ecumenical Foundations*, pp. 46, 131, for prominence of women *vis-à-vis* Edinburgh 1910.

[31] *EMC 1900*, I, p. 214.   [32] *Ibid.*, pp. 88–90.

attitude to the raising of money, but also in their emphasis on 'urgent proclamation' as the proper basis for missionary work, the faith missions, of which CIM was the model, with an immensely impressive record in China of primary evangelism (enhanced by its policy, following the Boxer Rebellion of 1900, of refusing all indemnities), were to cause observers like Warneck to mix caution and critical appraisal with admiration. Warneck could see that the CIM emphasis on preaching to as many Chinese of the interior as could be reached, never staying in one town too long in order to move on to the next, linked to a slogan like A. T. Pierson's about 'diffusion rather than concentration', could lead to a view of mission as a 'gospel-broadside'. Here there would be no deep rooting in the life of the people, which Warneck knew had been so important, for example, in the missionary work of the Middle Ages in Europe.[33] This tension between the so-called faith missions and the more established mission agencies and missionary thinkers would recur throughout the twentieth century.

EDINBURGH CONFERENCE 1910

Scotland had certain attributes and characteristics which made it peculiarly fitting for an epoch-making missionary conference to be held in its capital city. First, it had given to the nineteenth-century missionary movement in David Livingstone the figure who, above all others, represented missionary heroism to the wider world, whatever ambiguities of character and vocation twentieth-century critics might discern. Livingstone's example remained a potent symbol, not least for those who served in Africa.[34] One great Scottish mission in Africa, in which Donald Fraser, already mentioned, served from 1896–1920, was named after the explorer, the Livingstonia Mission of the United Free Church of Scotland. Again, Scotland had produced in Alexander Duff the first professor of missions,

---

[33] Warneck, 'Die moderne Weltevangelismus-theorie', *AMZ*, 24, (1897), pp. 307–11.
[34] See C. P. Groves' assessment in *The Planting of Christianity in Africa* (London, 1948–58), II, pp. 330–6. For the ambiguities of Livingstone's life and work see T. Jeal, *Livingstone* (London, 1973).

pre-dating Gustav Warneck. Duff had been both theorist and practitioner in India, where he had left a strong imprint on educational missions, with his attempts to reach the population through an approach to the cultured and highly educable Brahman caste.[35] Again, Scotland had a vigorous theological tradition, more akin to the German schools than was most of the Anglo-Saxon world. So, D. S. Cairns, Professor of Dogmatic and Apologetic Theology at the United Free Church's college (Christ's) at Aberdeen from 1907, had a direct impact on Edinburgh through his chairmanship of Commission IV on the relationship of the missionary message to the non-Christian religions. He stood in a tradition which produced at home such formidable theologians of the twentieth century as James Denney (who spoke powerfully at Edinburgh), James Orr, H. R. Mackintosh, John and Donald Baillie (the first of whom was among the stewards supplied by the SCM at the conference) and the brothers T. F. and J. B. Torrance, sons of Scottish missionaries in China: in the field, some of the most outstanding thinkers had been born or educated in Scotland, among them A. G. Hogg, J. N. Farquhar and Nicol Macnicol. Above all, in the context of the conference, J. H. Oldham provided a combination of Scots thoroughness, scholarship and Christian devotion, which, in harness with Mott's chairmanship, was the greatest single factor in making Edinburgh 1910 so unusually influential. Oldham had an almost uncanny prescience that Edinburgh was poised 'between the times' and that very great issues hung in the balance. Without prior knowledge of the catastrophe of 1914–18 in prospect, as a great divide between two worlds, his attitude and judgements might have been shaped by a prophetic vision of crisis to come.[36]

Oldham was the product of a devout Christian home, the eldest son of an officer in the British Indian army, who retired

---

[35] For Duff, see O. G. Myklebust, *The Study of Missions in Theological Education* (Oslo, 1955–7), pp. 19–24.

[36] *World Missionary Conference Report* (henceforth *WMC*), IX, pp. 322–9; Temple Gairdner, *Edinburgh 1910: an Account and Interpretation of the World Missionary Conference* (Edinburgh, 1910), p. 262. Oldham had a high opinion of Denney: see Oldham to

early to Scotland and spent much of his time in Christian
teaching, preaching and evangelism. Oldham added to this
deep piety a rigorous academic grounding at Oxford in the
classics, at New College, Edinburgh in theology and finally in
the study of missionary theory and practice at the University of
Halle, where Gustav Warneck taught. Like Cairns, who had
studied at Marburg, Oldham was in a position to appreciate
the concerns of the German mission theorists and the weighty
theological tradition in which they stood. At Oxford, Oldham
had been in Christian Union circles with others like A. G.
Fraser and W. H. Temple Gairdner, historian of Edinburgh
1910 and a missionary in Egypt of long service among
Muslims.[37]

Oldham had intended a career in the Indian civil service. In
the restrained wording of the *Dictionary of National Biography*,
'his objective changed as a result of religious conversion'.[38]
Temple Gairdner recorded more vividly that he and Oldham
attended the second student volunteer conference at Keswick
in 1894, when they heard R. E. Speer speak. Gairdner wrote:
'Speer simply God-inspired ... never heard anything like it.
Joe Oldham and I walk up the road and give ourselves to
God.'[39] Instead of the Indian civil service, Oldham went to
India in the service of the YMCA to work among students in
Lahore, after a year of service as the first full-time secretary of
the Student Christian Movement of Great Britain and Ireland.
Further study at New College, Edinburgh, and Halle was
followed by administrative work for his church, the United
Free Church of Scotland, and then appointment in 1908 as
secretary for the World Missionary Conference.

An important factor in Oldham's life was his deafness. This

Mott, 18 December 1913. On Oldham's prescience: Oldham to Mott, 23 September
1909: Mott Archive, Yale Divinity School.

[37] On Temple Gairdner, C. Padwick, *Temple Gairdner of Cairo* (London, 1929).

[38] *Dictionary of National Biography*, Supplement 1961–70, pp. 806–9. H. W. Oldham,
Lt.-Col. G. W. Oldham R.E.: a Memoir (London, 1926). Cf. W. R. Hogg, *Ecumenical
Foundations*, pp. 109–10. Oldham married Mary Fraser, daughter of the Lt.-
Governor of Bengal, Sir Andrew Fraser, and sister of A. G. Fraser the missionary
educator and Oldham's friend at Oxford.

[39] Ruth Rouse, *A History of the World Student Christian Federation* (London, 1948), p. 96.

was a handicap which, combined with his own modest temperament and manner, meant that he was at his best behind the scenes. As Gairdner reflected on Edinburgh 1910, however, Oldham was both entirely unobtrusive and yet all-pervading behind 'its ideals, aspirations ... hopes'.[40] Such a secretary was an ideal foil for Mott, with his strong public presence and command of large gatherings. The two men developed a deep bond of mutual respect, which was to give immense benefits to the missionary movement and to ecumenism. When Mott was under pressure, in 1909, to accept an appointment at Yale, Oldham, who had observed Mott's unusual capacity to pick and inspire able men and women for influential positions, raised the question whether the forthcoming conference might not result in a post for Mott which would free him to do this international service in the Christian cause, which for Oldham outweighed the claims of even a setting like Yale on Mott's life.[41] Once more, Oldham revealed remarkable prescience.

THE EDINBURGH COMMISSIONS: COMMISSION IV

Something of the careful preparation which Oldham set in motion for Edinburgh 1910 can be seen in the arrangements, for example, for Commission IV on the 'Missionary Message and the non-Christian Religions'. D. S. Cairns was put in charge of this section in 1908. A questionnaire was constructed which was sent to missionaries in the field, many of great experience, on such questions as points of contact between the Christian gospel and the non-Christian religions, those aspects which attracted and those which repelled the other religions and 'the chief moral and intellectual and social hindrances' to the acceptance of Christian belief.

The respondents were working in Muslim, Hindu, Buddhist, Confucian and animist contexts all over the world. Their

---

[40] W. H. Temple Gairdner, *Edinburgh 1910*, p. 65. *WMC*, IX, pp. 9–10; Lloyd, *Church of England 1900–1965*, p. 196.

[41] Oldham to Mott, 10 August 1909 and 23 September 1909: Mott Archive, Yale Divinity School.

responses were full, thoughtful and often perceptive and
provide a resource for reflection of early twentieth-century
inter-religious issues of great value.[42] The list of respondents is
a roll-call of the great missionary figures of the time: Temple
Gairdner, English missionary in Cairo, Dr Lepsius, a German
missionary writing from Potsdam, W. A. Shedd, the American
educational missionary writing from Persia and member of the
American Presbyterian Board of Foreign Missions, all working
in Islamic fields: C. F. Andrews, then serving with the Cambridge Mission to Delhi, to be Gandhi's friend and the most
widely known missionary figure in India, G. S. Eddy, J. N.
Farquhar, T. E. Slater and A. G. Hogg all writing from a
context of what Westerners call Hinduism: A. G. Fraser,
working at the time in Kandy, Sri Lanka (then Ceylon) in a
Buddhist environment: and, from basically animist settings,
Donald Fraser and W. B. Grubb, working in the Paraguayan
Chaco area; and, among Confucianist Chinese, Stanley Smith,
a member of the famous Cambridge Seven, working in Shansi,
A. E. Moule, brother of the English Bishop of Durham,
Handley Moule, and the great Timothy Richard of the Baptist
Missionary Society in northern China. There were responses
also from a number of indigenous Christians, often first-
generation converts, among them the widely known Indian
woman worker among young Hindu widows, Pandita
Ramabai, and clergy like Francis Kingsbury and Canon Nihal
Singh.

These and many others provided a large pool of material for
Cairns to digest. It was these well-informed responses to the
questionnaires which provided the essential background to
what Temple Gairdner described, with justice, as 'by common
consent' among the finest and even 'the most remarkable' of all
those presented at Edinburgh.[43]

---

[42] Copies at Christ's College, Aberdeen; the Missionary Research Library, New York;
the Day Missions Library, Yale Divinity School. See E. J. Sharpe's remarks in *Not
to Destroy but to Fulfil* (Uppsala, 1965), pp. 275–6 and notes 2 and 3.
[43] Temple Gairdner, *Edinburgh 1910*, pp. 134, 136; Hogg, *Ecumenical Foundations*,
p. 126. E. J. Sharpe, *Not to Destroy but to Fulfil*, p. 276 and note 6.

Fulfilment: 'yes' and 'no' towards other faiths

Two of Cairns' respondents may be taken as representing views which contrast on Christian attitudes to other religious faiths. Both, as it happens, were Scotsmen like Cairns. J. N. Farquhar (1861–1929) was born in Aberdeen and educated there before going on to Oxford, where a brilliant academic career culminated in double firsts. He went out to India with the London Missionary Society, but was recruited by John Mott for the YMCA after some years of service. By 1910 Farquhar had not yet written the book for which he is remembered, *The Crown of Hinduism* (1913), but he was already known as a representative of the 'fulfilment' school of thinkers, who saw Christian faith as a fulfilment of Hinduism even as it had fulfilled Judaism. In his response to Cairns he had written of 'a continuous unfulfilled search for a satisfying monotheism' as 'one of the most marked features of Hindu history'.[44] The Hindu soul, he wrote, 'longs for God and for fellowship with Him'.[45] Farquhar showed himself, here and elsewhere, to be deeply versed in the history and literature of Hinduism. Like C. F. Andrews, he had a great respect for the *Bhagavadgita* as expressing doctrines of grace, forgiveness and salvation and for the Hindu view of *bhakti*, that the truly religious man 'came into direct contact with God and lives in joyous love for Him and faith in Him'.[46] Farquhar stood for a view of Indian religion which said a firm 'yes' to much in it. This sympathy for other religious traditions was reflected broadly at Edinburgh, as was his desire for the accurate and intensive study of the great non-Christian religions. He would not, however, have dissented from Cairns' conclusion that 'this very charity and tolerance ... makes more impressive the agreement as to the uniqueness and finality of Christ', for he maintained that it was still possible to hold to the Lordship of Christ without compromise; and there are elements of his writing which indicate that, while he saw Christ

---

[44] Responses to D. S. Cairns, 'Hinduism', no. 154, p. 22 (see note 42 above).
[45] *Ibid.*, p. 35.
[46] *Ibid.*, p. 35.

as bringing the best of Hinduism to fulfilment, the relationship was also one of supersession and replacement.[47]

By contrast to Farquhar, A. G. Hogg was critical of fulfilment ideas. Hogg was a brilliant and rigorous thinker, who had been trained in philosophy at Edinburgh under Pringle-Pattison and in 1904 had been appointed as Professor of Philosophy at the United Free Church of Scotland's Madras Christian College. By 1910 Hogg had already acquired a reputation in the realm of Christian approaches to Hinduism with his book *Karma and Redemption* (1909).[48] Hogg was a personal friend of Cairns, who owed much to Hogg's father, a missionary doctor in Cairo. Cairns appears to have repaid his debts to the Hogg family when standing by A. G. Hogg when he was afflicted with a similar crisis of faith as Cairns when a student.[49] In his response to Cairns' questionnaire, Hogg described how when he first went to India he had arrived with a vague theism, prepared to surrender 'alleged facts of the New Testament narratives – even the resurrection itself' provided that the 'general impression' of 'Jesus' personality was not affected'. But 'I had not long been in India when a radical change began to be effected in the tendency of my teaching.' He came to think that God as active will, self-expressed in history and supremely in Jesus Christ was central, with the need to 'break root and branch' with the 'conception of merit' over against the Hindu doctrine of *karma*, essentially worked out in terms of desert, often linked to reincarnation. For Hogg, 'Christian doctrines are not the fulfilment of Hindu doctrines': 'outside the realm of vague abstraction what does it [fulfilment] mean?' Certainly, Hindu satisfaction 'proves that

---

[47] *WMC*, IV, p. 181; Cf. Sharpe, *Not to Destroy but to Fulfil*, pp. 205, 262, 336. Cairns included a good deal of Farquhar's response in his digest: see *WMC*, IV, pp. 181–2, 267–8. Farquhar's books *Modern Religious Movements in India* (New York, 1915) and *An Outline of the Religious Literature of India* (Oxford, 1920) illustrate the efforts which he made, with other missionaries, to extend knowledge of Hinduism. See Sharpe, *Not to Destroy but to Fulfil*, p. 304.

[48] See the accolade from H. A. A. Kennedy in *WMC*, IX, p. 179; a 'masterly study'; and from the Scottish dogmatician, H. R. Mackintosh, in the preface to Hogg's book *Christ's Message of the Kingdom* (Madras, 1911), p. v.

[49] Sharpe, *Not to Destroy but to Fulfil*, pp. 282–3.

Christian beliefs fulfil the yearning of the Hindu consciousness, thrown out of equilibrium by Christian influence but not that Christianity is a fulfilment to ... the typical undisturbed Hindu consciousness'. For Hogg, 'Christianity is the solution of a religious problem which the typical Hindu does not feel but which under favourable conditions he may be made to feel.' So, he concluded 'if this be the real relation of Christianity to Hinduism, to call it one of fulfilment may be ... permissible but the description obscures the fact that it fulfils by, at least partially, destroying'.[50]

Hogg will reappear in this record. Here he represented the 'No' to heavy emphasis on religious continuity between Indian religion and Christianity; but, as we shall see, this did not mean that he discounted Indian claims to an authentic experience of God within their own religious tradition.

EDINBURGH 1910 AND THE FUTURE

Cairns' report laid out one very significant area of understanding, an approach to the non-Christian religions which was to be sympathetic and charitable while holding to the claim of finality and 'absoluteness' (his choice of word) for Christ. Certain other directions for the future were also present in the reports. First, a widespread fear of advancing Islam was expressed in 1910. Mott articulated it both in Commission 1 and in identical words in his book following Edinburgh, *The Decisive Hour for Christian Missions* (1910): 'the greatest solidarity and the most activity and aggressiveness' among the non-Christian religions was shown by Islam, and 'if things continue as they are tending Africa may become a Mohammedan continent'.[51] Gustav Warneck also noted the advance of Islam and gave his opinion that 'the new battle against Mohammedanism in the immediate future will be fought on

[50] Responses to Cairns 'Hinduism', no. 176, p. 14. For A. G. Hogg, see J. L. Cox, 'The development of A. G. Hogg's theology in relation to non-Christian faith', unpublished Ph.D thesis (University of Aberdeen, 1977).

[51] *WMC*, 1, pp. 20, 18–21, 405–6; Mott, *The Decisive Hour for Christian Missions* (London, 1910), pp. 57, 60.

East African soil' in a letter he wrote to Mott.[52] Edinburgh had
a view of Africa which saw it as broadly Muslim in the north,
pagan in its great central areas (where Christianity and Islam
were seen to be in competition for the souls of animists) and
Christian in the southern tip.[53]

Secondly, there was a longing for unity. In a message to the
conference, King George V had expressed the hope that it
would 'promote unity among Christians'[54] and Theodore
Roosevelt had added an influential American voice on the
theme: 'it is important to remember that a divided
Christendom can only imperfectly bear witness to the essential
unity of Christianity ... one of the lessons ... particularly
impressed upon me by what I have seen of Christian work in
Africa'.[55] It had been a notable achievement by Oldham, the
significance of which he was well aware, to have added to the
predominantly Protestant character of Edinburgh certain
churchmen who stood firmly in the Catholic tradition of Anglicanism, such as Bishop Gore, W. H. Frere, Father H. H. Kelly
and Bishop Montgomery, then secretary of the Society for the
Propagation of the Gospel. Gore and others had insisted before
the conference on due recognition for the Roman Catholic
church by the exclusion of Latin America as a mission field
from its purview: other Anglicans present all pleaded for a
wider unity. These included Bishop Talbot of Southwark,
Bishop Montgomery and Eugene Stock of the CMS; and
although James Denney, in a powerful speech on the exclusiveness of the gospel which should never be cheapened, cast a
critical eye over organic unity, the desire for it was backed up
by those who had seen the harmful effects of the lack of it in the
field. H. T. Hodgkin, a widely respected Quaker missionary in
China, reminded the conference that 'we are being brought up
to this question of unity ... in an atmosphere where unity
means more than it means here in the West';[56] while Sherwood
Eddy, from his experience of the YMCA in India, made a

---

[52] *WMC*, I, p. 435.   [53] *Ibid.*, pp. 405–6.   [54] *Ibid.*, IX, p. 141.
[55] Temple Gairdner, *Edinburgh 1910*, p. 46.
[56] *WMC*, IV, pp. 321–2: for the other speeches VIII, pp. 201–14.

typically rhetorical appeal for unity, at home as well as on the
mission field, where he noted that the South India United
church had set an example by bringing together 150,000 Christians.[57] The younger churches, the conference report noted,
'may see with a clearer vision and act with a bolder purpose'
than the churches of the sending countries.[58]

Nationalism was an inescapable reality for the missionary
movement to notice. The success of Japan in the war with
Russia of 1905 had a considerable effect on the Eastern nations,
as the conference observed.[59] There was a recognition, as in
Oldham's case, of the crucial nature of the immediate future in
relation to the nations of China, India and Japan. 'The plastic
condition of the nations will not long continue': China was a
'plastic metal' which, once shaped, might set in a mould which
could not be changed again.[60] There was growing racial
antagonism in India.[61] 'Many missionaries report their conviction that if the tide is not set towards Christianity during the
next decade both in the Far East and the Near East, it may be
turned against us in the decade following',[62] which showed that
Oldham was not alone in seeing a time of crisis. Mott's Commission 1 asked: 'these nations are still plastic. Shall they set in
Christian or pagan moulds?' and the sense of specially forma-
tive, if fleeting, opportunity was struck again by Mott when
presenting the report.[63] Bishop Honda of Japan urged the conference to recognise nationalism and to form a national Christian church:[64] and the danger of 'de-nationalising' converts was
noted and addressed.[65] Christ, it was said, 'never by teaching or
example resisted or withstood the spirit of true nationalism'.[66]
In terms of the indigenous church, the Anglican Bishop Tucker
of Uganda had held up as an ideal 50 European men and
women matched by 3,000 indigenous church workers.[67]

[57] *Ibid.*, IX, pp. 320–1.   [58] *Ibid.*, II, p. 35.
[59] *Ibid.*, I, p. 32. In a war of 1904–5 Russia was defeated on land and sea and ceded
Port Arthur to Japan. The first defeat of what was viewed as a 'Western' nation by
an Eastern nation made a great impression in the East.
[60] *Ibid.*, pp. 27–8, 107.   [61] *Ibid.*, p. 143.   [62] *Ibid.*, p. 29.
[63] *Ibid.*, p. 362.
[64] *Ibid.*, II, pp. 349–50.   [65] *Ibid.*, p. 6.   [66] *Ibid.*, I, p. 33.
[67] *Ibid.*, p. 238.

Finally, and reverting to the theme of expansion and extension as a category for Christian mission, the emphasis at Edinburgh on the need for a 'comprehensive plan for world occupation',[68] expressed often in militaristic metaphors, was strongly present in Commission I, 'Carrying the gospel to the non-Christian world', but not only there. Mott's fondness for military metaphors has been noticed elsewhere;[69] and Commission I, which he chaired, was studded with them: the church was engaged not in 'guerrilla warfare [but] in a unified spiritual campaign',[70] though the 'far-flung battle line' of the 'army of God' was 'perilously slender'.[71] It would be disloyalty to Christ to 'neglect the great citadels of the non-Christian world':[72] 'it is high time ... deliberately and resolutely [to] attack some of these hitherto almost impregnable fortresses'.[73] In fairness to Mott, he was not alone in the language of conquest. Gustav Warneck, as we have seen, had written of the battle,[74] the Methodist Bishop Bashford used the language of crusade[75] and R. F. Horton of world conquest.[76] Speaker after speaker was to use the term 'aggressive' as correct policy.[77] It is important to remember that even those most sympathetic to non-Christian religions and cultures, like J. N. Farquhar, still saw Hinduism as to be fulfilled in part by supersession, while the 'philosophical disintegration' of Islam was confidently predicted.[78]

Considering all that had gone before, Mott's closing address struck a note of firm resolve rather than any optimistic triumphalism, though even here the note of world conquest was present. Perhaps he remembered David Livingstone's appeal, 'the end of the geographical feat is the beginning of the missionary enterprise' in his opening remarks: 'the end of the

[68] *Ibid.*, p. 288.
[69] See Clifton Phillips in J. K. Fairbank (ed.) *Missionary Enterprise*, p. 102. Mott's closing address at the SVM meetings of 1898 had been 'full of the metaphors of the battlefield'.
[70] *WMC*, I, p. 190.   [71] *Ibid.*, p. 288.   [72] *Ibid.*, p. 296.   [73] *Ibid.*, p. 296
[74] *Ibid.*, p. 435.   [75] *Ibid.*, IX, p. 250.   [76] *Ibid.*, p. 341.
[77] *Ibid.*, III, p. 417 where the policy of aggression is contrasted favourably with the policy of creating a Christian atmosphere. See *ibid.*, p. 410, and *ibid.*, VI, p. 169.
[78] *Ibid.*, I, p. 13.

conference is the beginning of the conquest. The end of the
planning is the beginning of the doing.' Certainly Scottish
poetry was quoted to effect: 'time worketh, let me work too'.
The call was to a life of religious reality, for which 'our best
days are ahead of us'. He reminded the conference of the
Archbishop of Canterbury's closing words to them (how glad
Oldham had been to secure him after long hesitations)[79] to the
effect that the kingdom of God might come with power before
many present tasted death: this might prove a splendid proph-
ecy.[80] Meanwhile, in response to requests from Lord Balfour of
Burleigh,[81] Julius Richter, the German academic[82] and
others[83] there was to be a continuation committee, with Mott
as chairman and Oldham as secretary by unanimous acclaim.
It would become the International Missionary Council
(IMC). As Lord Balfour had hoped, Edinburgh would thereby
leave behind 'some permanent body which will speak for you'
with something of the same continuity as governments pos-
sessed, over against quickly dissolved conferences.[84]

So ended a conference which had been, *par excellence*, a
conference on expansion and extension. Great speeches had
been made by nationals like Cheng-Ching-Yi and V. S.
Azariah, with his appeal to the sending churches to give
Christian friends as well as sacrificial service; by the American
Bishop Brent of the Philippines, who glimpsed unity as attain-
able by the end of the century;[85] by Bishop Gore, with his
intense admiration for the missionary participants and missionary educators in the field,[86] by R. E. Speer and Mott himself.
To the Germans, 'Edinburgh became a milestone'.[87] While
they continued to be critical of some of the American methods
and slogans,[88] which they viewed still as a confusion of human
efforts with God's initiatives, they were also reassured: if their

[79] G. K. A. Bell, *Randall Davidson* 2 vols. (London, 1935), I, pp. 572–4; Tissington
Tatlow, *The Story of the Student Christian Movement* (London, 1933), p. 309.
[80] *WMC*, IX, pp. 347–51, 150.   [81] *Ibid.*, VII, p. 185.   [82] *Ibid.*, I, pp. 432–3.
[83] *Ibid.*, p. 297; *ibid.*, VIII, pp. 144–7 and 206.   [84] *Ibid.*, VII, p. 185.
[85] Hogg, *Ecumenical Foundations*, p. 134.
[86] *WMC*, III, pp. 405–6.   [87] Hogg, *Ecumenical Foundations*, p. 135.
[88] *WMC*, VI, p. 144 on the use of 'decision' cards and on the SVM; *ibid.*, VIII,
pp. 216–17 on the watchword.

contribution was to be 'solidity' and 'objective thoroughness'
there had been no lack of either in the preparations set in hand
by Oldham, while Cairns, Gore, Frere and others had supplied
plenty of theological ballast from the side of the Anglo-
Saxons.[89] Meanwhile, in the wings as stewards and members of
the SCM were such figures as William Temple, William Paton,
John Baillie, Kenneth Kirk, William Manson and Neville
Talbot, men of great future influence, ecclesiastical, theological and ecumenical, who here caught a vision of a world
church, with Indian, Chinese and Japanese leaders of stature;
the phenomenon William Temple would one day refer to as the
'great new fact of our time'.[90]

[89] Hogg, *Ecumenical Foundations*, p. 135.
[90] W. Temple, *The Church Looks Forward* (London, 1944), pp. 2–3; see S. C. Neill, *A History of Christian Missions*, p. 15 and note 1.

CHAPTER 2

Mission as the church of a people ('Volkskirche') 1910–1920

In the approach to the decade following Edinburgh 1910 the main focus will be on German missions; and, in particular, on the work of two German missionaries, both of whom worked in tribal settings and whose reflections upon those societies gave rise to much debate on what was termed the *Volkskirche* approach to mission. Both Bruno Gutmann and Christian Keysser were missionaries in the field until 1920, at which date they were repatriated to Germany under the conditions which obtained after the 1914–18 war and the Treaty of Versailles of 1919. This treaty had wide repercussions in the mission field, especially upon German missions, despite valiant attempts to limit the damage, in part successful, made by J. H. Oldham, assisted by Randall Davidson, Archbishop of Canterbury.[1] Gutmann was to return for a further spell of service in what had been German East Africa but Keysser was unable to renew his work in New Guinea.

BACKGROUND TO A GERMAN THEORY OF MISSION

Mission theory has taken various forms in the modern era. Prominent in the last chapter was the emphasis on individual conversion. In the German tradition, Moravian missionaries from the Herrnhut community on Count Zinzendorf's estate

---

[1] For Oldham and the Treaty of Versailles, see W. R. Hogg, *Ecumenical Foundations*, (New York, 1952), pp. 184–7; G. K. A. Bell, *Randall Davidson*, 2 vols. (London, 1935), II, pp. 933, 944–50; A. C. Hastings, *A History of English Christianity*, (London, 1991), pp. 95–6.

sought such conversions as 'trophies for the Lamb';[2] but this was combined with a practice of mission emerging from and creating the kind of warm community of believers which Herrnhut itself represented. In this sense there was an emphasis on the church, even if Zinzendorf himself was wary of what he judged to be the formality and lack of Christian vitality of the Lutheran church as he knew it.[3] For Moravians it was still true that mission was 'always an enterprise of the community'.[4] An ecclesiocentric approach to mission had certainly been the effect of the writings of the two missionary strategists of the Anglo-Saxon world in the nineteenth century, Rufus Anderson of the American Board of Commissioners for Foreign Missions and Henry Venn of the English CMS. Here, the pietist stress on individual conversion was still present but the weight was laid on church planting, of groups of believers formed into indigenous churches which were to become self-governing, self-supporting and self-extending. An equivalent figure to Anderson and Venn in German mission theory was Karl Graul (1814–64), a Lutheran and first director of the Leipzig Society. He and a contemporary called Wilhelm Löhe 'regarded mission as the responsibility of the church',[5] which was also to plant churches. Graul went further. The need was to build national churches, which took into their congregational life as much of the 'natural' and national custom as was possible. Such national churches would thereby be truly rooted in the soil (*bodenständig*).[6] Such ideas contributed substantially to the so-called *Volkskirche* approach to mission, where the aim was to create the church of a people, expressing the particular individuality of that race or ethnic group.

Gustav Warneck, whose influence as a formative missiologist has already been noted, combined a number of these themes in

[2] G. Warneck, *Outline of a History of Protestant Missions* (London, 1906), p. 51, quotes Zinzendorf: 'look to it whether you are attracting some souls for the Lamb'.

[3] D. Bosch, *Transforming Mission: Paradigm Shifts in Theology of Mission* (New York, 1991), pp. 253–4.

[4] Heinz Motel, 'Zinzendorf', in *CDCWM*, p. 680.

[5] D. Bosch, *Witness to the World: the Christian Mission in Theological Perspective* (London, 1980), p. 170; for Graul see *RGG*, II, p. 1832.

[6] J. C. Winter, *Bruno Gutmann 1876–1966*, (Oxford, 1979), p. 39.

his writing. He wrote appreciatively of Karl Graul as man, churchman and missionary thinker.[7] Where Graul's theories had aroused debate and opposition, not least among those who wanted above all to emphasise the conversion of individuals, Warneck sought to achieve a resolution of this tension in his writings. By contrast to any attempt to polarise these two methods of mission, Warneck pointed to the need for individual conversions as a necessary stage towards the christianising of a whole people.[8] Like Graul, Warneck too wanted to emphasise the need to take up those aspects of the culture of a people which expressed their national life. So, he wrote, every 'natural social institution and especially the family as the foundation of the national community [*Volksgemeinschaft*] should be regulated and taken into Christian care'.[9] Mission has as its aim 'to bring the greatest possible segment of the people into the orbit of the church. This should be done in such a way that the church in every nation conveys the native traits and characteristics and sways the whole ethnic life ... the folk church [is] the school in which mankind [as] ethnic groups is brought to the discipleship of Christ'.[10]

The German term *Volk* is a difficult one to define but it is one which has carried great power and importance in German thought. Alan Bullock, in his life of Hitler, regarded it as 'a difficult term to translate: it combines the idea of nationalism and that of race (the *Volk*)'.[11] In the hands of the National Socialists of the 1930s this was to include ideas of racial purity and anti-Semitism: the German *Volk* was thought of as purely Aryan in extraction and as a *Herrenvolk*, a master race. Such ideas were entirely absent from Warneck. For Germans of his time, the inheritance of the word came from a period when French dominance of Europe at the time of Napoleon had led

---

[7] G. Warneck, *Outline of a History*, pp. 101–2.
[8] G. Warneck, *Evangelische Missionslehre*, 5 vols. (Gotha, 1897–1903), III:1, p. 245, 'every period of mission leads to the christianisation of the ethnic group ... and every period of mission begins with the conversion of individuals'.
[9] *Ibid.*, p. 271; J. C. Winter, *Gutmann*, p. 40.
[10] G. Warneck, *Missionslehre*, III:1, p. 269.
[11] A. Bullock, *Hitler: a Study in Tyranny* (London, 1952), p. 123 note 1.

German thinkers to assert the German character before there was any unified German state. J. G. Herder (1744–1803) and a stream of thought in German romanticism wanted to assert a specifically German consciousness, with radical characteristics, culture and social formation. Herder stressed that through a shared language a nation established its identity and developed its character; so the concept of *Volk* 'infinitely vaguer and at the same time much more powerful than "citizenship"'[12] was used by Herder and other German romantics to meet a need – German racial, political and cultural identity. *Volk*, like the terms *Blut* (blood) and *Boden* (earth), had powerful resonances and association in German thought: but neither in the writings of Warneck, who died in 1910, nor in the main writings considered here of Bruno Gutmann and Christian Keysser, written before 1930, were the Nazi associations of the 1930s a possible context, their chief works having gestated in their first periods of missionary service, reflections on which were published in 1925 (Gutmann) and 1926 (Keysser). As will be seen, however, a thinker like Gutmann, standing in the *Volkskirche* tradition, could use language and phraseology sufficiently similar to that used by Nazis like Alfred Rosenberg to be accused of being sympathetic to, and even ideologically supportive of, such views in the crucial German decade of the 1930s.

GERMAN MISSIONS

At the New York Conference of 1900, Dr Schreiber, Inspektor for the Rhenish Missionary Society, had described the progress of German missions during the first half of the nineteenth century. So, in addition to his references to the Moravians and the Basel Society, founded by Germans but based in Switzerland, his own Rhenish Society had worked in South Africa in

[12] D. Bosch, *Transforming Mission*, p. 299; cf. E. Jaeschke, *Bruno Gutmann: His Life, His Thoughts and His Work* (Erlangen, 1985), p. 258: Graul and others had 'determined that the object of missions must be the "nations". German romanticism and the rising national consciousness used the term "folk" with a certain glorified mystic content.'

its western areas, in the Dutch East Indies and in South China; the North German Society had worked on the west coast of Africa; the Gossner society among the Kols of Bengal; the Herrmannsburg Society on the east coast of British India and also in South Africa; and the Leipzig Society in Tranquebar, the scene of a notable visit by Karl Graul, its director, which he turned into five volumes of reflections between 1854–6.[13] This list is a reminder that, whereas the North American societies were mainly from denominational churches and English missions were either denominational or representing distinctive strands of tradition in the Church of England (SPG, CMS, UMCA), in Germany the societies were territorially based and drew missionary recruits from the regions where they were based. An important late-nineteenth-century development which brought all these societies together in conference was the creation in 1885 of the 'Ausschuss', described by one authority as the 'prototype of all national missionary councils'[14] and long pre-dating, for example, the Conference of British Missionary Societies. It became a kind of standing committee for all the societies and carried great influence and authority.

In the late nineteenth century also, the Leipzig Society began a work in modern Tanzania. German influence in East Africa had developed rapidly after the intervention of Karl Peters, an adventurer and patriot of somewhat similar stamp to Cecil Rhodes in his vision of a national destiny in Africa for his homeland. As a young man of 28, Peters had achieved German control of large areas of land in the 1880s, a political dominion hotly disputed by the Sultan of Zanzibar, who regarded the area as his own zone of influence. The Sultan had to bow, however, when Peters' initiatives were given national backing by Bismarck in 1885, made evident to the Sultan by the appearance of the German battle fleet within range of Zanzibar. Despite a revolt in 1905–6, German colonial rule, established in the 1890s, remained effective. German East Africa

---

[13] *EMC*, II, p. 413; G. Warneck, *Outline of a History*, pp. 95–106; K. Graul, *Reise nach Ost-Indien*, 5 vols. (Leipzig, 1854–6).

[14] W. R. Hogg, *Ecumenical Foundations*, p. 16, and on the cooperation between the government and the Ausschuss, p. 72. The full title of the body is 'Ausschuss der deutschen evangelischen Missionsgesellschaft'.

was to be the scene of a brilliant defensive campaign in the
1914–18 war by the German general von Lettow, admired by
his military opponents with some of the professional respect,
amounting to awe, which was later accorded to Rommel in
1939–45. After the internment of German missionaries,
German missions were further depleted in personnel under the
terms of the Treaty of Versailles. The territory then became a
British mandate of Tanganyika under a ruling of the League of
Nations. The work of the Leipzig mission, begun in 1893,
nevertheless continued in the area of Mount Kilimanjaro in the
north of the country.[15]

BRUNO GUTMANN (1876–1966)

Gutmann was born in Dresden one year later than that other
German-speaking missionary from Alsace, Albert Schweitzer,
who also went to Africa (in his case to the West Coast) and who
has remained for many, who know little else about Christian
mission, one of the heroic figures of Christian history. His work
for medical missions among Africans made a considerable
impression and is described in his book *On the Edge of the Primeval
Forest*, 1921.[16] Unlike Schweitzer, Gutmann was not the child
of the manse: his childhood had in fact been clouded by his
father's business failures and his brother's death in 1883. He
was brought up by devoted grandparents, to which circum-
stance he later related his own independence and imagination.
In the light of the last chapter, with its emphasis on North
American initiatives, it is interesting to note that the young
Gutmann's call to missionary work came through the influence
of the YMCA, a favoured leisure-time resort while he was
working as a municipal clerk after leaving school in his teens.
At 18 he applied to the Leipzig Society for admission to their

---

[15] Judith Listowel, *The Making of Tanganyika* (London, 1965), pp. 54–65; C. P.
Groves, *The Planting of Christianity in Africa*, 4 vols. (London, 1948–58), III,
pp. 15–18.

[16] Schweitzer's theological *tour de force*, published in England as *The Quest of the
Historical Jesus*, appeared in 1906. The German titles of the two books were *Von
Reimarus zu Wrede* (Tübingen, 1906; Eng. trans. London, 1910) and *Zwischen Wasser
und Urwald* (Berne, 1921; Eng. trans. London, 1922). His surrender of a brilliant
academic career and acclaim as a musician and interpreter of J. S. Bach to work in
Africa in 1913 was widely admired.

missionary seminary, which he entered in 1895. As a student there he came under the influence of an anthropologist called Wilhelm Wundt (1832–1920). Wundt wrote on the psychology of peoples (*Volkspsychologie*) and Gutmann was to revert to these theories later in life. Another intellectual influence for Gutmann was a professor of social history, W. H. Riehl, described as a contributor to the 'typical German myth of the *Volk*'.[17] In terms of mission theory, Gutmann was indebted to Karl Graul, director of the same society to which Gutmann belonged: Graul's visit to India and his meeting with the problems of caste had caused him to conclude that it was through and in the church and its life that national character-istics could be purified, but only if the church was 'completely attuned to the people and deeply rooted among the people'.[18] It may have been through Graul's writing on India that Gutmann had first looked in that direction for his missionary service, to which end he had studied Sanskrit; but, in a quix-otic gesture to help a fellow student assigned to Africa which, the man held, his fiancée would find unhealthy, Gutmann accepted relocation. He arrived in East Africa in August 1902.

Gutmann joined the Leipzig Mission's work among the Chagga people. Between 1902 and 1920 he studied this people, their language, customs, proverbs, social structures and tribal society as a whole, with great thoroughness. He gained a considerable reputation as an anthropologist because of his understanding of Bantu society as exemplified in this people by way of his writings, which were extensive and on all aspects of Chagga life.[19] He remained a missionary, however, and in further books he described his understanding of Christian mission in a way which sought to combine anthropological insight with a highly individual missionary vision. Chief of these books was *Gemeindeaufbau aus dem Evangelium* (Structuring

[17] J. C. Winter, *Gutmann*, pp. 31–7; E. Jaeschke *Bruno Gutmann*, pp. 5–10; for Wundt, *RGG*, v, p. 2053.
[18] E. Jaeschke, *Bruno Gutmann*, p. 9.
[19] They were *Dichten und Denken der Dschagganeger* (1909), *Volksbuch der Wadschagga* (1914), *Das Recht der Dschagga* (1926); and later a three-volume work, *Die Stamme-slehren der Dschagga* (Tribal Teachings) (1932–7).

the Congregation on the Basis of the Gospel): the sub-title included a reference to the home church, by which he indicated that he believed that he had found principles for church life which had an equal application to the Lutheran Church at home as to the conditions of the mission field. It has to be said that this book is often exceedingly opaque, and German scholars have complained of Gutmann's writing, which can be highly metaphorical, poetic and involved. Nevertheless, the main lines of his thought, reiterated as they are again and again, can be discerned despite the obstacles to comprehension in his style and expression.

Basic to tribal society, as Gutmann observed it, were what he called the 'primal ties' ('urtümliche Bindungen'). Family, in its extended African form, age groups (especially those associated with puberty in tribal life, known among the Chagga as 'shield groups', because of the value of loyalty in battle among young men) elders, neighbourhood, clan and tribe formed a network of relationships which was fundamental to all forms of life. Gutmann discovered early on what other later commentators have expressed: in African society 'I am, because I participate' (J. V. Taylor) or 'I am, because we are' (John Mbiti).[20] In his own phrase, 'what you are, you are only through connectedness'.[21] Such primal bonds and groupings are part of the creation. Because they are God-given, they are to be fostered and strengthened. Along with this perception of society, Gutmann believed in a kind of vitalism, whereby society was built up by its living cells of life. The church, like primal society itself, was a source of such vitality. The missionary's aim should be so to integrate church and society that the God-given and God-sustained social relationships and cellular life should be re-vitalised by the life of Christ. So, he wrote, the primal bonds between people are from God and provide the 'body cells' for the building of the life of Christ; one might say that they provide the basic building-blocks for the congregational life.

---

[20] Gutmann, *Gemeindeaufbau* (Leipzig, 1925), p. 7; J. V. Taylor, *The Primal Vision* (London, 1961), pp. 50, 65, 117–21; J. Mbiti, *African Religion and Philosophy* (London, 1969), pp. 108–9.
[21] Gutmann, *Gemeindeaufbau*, p. 15 and see p. 145.

This made Gutmann the sworn enemy of individualism as mediated by Europeans and with it the cult of individual personality. As a strongly Lutheran churchman and admirer of Luther, he believed that Luther had been radically misunderstood as the apostle of the individual. By contrast, in Gutmann's view of Luther in the struggle with the Roman Catholic church, Luther had stood for the relationship between a people (he means the German people) and the gospel. Luther was not one to forget the corporate aspect of Christian faith: his emphasis on the organic bonding of a people, who must be prepared to suffer and fight as a *Volk*, showed that this was the case.[22] With Warneck, Gutmann recognised that the winning of individuals was necessary, but in order to build a Christian community.[23]

This in turn should provide a bridge to the whole of a people, so that individual repentance and faith should lead to the creation of a godly community, which would provide the groundwork, by being rooted in the gospel, for the whole society and its transformed consciousness. To this end, Gutmann took over the tribal understandings of eldership and used them as a structure for the church's community life. Elders settled quarrels, led acts of worship, cared for the sick and dying and took responsibility for the community's life by meeting in council, as tribal elders also did.[24] The community needed to discover its own powers of corporate life over against another power in its midst, the intellectual individualism of the white man, whose Western, even seminarian, learning could set him over against the community spirit and its primal bonds.[25]

If Gutmann was the sworn enemy of Western individualism, he was equally severe on what he termed 'civilisation', what might be characterised as the whole Western cultural package, with its corrosive effects on traditional cultures. Such 'civilisation' deals either with people as individuals only, with the

---

[22] *Ibid.*, p. 17; on the cult of personality in the West, p. 152; on the misunderstanding of Luther, p. 174.
[23] *Ibid.*, p. 115.   [24] *Ibid.*, p. 120.   [25] *Ibid.*, pp. 121-9.

destructive effects described already, or in the mass. Westerners have discerned too late that to be free of the primal bonds
of primitive society is to be part of the doomed situation of a
soul-less 'civilisation'.[26] Gutmann saw it as the special task of
the German Lutheran mission to renew the irreplaceable
social organisms of African life. Both Scots missions and
American missions in Africa were seen by him as stronger at
certain points; but this calling to the renewal of tribal life was
to be the special work of the Lutheran church in Africa.[27]

To anticipate at this point criticisms aimed later at
Gutmann, not least by Karl Barth in the 1930s and again by
Johannes Hoekendijk in the 1940s, there can be no gainsaying
that his mission theory laid heavy emphasis on creation and
God's activity already present in communal life, not least
through the 'primal ties'. In this context, he did indeed use
what later became danger words, *Blut* and *Boden*. The first
pointed to the all-important place of kinship in African life, its
understandings of the responsibilities of the wider family, often
carefully defined in respect of certain particular relationships;
in the case of the earth, not only was it stressed as the essential
basis for the life of an agricultural people, but also for its connection with the ancestors who had gone before and were
understood still as part of the communal life of the tribal
society. *Blut*, *Boden*, *Alten* (elders) were fundamental to tribal
life, which then expressed itself in the wider network of
relationships in the neighbourhood (that is, where neighbour-
_____ and to be experienced), the 'age sets', the
_____. Far from breaking down such a carefully
_____ unity, the church's life and message should
_____ nding already given by God, protecting the
_____ m individualism and the onset of a materia-
_____ The need was to infuse fresh life into the exist-
_____ sms with the church's own cells of vitality,
_____ ewness and power springing from Christ

_____ ssary to return to Gutmann's critics. First we

Ibid., p. 147. See p. 146 for Scots and Americans.

must turn to his fellow missionary and thinker, Christian Keysser.

CHRISTIAN KEYSSER (1877–1961)

Where Gutmann had a farming background, Keysser was the son of a forester in Bavaria. He too joined a German missionary society, the Neuendettelsau Mission, and trained at its institute. This mission had a work on the north coast of New Guinea, pioneered by Johannes Flierl (1858–1947), a man of remarkable courage and steadfastness, who had encouraged the mission to allow him to enter an untouched area, by then formally part of the German colony of north-east New Guinea. As the Papuans were unfamiliar with white men, had head-hunting tribes and many recorded instances of cannibalism in their recent history, Flierl's bravery in landing and establishing himself at Finschafen in 1885 on the north coast of New Guinea was beyond question. In 1892 he established a mission station at Sattelberg among the Kate people and it was to this station that Keysser came in 1899, the year of the first baptisms among this tribe.[28]

Something of the pre-Christian savagery of these tribes (and the courage of the first European evangelists) is indicated by the pre-baptismal confessions at a later date. Among 259 adults, there were confessions of 867 murders (more than 400 of them by four individuals). Cannibalism was considered a duty upon all in order to restore the 'life force' of the people.[29] It was hardly surprising that Flierl and Keysser and their missionary colleagues found themselves confronted by a society dominated by fear, both of the unseen spirit world and the power of the sorcerer to will anyone to death; and also of the ever-present danger of revenge killings.

Keysser did not aspire, as Gutmann had, to the role of scientific anthropologist, but he was a very perceptive observer

[28] J. Flierl, *Christ in New Guinea* (Tanunda, South Australia, 1932); H. Wagner and H. Reiner (eds.) *The Lutheran Church in New Guinea: the First 100 years 1886–1986* (Adelaide, 1986), pp. 31–41; *RGG* III, p. 1263.
[29] G. Vicedom, *The Church in New Guinea*, (London, 1961), p. 9.

of Papuan life with an imaginative and intuitive understanding of their world-view and an extraordinary flair for communication, both to tribal culture and to the reading public at home in Germany after his return in 1920. His book *Anutu im Papuagemeinde*, published in 1926, gave a vivid account of his experiences among the Kate and Hube people, backed up by photographs, on a year-by-year basis between 1901 and 1920. 'Anutu' was the name used by the missionaries for the God whom they proclaimed. With Keysser we are in a very different literary genre from Gutmann's, for Keysser was accessible to the general reader, with an eye for description comparable to St Luke's: here we meet a tribal chieftain, Sane; a Papuan friend of Keysser's called Zake, whose help was needed to deal with the problems of the sorcerers; and a young catechumen called Jakabanga, whose name translated delightfully as 'sweet potato mountain'. It was a world, like Luke's, of dreams, earthquakes and magicians. Keysser is a master, in the style of Bede, the great historian of the English missions of the sixth and seventh centuries, of the setpiece description, as in the festival gathering called by him and Zake in 1903, where, after a whole night of festivity, he was in a position, by tribal custom, to speak a decisive word against the sorcerers, leading to fireside confessions and changes of heart.[30] Such an occasion was 'echt papuanisch' (truly Papuan). It showed the master missionary at work, with the same remarkable insight into the ways of the culture as in a later incident when, after two weeks of 'palaver', the tribal mind was expressed by the dragging of a tree stump (representing the old ways) to the side of a precipice, and its corporate heaving over into oblivion as the symbolic ending of the past;[31] or, again, when he demonstrated to a group around the fire that they were running away from the

---

[30] Keysser, *Anutu im Papuagemeinde* (Nuremberg, 1926), pp. 27–9; Vicedom, *New Guinea*, pp. 17–18; on Keysser's 'magical' effect on the German public as a writer about the New Guinea mission see H. Fontius, *Mission, Gemeinde, Kirche* (Erlangen, 1975), p. 114 n. 341.

[31] Keysser, *A People Reborn* (Pasadena, 1980) pp. 8–9 (the German title of the original was *Eine Papuagemeinde*).

Christian faith by snatching a burning brand and running off with it,[32] so destroying the fire.

Nevertheless, whatever differences there may have been over literary approach or anthropological expertise, Keysser produced many of the same insights as Gutmann into tribal society. He, too, realised the weakness of a Western individual approach to a people of this kind. He noted in *Anutu* that the early baptisms of 1904 did not result in a 'forward movement for the whole *Volk*' and that what was needed was 'to grasp the *Volk* as a whole'. Even repulsive relationships, which he found some of them to be, were still relationships and the aim must be for the whole group to turn.[33] Eventually, his faith and zeal were rewarded by such a corporate movement. This remained 'completely prosaic', with little of the accompaniments of a religious revival, but it was real enough: the important part of the response was 'we are all together'.[34] In a celebrated case of 1914, Jakabanga was refused baptism, although considered by Keysser as fully ready for it, because the assembly of Christian elders, which Keysser had brought into being, over-ruled him: the catechumen must prove himself by going back to his own people and persuading them to receive baptism also: if not, his position would be too vulnerable as a lone Christian. Jesus, it was said, must not appear as the destroyer of family solidarity or the destroyer of the *Volk*.[35] In due course, on Keysser's account, the baptism of this man and another made a very great impression and was used as a demonstration for the end of heathenism in the whole tribe. Challenged to own this decision, the same acted demonstration of taking brands from the fire was employed as a willing demonstration of the whole *Volk*,[36] accompanied by a kind of 'Amen': 'Oong – yes, so it is';[37] 'the old heathen fire is extinguished. Anutu will kindle a new one.' Hube baptisms were 7 in 1905, 110 in 1908 but 1,000 in 1918, evidence, regardless of differing views on the delay of

[32] *Ibid.*, pp. 70–1.   [33] Keysser, *Anutu*, pp. 31ff.   [34] *Ibid.*, pp. 48–9.
[35] *Ibid.*, pp. 133–4.
[36] *Ibid.*, p. 142.   [37] *Ibid.*, p. 143.

baptisms, that Keysser's search for a corporate response was rewarded.[38]

Keysser laid great emphasis on the corporate life of the congregation, not only for worship but for discipline. The whole clan was included in the congregational meetings, which were 'a necessary organ of congregational life'. Like Gutmann, Keysser called Luther in aid as an authority for a corporate approach. It was, after all, the congregation as a body which chose bishops in Luther's understanding and who together resolved hard cases (Matt. 18:19ff) and gave the final judgement. The Sattelberg congregation 'is a tribal congregation': in this respect it was set over against any understanding of church life as a 'little flock' of the saved.[39] In a comment on the revival movement, which happened after he had left the field, he described how the people had felt and expressed a corporate responsibility for their wrong-doing and added 'everything in our European individualism is so entirely different'.[40] He discerned a corporate, congregational soul, as there was a family or national soul: it was of great importance to treat the congregation as an organic unit, for which indigenous elders must be made fully responsible and for which the congregational meeting was 'absolutely indispensable'. On the subject of addressing a whole people, he was able to call on the testimony of Johannes Warneck, son of the missiologist, who had worked among the Bataks of Sumatra in the footsteps of the great German nineteenth-century pioneer, Ludwig Nommensen. On the question of 'christianising' over against 'individual conversions', Johannes Warneck judged that 'history has answered the question decisively. Modern missions in the beginning rejected this goal ... but the hesitations did not stop the course of history. The development was in the direction of people-christianising' regardless of such objections.[41] For Keysser, 'the folk church or tribal church is the goal of mission endeavour as pursued by Lutherans and as distinguished from the pietistic

---

[38] *Ibid.*, p. 143; p. 75 for baptism details.
[39] Keysser, *A People Reborn*, pp. 54, 195, 213.
[40] *Ibid.*, p. 217.   [41] Quoted in *ibid.*, pp. 24–5.

goal of soul-winning. The goal of the folk or people church does not exclude soul-winning but includes it. Do not consider the folk or people church as evil but as being the will of God (see the Great Commission) and a vital necessity'.[42]

Keysser's missionary career was to end tragically. Like other missionaries during the First World War he had taken an oath to the new Australian administration in New Guinea that he would not assist compatriots who were combatants. He adhered to this: but when a fugitive German officer appealed to him for essential medicines and food he gave humanitarian aid. This was discovered by the authorities and Keysser was not only repatriated in 1920 but forbidden to return. Like Gutmann, Keysser's theories had been disputed in the field: Gutmann's colleague, J. Raum, had disputed his theories in the Leipzig mission, debates which may well be reflected in his son Otto Raum's account of Gutmann in an article in the *IRM* of 1937.[43] Keysser's theories, and disputes about them, reached something of a crux at the time of Inspektor Steck's visit to New Guinea for the Neuendettelsau Mission. The debate was compared by one missionary to that in Acts 15 (the Council of Jerusalem); and, if anything, the fact that Steck put his weight behind Keysser's methods and their missionary flexibility to the prevailing cultural norms simply intensified the struggle in 1915–16 and after. Perhaps the final comment on Keysser's career may be given in a quotation from a fine historical essay on the early New Guinea mission:

his missionary pioneering was marked by . . . extraordinary sensitivity towards Melanesian culture; and so was his concept of building up a living Christian congregation in a genuine New Guinean setting. Even Senior Flierl thought he had to defend himself against Steck and Keysser. The outcome of the long drawn out and often exaggerated discussion, however, is [that] since 1928, where new Neuendettelsau staff have come to New Guinea [his] guidelines for mission work and congregational organisation had been accepted as the 'Neuendettelsau approach'; for all missionaries sent out by Neuendettelsau since World War I were students of Keysser at the Missionary Seminary. In this way Keysser's experiences and insights

[42] *Ibid.*, p. 304.   [43] *IRM* vol. 26, no. 104 (October 1937), pp. 500–7.

continued to bear fruit in the New Guinea Mission even though the Australian administration refused to let him return to his former field of work.[44]

THE THEOLOGICAL DEBATE: KARL BARTH AND THE 1930s

It is of importance to remember the historical background in Germany to which both Gutmann and Keysser returned in 1920; and, with this, the theological context which turned Karl Barth into a critic of Gutmann in the 1930s. Hitler's attempt at a *putsch* in Munich failed in 1923 and at this stage the Nazis were still a comparatively negligible force politically: but he was to play with increasing success on the theme of the terms of the Treaty of Versailles, under which many in Germany were still smarting. Karl Barth moved from the parish of Safenwil in Switzerland, where he had written the famous commentary on the Epistle to the Romans (the first blast of the new dialectical or crisis theology), in 1921, to be a professor of theology in Germany, first at Göttingen and Münster (1921–30) and then at Bonn. Barth admitted that at first he had been unable to take the Nazis seriously but before long he realised that the church in Germany was engaged in a life and death struggle with a neo-paganism, all the more dangerous because many churchmen seemed unaware of the issues at stake. This was the time of the rise of the 'German Christians', who identified with the nationalism of the Nazis under Reichsbischof Müller, who was given full powers over the church's affairs by Hitler in April 1933: it was also the time of the resistance to this mood by the 'Confessing Christians', to whom Barth became the most formidable theological leader and resource.

This was the context, in the words of his biographer, in which Barth challenged Christians to say farewell finally 'to all and every kind of natural theology and to dare to trust only in

---

[44] H. Wagner, 'Beginnings at Finschafen' in *The Lutheran Church in New Guinea*, pp. 31–98, quotation from p. 74. One missionary described Steck's backing of Keysser's methods as a 'bomb' in its effects on the fraternity: see H. Fontius, *Mission, Gemeinde, Kirche*, p. 96.

the God who has revealed himself in Jesus Christ'.[45] This
rejection of natural theology and its capacity to draw on the
created order for reflection on God was both a theological
bulwark against the Nazi doctrines of *Volk, Blut, Boden* and of
any understanding of God-given racial purity by way of 'orders
of creation', which could lead directly to anti-Semitism; and
also meant, inevitably, that Barth must look askance at Gutmann's views of mission, which leaned so heavily on the God-
givenness of the 'primal ties' and the need to strengthen them
through the gospel. Indeed, Gutmann used the term which
Barth so vehemently repudiated in his dispute with Brunner,
the 'point of contact' (*Anknüpfungspunkt*) between the created
order and the gospel message. God Himself, alone, by the
direct activity of the Holy Spirit, could provide such a point of
contact: and to take any other view, even so marginally different as Brunner's (as an outsider might view it) was to open the
door to all the errors of the day. Barth's only response could be
Nein!

Ernst Jaeschke, who followed Gutmann as a missionary at
Kilimanjaro and became something of a disciple, expositor and
advocate of his missiology and *praxis*, has pointed out, with
justice, that it was tragic that Barth and others so misunderstood the great missionary. For Gutmann, the primal ties were
'containers, the soil in which the Spirit of God works: then the
individual can become part of the body of Christ', but he
realised that the 'ties have to be redeemed and sanctified in
Christ': that is, there is an element of newness and of in-
breaking of the life of Christ, the very thing for which Barth
was contending. Indeed, Gutmann can use the phrase 'ganz
anders' (quite other, different) of this new life. To Barth,
however, both in a public lecture[46] and in *Zwischen den Zeiten*,
his journal used in part to stiffen the theological resolve of the

---

[45] E. Busch, *Karl Barth* (London, 1976), p. 224, see p. 190 for Barth's early view of the
Nazis as 'absurd'.
[46] Bosch, *Witness to the World*, p. 166. The lecture was to the Brandenburg Missionary
Conference in 1932; for Gutmann's use of the term 'ganz anders', see *Gemeindeaufbau*,
p. 46 and compare p. 64; p. 159 for 'Anknüpfungspunkt'. *Nein!* was the title of
Barth's response to Emil Brunner.

Christians in Germany in the 1930s, the issue was clear: 'does not the truly prolific Gutmann literature sound all the way through like a single variation of the seductive song of the serpent: *gratia non tollit supponit et perficit naturam* (grace does not overthrow but completes and perfects nature)'.[47] In fact, as Jaeschke argued, both were engaged in parallel tasks, which revolved round the same axis: how is the Lordship of Christ to be asserted in a society which is apart from him?

The church at home was engaged in conflict against the theological misunderstanding of the 'basic social orders', which confronted Gutmann in quite a different context among the Chagga – namely, in ... preparing for the new being in Christ. A church which had to call upon its ultimate resources to resist inch by inch the challenge of the syncretistic commingling of gospel and national myth could not in such an extremity give ear to ... the missionary who not only had interest for the primal ties but even found them relevant for his missionary task. If Karl Barth saw in Gutmann's contribution 'that ancient serpent' rearing its head, it was a carry-over of his own experience with a heretic and degenerate nationalism ... As a matter of fact both were engaged on the same front, except that they fought in opposite directions. How can Christ become also Lord of the nation ...? For Gutmann the answer was: Christ assumes Lord-ship over the 'primal ties' not by destroying them, replacing them or ignoring them, but by converting them and receiving them into the new reality of his body.[48]

Jaeschke was himself one of the Confessing Christians,[49] for whom Barth's theology did so much under the intense pressures of the period to clarify that 'the fellowship of those belonging to the church is not determined by blood, therefore not by race but by the Holy Spirit and baptism': a quotation which continues with explicit reference to the Jewish question: 'if the German Evangelical Church excludes Jewish Christians, or treats them as of a lower grade, she ceases to be a Christian church'.[50] Jaeschke stated categorically, on the basis of his own

[47] Barth in *Zwischen den Zeiten*, vol. 10, no. 3 (1932), pp. 211–12.
[48] Jaeschke, *Bruno Gutmann*, pp. 244–5.
[49] *Ibid.*, p. 311.
[50] Barth in the *Round Table* of 1934, vol. 24 (Dec. 1933 – Sept. 1934), pp. 326–7; one may compare the words of the Barmen Declaration of the same year in J. H. Leith,

knowledge of Gutmann in personal friendship, that he had no love for the Nazis. They spoke together at the time of Hitler's ruthless liquidation of Roehm, Hitler's chief henchman in the 1920s, which signalled for those who could see that the constitutional government, to which Hitler had acceded in 1933, was subject to total disregard now the Nazis held power. Gutmann had expressed distress then and had never been a Nazi.[51] The sad truth was that the terms which occurred in Gutmann's writings had been filled with a new and sinister content. His friend was also able to recall Gutmann's vigorous defence of his ideas before a large gathering of Barthian-inspired church and mission leaders at Halle in the early 1930s, when he faced the violence of his critics 'like an erupting volcano', but speaking with clarity, as well as force, in his own defence.[52]

Still, the theological issue remained a real and pressing one, having to do with the relationship of nature and grace. Barth here and elsewhere was to dismiss nature and with it, as will become clear in the work of those who followed him in the next chapters, natural religion as a *locus* for the presence of God. Gutmann saw God present in tribal relationships, indeed in all relationships, as the title of one of his books, *Gott zwischen uns* (God Between Us) indicated. God was in the bonds which bound human society together. This was as true in the church as it was in the pre-Christian society. Later authorities than Barth were to give Gutmann credit for this emphasis as legitimate and missiologically appropriate to the context of African life:

if nature and grace cannot simply be separated, then Gutmann was correct when he related the gospel to the religion of his Chagga and did not simply disregard it. Their communal forms and associations are implied in their religion ... perhaps his terminology may be unacceptable to us ... and his theology may later have been appro-

Creeds of the Churches (Oxford, 1973), pp. 517–22; also Barth's book on the German Christians issue of 1933, *Theological Existence To-day* (Munich, 1933), pp. 51–2.

[51] Jaeschke, *Bruno Gutmann*, pp. 310–16.

[52] *Ibid.*, pp. 25–6. Jaeschke recalls Gutmann as having infinite patience with Africans. The reference to a volcano, as the African mothers warning about him (as a young missionary), 'the leopard is coming', indicates that he was a rare blend of severity and kindness.

priated by others in the service of their 'German Christian' heresies. It nevertheless remains to Gutmann's credit that he thought through theologically the confrontations of the gospel with the African communal associations ... It was Gutmann's fate that his work became a victim of the theological *Zeitgeist*. When the smoke from the ruins of the 'folk-faith' are finally dissipated the debate ... [can] again be resumed with profit ... for theology as well as for missiology.[53]

GUTMANN AND KEYSSER APPRAISED SINCE BARTH

Gutmann had succeeded 'with forceful single-mindedness' in isolating this one problem 'the use of the indigenous structures for the building of a national church', the question which 'from the time of Karl Graul until the Second World War was the ... centre of the German idea of *Volkskirche*'.[54] The debate did not end with Barth or with 1945. Other critics in the 1920s and 1930s asked if Gutmann wanted to ignore the fallenness of humanity; others if the Cross (and so redemption) was no longer central in his version of Lutheranism; and whether, in another case, he had not heard the Lord of the gospel-sayings cut through all family relationships to build his church?[55] Was this emphasis on blood ties legitimate when discipleship included 'hating' one's father and mother?

After 1945, Johannes Hoekendijk, who had experienced the Nazi occupation of Holland during the war, published an important missiological study in which the whole *Volkskirche* approach was subjected to extensive scrutiny.[56] Here, Gutmann was held to have misunderstood Christ's command to disciple 'all people' (Greek: *panta ta ethnē*): this was not a reference to tribal societies but to the whole inhabited world

[53] H. Burkle, quoted by Jaeschke, *Bruno Gutmann*, pp. 373–4, from *Missionstheologie* (Stuttgart, 1979), p. 67.

[54] P. Beyerhaus, *Die Selbständigkeit der jungen Kirchen als missionarisches Problem*, (Uppsala, 1956), pp. 88ff.

[55] Roehl in *IRM*, 15, no. 59 (1926), pp. 601–2; Kellerhals in *EMM*, 79, no. 4 (April 1935), pp. 117–24; and Nitsch, cited in Jaeschke, *Bruno Gutmann*, p. 234.

[56] J. Hoekendijk, *Kirche und Volk in der deutscher Missionswissenschaft* (Munich, 1967): see sections on Gutmann (pp. 130–77) and Keysser (pp. 177–208). This is the German edition of the book originally published in Dutch as *Kerk en Volk in de Dvitse Zendingswetenschap*.

(Greek: *oikoumenē*).[57] Gutmann had read his *volksorganisch* views (organic views of peoples) into the Bible rather than out of it.[58] He had ended up by 'socialising' the gospel and Christian faith and so losing the heart of both in his concern with society. Hoekendijk recalled the story of Esau and Jacob and asked: 'has Gutmann traded his birthright for a bowl of cultural-philosophical lentils?'.[59] In writing of Keysser, Hoekendijk was able to point out that Keysser had admired the Nazi emphasis on *Volk*, over against individualism. This fitted with Keysser's later advocacy of the collectivist nature of much of the Old Testament, which he wanted to see reflected in both mission field and home church and nation. Keysser had named Hitler as a fellow fighter in this respect in 1933 and had given a welcome to the Nazi ascendancy in 1934: 'heute regiert, Gott sei dank, der National-socialismus' (today, thank God, National Socialism rules). Emil Brunner had pointed to a common collectivism of appeal between the mission in New Guinea and National Socialism.[60] Despite all this probing of the two greatest practitioners of the approach, Hoekendijk concluded: 'so long as the approach is treated as one of the possibilities [of mission] there is nothing sinful in talking about *Volkskirche*'.[61]

Some have judged that the whole approach was overtaken by history. So, it was argued, Gutmann's hated 'civilisation' was bound to advance and the approach would become outmoded.[62] Of course there is truth in this position. Edwin Smith in the 1920s and J. V. Taylor after 1945 saw it to be so.[63] Nevertheless, this chapter should close with reflections which show that this approach, in terms of its emphasis on community and communal relationships, is still valid: first, as the

[57] *Ibid.*, pp. 157–8.   [58] *Ibid.*, p. 175.   [59] *Ibid.*, p. 188.
[60] *Ibid.*, p. 159.
[61] *Ibid.*, p. 280. See J. Verkuyl, *Contemporary Missiology: an Introduction* (Grand Rapids, 1978), p. 51, on Hoekendijk and the whole cluster of ideas round *Volkstumideologie*.
[62] H. W. Gensichen, *Glaube für die Welt* (Gütersloh, 1971), p. 146; Jaeschke, *Bruno Gutmann*, pp. 384–7.
[63] J. V. Taylor, *The Primal Vision*, p. 112. 'Urbanization and a cash economy have smashed the intricate balance of dependence ...'

writings of Vincent Donovan have shown, in tribal societies the communal approach is still a necessity: wisely Donovan approached communities with thoughts of baptism and then, like Keysser, left them to think over the implications communally. Their response became 'either you baptise us all or none' in at least one instance.[64] Such an approach is still required in areas of Africa, as Bishop David Gitari of Kenya suggested to the 1988 Lambeth Conference of Anglican bishops.[65] Secondly, in responding to the frequently levelled criticism that individual conversion was insufficiently stressed in the approach, it is interesting to find a conservative evangelical like Donald McGavran, who is not likely to underplay conversion, writing in the preface to the English translation of Keysser's book *Eine Papuagemeinde (A People Reborn)* that 'the discovery ... that group decisions, which preserved the corporate life of the society and enabled men and women to become Christians without social dislocation, was the route by which most humans have moved to Christian faith and *was a good route*'.[66] McGavran also noted rightly that Gutmann and Keysser were shaken on their return to Germany to find a lack of congregational responsibility.[67] That such a corporate approach to mission is not to be confined to tribal societies has been shown in the so-called advanced societies: to give one example, Bishop David Sheppard and his fellow worker George Burton found that in working among unchurched youth in the conditions obtaining in south London in the 1950s and 1960s, group decisions rather than individual

[64] Vincent Donovan, *Christianity Re-discovered* (Indiana, 1978), pp. 91–3.
[65] D. Gitari, essay in C. Wright and C. Sugden, (eds.), *One Gospel, Many Clothes* (Oxford, 1990), pp. 60–70, originally a paper delivered to the Lambeth Conference of 1988. Note the quotation from J. I. Packer at p. 69, note 2: 'An atomic individualism, really a product of European rationalism and romanticism two centuries ago, has crept into our thinking about individuals before God, making us unable, it seems, to take seriously the family ... national and Adamic solidarities which scripture affirms as part of the created order ... which the so-called "primitive" mind grasps so much better than most of us'.
[66] D. McGavran in his preface to Keysser, *A People Reborn*, p. xii: see also pp. xiii, xiv, xx, xxi.
[67] *Ibid.*, pp. xii–xxii.

conversions were a necessary process if Christianisation was to be achieved.[68] Finally if Gutmann, in particular, who was in the field long after Keysser, is to be judged on the dominical principle of 'by their fruits you shall know them', the Moshi mission, main site of his labours among the Chagga, showed remarkable growth, and increase of 450 per cent between 1919 and 1959, which Jaeschke justly calls 'a vindication of Leipzig mission work and of Bruno Gutmann's part in it'[69] and this despite the Moshi congregation being more subject to the influence of 'civilisation' than any of the surrounding congregations of Kilimanjaro.[70] If, in cross-cultural mission, the essence of the missionary task is flexibility and sensitivity to context, perhaps the lesson of Gutmann and Keysser to modern mission is, as Hoekendijk suggested, that so long as this approach is not exalted as the only way, it has a true and lasting validity, for human beings will always live in community and in relationships, in neighbourhoods and extended social settings, with structures which can be penetrated and employed in the propagation of the gospel and the building of Christian community. In conditions as widespread as those in Moshi in Tanzania, Sattelberg in New Guinea, and in Kenya among the nomadic people like the Maasai, as well as Canning Town in south London, there will be times when the approach to the group is very much more productive than an individualism which ignores the social contexts to which the gospel is addressed.

68 D. S. Sheppard, *Parson's Pitch* (London, 1964), pp. 183–4, and see also his *Built as a City* (London, 1974); G. Burton, *People Matter More than Things* (London, 1965), pp. 79ff.
69 Jaeschke, *Bruno Gutmann*, pp. 346–8.   70 *Ibid.*, pp. 236–7.

CHAPTER 3

Mission appraised (1): 1920–1940

It should occasion no surprise that, in the two decades which
followed the First World War, missionary work, along with
many other aspects of Western life and culture, should have
been subjected to extreme and searching scrutiny. In so far as
the canvas now becomes the world setting for an increasingly
universal phenomenon, Christian world mission in every continent, it is important to be reminded of the world of 1920–40.
The Russian Revolution of 1917 had launched on the world a
vigorous competitor for Christian mission and the presence of a
trained Communist revolutionary like Borodin in China in the
period was a reminder that Russian Communist tentacles
stretched into the Orient. Lenin died in 1924, but for the
Russian people, already the recipients of political terror post-
1917, his death served only to usher in the régime of Stalin,
whose efforts at social reconstruction have been estimated to
have cost the rural population of the then USSR some 10
million deaths by famine or 'elimination' of peasant farmers. In
the late 1920s, Hitler became a growing force until his access to
power in 1933 and the neo-pagan doctrines, already noted, in
due course were to issue in the horror of the Holocaust, in
which 6 million Jews were to die. Against this backcloth of the
dictators, to whom Mussolini must be added as a less evil but
powerful enough figure to absorb the ancient Christian
kingdom of Abyssinia (Ethiopia) in 1935, Christian missionary
leaders became aware of pressures upon the church, upon the
Jewish people (a special branch of the International Missionary Council tried hard to alleviate the effects of anti-
Semitism), upon funding after the Wall Street Crash of 1929

57

and upon missionaries in the field. This was true, for example, through Communist-inspired riots in China in the 1920s, when some missionaries lost their lives. If the Christian mission was a light to the nations, it was a light shining in profound darkness in the early twentieth century.

In chapters 3 and 4, while returning to the mainly Anglo-Saxon stream of mission, which continued after the Edinburgh Conference of 1910 under the leadership of men like J. R. Mott and J. H. Oldham, the emphasis will be, first, on the general appraisal of mission, covered in this chapter; and in the next, with special focus on the relationship to the other great faiths of Hinduism, Islam, Buddhism and Confucianism as reflected in the missionary movement. Each chapter, as each decade, will examine one of the great world missionary conferences which followed Edinburgh, the conference at Jerusalem in 1928 and the one planned for Hangchow (Hangzhou), but, because of conditions of war between China and Japan, held eventually at Tambaram, Madras, in 1938. An invaluable source for the period can be found in the *International Review of Missions*, begun in 1912, whose first editor was J. H. Oldham (from 1912 to 1927), followed by William Paton (editor 1927–1943). Paton had served as missionary secretary of the SCM, worked with the YMCA in India and acted as the first secretary of the National Christian Council of India, Burma and Ceylon from 1922–7. Mott was to say of the *IRM* at the Jerusalem Conference:

cooperation among those of different nationalities and races invari-ably results in stimulating one another to good and better intellectual works. Every number ... is an illustration of this fact. This scholarly journal, going as it does to thousands of the most thoughtful persons in all parts of the world, makes available to all some of the most fruitful and constructive work of thinkers and scholars who otherwise might be comparatively isolated.'[1]

Oldham's editorship, conducted often under great difficulties, deserved no less a meed of praise than this: by 1928 he had

---

[1] *International Missionary Council, Jerusalem Report*, 8 vols. (London, 1928) (hereafter *IMC/J*) vol. VII, p. 5.

made the *IRM* essential reading for all who reflected on world mission and had managed to involve Americans, Germans, Scandinavians, French, British and Dutch alongside contributors from the 'young churches', Chinese, Indians, Japanese, Africans. Beyond his influence at Edinburgh, it was a further remarkable achievement by a remarkable figure.

Finally, a major part of this chapter will be devoted to what became the most extensive enquiry ever made into the Christian mission by Protestants, the Laymen's Foreign Missions Inquiry of 1930–2.[2] Here the concentration was on the great nations of the Orient, Christian missionary institutions, personnel and overall impact in China, India (with Burma) and Japan. A large quantity of data was accumulated on every aspect of missionary endeavour, educational, medical, evangelistic, agricultural. The enquiry also revealed growing theological tensions, not least in China, between the conservative and liberal wings, the kind of debate which, for one example in a 'sending' country, had resulted in England in the split between the CMS and what became the Bible Churchmen's Missionary Society in 1922.[3] Differing views on the Bible and its authority led to divisions not only at home but in the field, so that a firmly conservative body like the CIM, the largest protestant missionary force in China, decided to withdraw from the NCC of China in the 1920s, one of the national councils which had resulted from Mott's world tours after Edinburgh.

ALLEN AND FLEMING

Before turning to the Jerusalem Conference of 1928 and the Laymen's Foreign Mission Inquiry (LFMI) which followed it, two writers and thinkers who carefully scrutinised current mission practice deserve notice. The first of these was Roland

---

[2] A single-volume digest was produced as *Rethinking Missions*, ed. Hocking (New York, 1933): subsequently a Supplementary Series (7 vols.) was published in New York, 1933.

[3] See G. H. G. Hewitt, *The Problems of Success: a History of the Church Missionary Society 1910 – 1942* (London, 1971), vol. I, pp. 461–73.

Allen (1868–1947), the son of an English clergyman. His father
had died when serving as a chaplain in Belize (then British
Honduras).[4] Whether or not influenced by his father's overseas
service, Allen offered himself to the SPG and served in North
China for eight years (1895–1903), during which time he
experienced the violence of the Boxer Rising of 1900 from the
comparative safety of the British Legation in Peking (Beijing),
to which he was chaplain and about which he wrote his first
book, *The Siege of the Peking Legations*, in 1901. Allen's observation of missionary work as it had developed in the sixty years
since the opening of the treaty ports to Western influence in
1842 led him to reach radical conclusions on the way Christian
mission was practised. After his return home in 1903, these
resulted in writings such as *Missionary Methods: St Paul's or Ours?*
(1912) and *The Spontaneous Expansion of the Church* (1927), which
have continued to exercise considerable influence into our own
day and were widely read and debated at the time.

Allen had discerned, while in China, what became an
increasingly important and central question for the missionary
movement: 'are we actually planting new churches or merely
perpetuating a mission?'[5] The relationship of the mission, often
administered from a home base in a 'sending' country, with the
local church was to loom large in these years: further, the
relationship of the expatriate leadership to the local church
and its leaders was of crucial significance as the younger
churches developed. In *Missionary Methods*, his first explosive
essay in missiology, on which we concentrate here, Allen
insisted that St Paul was very much wiser than modern missionaries; and this largely because he trusted in the Holy Spirit,
present in the local church, to create and equip leaders. Unlike
modern missionaries, St Paul spent comparatively little time in
each place he evangelised: perhaps six months in Lystra, five

---

[4] Ake Talltorp, *Sacrament and Growth: a Study in the Sacramental Dimension of Expansion in
the Life of the Local Church as Reflected in the Theology of Roland Allen* (Uppsala, 1989);
D. Paton (ed.), *Reform of the Ministry: A Study in the Work of Roland Allen* (London,
1968); *CDCWM*, p. 14; *IBMR*, 13, no. 2 (April 1989), pp. 65–70.
[5] R. Allen, *Missionary Methods: St Paul's or Ours?*, (London, 1912; new edn London,
1960) p. v., preface by K. G. Grubb.

months in Thessalonica (Salonica), eighteen months in Corinth.[6] His practice was to appoint elders and then to move on, thus ensuring that his own potentially stifling presence was removed and the local church was left to its own leadership under the guidance of the Holy Spirit. Modern missionaries, by contrast, confronted by highly educable indigenous Christians, not 'destitute of natural ... ability to lead', whether 'in the South Seas, in Papua, in New Zealand, in Central, South and West Africa and among the lower castes of India', had failed to apply the lessons of St Paul. Instead they had argued against independence on the grounds of a lack of capacity in the converts.[7] For Allen, the very brevity of St Paul's visits 'may have accounted in no small measure for [his] success. There is something in the presence of a great teacher that sometimes tends to prevent smaller men from realising themselves. They more readily feel their responsibility, they more readily ... exert their powers, when they see that, unless they come forward, nothing will be done.'[8]

Allen's deep belief in the inner vitality and giftedness of the local church made him suspicious, equally, of large 'national' churches (this may have been a factor in his resignation from incumbency of an Anglican parish in 1907, though the ostensible reason was the practice of infant baptism 'on demand') or of the imposition of forms of orthodoxy, whether of practice or doctrine, by missions as external authorities. St Paul merely gave guidelines to his communities, in Allen's view, before leaving them to the Holy Spirit and their Christian reason. He did not, specifically, set up the church at Jerusalem as an authority for Christian norms or for the imposition of an external form of unity. For Western Christianity, however, there must be 'a highly centralised organisation ... the Roman system, a system which has so dominated the modern world that even those who repudiated the papal claims ... adopt it'.[9] This imposition of external authority by 'foreign guides' may

[6] *Ibid.*, p. 84: Allen used Sir William Ramsay's chronology of Paul's journeys.
[7] *Ibid.*, p. 25.
[8] *Ibid.*, p. 93.   [9] *Ibid.*, p. 130.

persuade indigenous Christians to obey, but it is the 'way of
death not of life; it is Judaism, not Christianity; it is papal not
Pauline'.[10] St Paul's alternative was trust in the authority and
unifying activity of the Holy Spirit within that all-important
unit of Christian mission, the local church. Allen criticised
Rufus Anderson and Henry Venn for regarding self-support,
self-propagation and self-government as a goal to be aimed at:
independent life was instead to be seen as present from the
beginning in every Christian community.[11]

Such Christian radicalism, whether early in the century or
today, will command a hearing. Allen was writing into a
context where, for example, in the Japan of the 1920s even
friendly observers could judge that the day of the missionary
was done.[12] Hard-worked missionaries in the field and heavily
burdened missionary administrators at home might, however,
find Allen's an idealistic application of New Testament patterns to their situation, often one very different from churches
brought up in the general penumbra of the Jewish synagogues
of the Mediterranean world. Easy comparisons with the apostolic missions had been warned against by Gustav Warneck,
who was quoted at the Jerusalem Conference, perhaps with
Allen in mind. Other criticisms of Allen's positions found their
way into the *IRM*.[13] There was an element in Allen which
seemed to need to protest. To say this should not detract from
appreciating the vigour and penetration of his missionary
critique. Nevertheless, his resignation from the national
Church of England, his advocacy of non-stipendiary or 'voluntary' ministry as the only Christian form, his lack of enthusiasm
during his association with the World Dominion Trust of
Sidney Clark for undertaking the kind of down-to-earth

[10] *Ibid.*, p. 118.
[11] R. Allen, *The Spontaneous Expansion of the Church and the Causes Which Hinder It* (London, 1927; new edn 1960) pp. 8–43.
[12] *Laymen's Foreign Missions Inquiry* (Supplementary Series) 7 vols. (New York, 1933), vol. VI, p. 305.
[13] *IMC/J*, vol. III, p. 33; *International Review of Missions* (hereafter *IRM*), 16, no. 64 (October 1927), p. 597 (F. J. Western), cf. *IRM*, 16, no. 62 (April 1927), pp. 262–70 (Allen); *IRM*, 13, no. 49 (January 1924), pp. 3–25 (W. H. Temple Gairdner); *IRM*, 9, no. 36 (October 1920), pp. 531–43 (Allen).

surveys envisaged for him,[14] his restless wandering, which finished in Kenya; and, perhaps most strikingly for one who put great emphasis on the eucharist and its expression in the local church, his retreat into a 'family rite' with himself as the celebrant,[15] seem to be signs of a radical spirit, who found the discipline of any structures at odds with the individualism of his vision. He remained and remains, however, a disturbing and arresting voice for modern missiology: in Lesslie Newbigin's words 'slowly but steadily the number of those who found themselves compelled to listen has increased'.[16]

The second missionary thinker was an American, Daniel Johnson Fleming (1877–1969). Fleming had spent time in India as a young man, without any original intention of missionary commitment; but teaching at Forman Christian College in Lahore so fired his vision that his aim of returning to the US to train as a lawyer was surrendered. In 1904 he went back to India as a missionary, to serve again at Lahore until 1912. Medical and family factors caused a furlough to turn into a fresh direction for Fleming. He became one of the most widely respected writers and thinkers in the North American missionary world, teaching at Union Theological Seminary from 1915, in the faculty of which he became Professor of Missions from 1918–44.[17]

Fleming was a fluent writer, with an easy and accessible style; but this did not disguise the probing nature of his books. The titles reveal his preoccupation with important questions for Christian mission: *Contacts with Non-Christian Cultures*, *Whither Bound in Missions?* and *Attitudes Towards Other Faiths* all appeared in this decade. The last will be noted in the next chapter. Here *Whither Bound in Missions?* should be noted for its attack on missionary or Western 'superiority': 'just as we have given up the idea of the divine right of kings and are giving up the idea of male superiority, we will very likely have to give up

---

[14] Talltorp, *Sacrament*, p. 17.   [15] *Ibid.*, pp. 56–7.

[16] Allen, *Spontaneous Expansion* (1960 edn), p. iii: preface by Lesslie Newbigin.

[17] L. H. Hoyle 'The Legacy of Daniel Johnson Fleming', *IBMR*, 14, no. 2 (April 1990), pp. 68–73, with bibliography.

the flattering delusion of decided racial superiority'.[18] While Fleming was prepared to regard Christ himself as the greatest gift for East or West, far from this denoting any 'superiority' in the 'sending' countries it showed rather that the West's guilt was greater 'because it has had access to Christ for so long'.[19] A 'pervasive humility' was required of Christians: any missionary work had to be accompanied by a 'deep sense of national and racial repentance'.[20] In a story which recalled V. S. Azariah's appeal at Edinburgh for not only self-sacrifice but friendship on the part of missionaries, Fleming recounted how 'an Indian Christian saint of great spiritual penetration had said of European Christians: "you know, you make us feel that you want to do good to us but you don't make us feel that you need us"'.[21] The separation of Western culture from forms of indigenous Christianity was also an essential goal for Fleming.

He was to be an important member of the LFMI team, but it is clear from this work of 1925 that he was already aware of the groundswell of discontent in the younger churches, not least in China. He quoted the Chinese leader, Cheng Ching-Yi, a participant at Edinburgh and secretary of the NCC formed in 1922, telling missionary leaders in 1923: 'may we say with all kindness that the missions have been altogether too fearful of surrendering their control ... the time has come for a thoroughgoing reconsideration of the whole situation.'[22] As Fleming sought to prepare minds for new attitudes in the mission field, so he sought to make North American Christians sensitive to what mission could mean to nationals. In an article entitled 'If Buddhists Came to Our Town'[23] he used a neat device of rôle-reversal to invite North American Christians to enter into the experience of the 'missioned', as imaginary Buddhists discussed missionary approaches to Americans. Fleming also tried to reform missionary terminology: words like 'heathen' or 'native', with their pejorative overtones, must

[18] D. J. Fleming, *Whither Bound in Missions?* (New York, 1925), p. 15; see *IRM*, 12, no. 1 (January 1923), pp. 112–21.
[19] Fleming, *Missions*, p. 47.   [20] *Ibid.*, p. 64.   [21] *Ibid.*, p. 27.
[22] *Ibid.*, p. 162.
[23] *Christian Century*, 46, no. 9, (28 February 1929), pp. 293–4.

be replaced. In this respect and others 'Fleming's writings of the 1920s were laced with gentle protests against the old-time vocabulary of conquest and condescension.'[24]

JERUSALEM CONFERENCE 1928

Allen and Fleming were not the only critical intelligences at work prior to the Jerusalem Conference. There was unease among Continental thinkers also, but of a different kind. The Continuation Committee of Edinburgh 1910 had turned into the IMC in 1921 at a meeting at Lake Mohonk in New York State. Although the name might change, the *dramatis personae* of Mott as chairman and Oldham as secretary did not. Under pressure from 'Continental' representatives, as the Germans, Dutch and Scandinavians were termed, Mott agreed to a meeting held in Cairo in 1927 to thrash out the deeply held theological reservations over the shape of preparations for the conference. Great anxiety was being expressed that in the handling of the issue of the Christian message and its relation to other faiths, there was a discernible shift into syncretism and that the missionary movement was in danger of moving towards the 'social gospel' position, then widely adopted in North America.[25] Their fears were expressed by a German professor of theology, Karl Heim: 'the kingdom of God means nothing more than the League of Nations, democracy and the coming of militant capitalism'.[26] Mott himself invited an American Quaker, Rufus Jones, to give his widely discussed paper on the Christian message, and it was Oldham who managed to insist that, as well as other faiths, the issues raised by secularism in the modern world should be discussed.

The Jerusalem Conference differed sharply from the Edinburgh Conference in character, and still more from the kind of demonstration which the New York Conference of 1900, or, more recently, the Washington Conference of 1925, had

---

[24] W. R. Hutchison, *Errand to the World*, p. 155.
[25] W. R. Hogg, *Ecumenical Foundations*, pp. 240–2.
[26] *Ibid.*, p. 416 note 13.

represented, where again a President of the United States, Calvin Coolidge, had addressed a gathering of 3,500 delegates. Jerusalem, as William Paton pointed out in a preparatory pamphlet, was not a conference but a meeting of a council.[27] Attendance was carefully restricted to 250. Instead of the sprinkling of Christians from the younger churches, like V. S. Azariah and Cheng Ching-Yi at Edinburgh, more than fifty of the total were nationals.[28] Among them were leading Indian Christians such as K. T. Paul, P. Chenchiah, P. O. Philip and S. K. Datta; Chinese in T. C. Chao, David Yui and Cheng Ching-Yi once more; and, from Japan, a Methodist, Bishop Uzaki. Mott once again chaired the conference and, although Oldham was not present, it was he who had secured the attendance and contributions of such a significant contributor as R. H. Tawney, the Christian economist, whose paper was a masterly piece of advocacy for Christian commitment to the economic and social structures of national and international life, that emphasis on the 'comprehensive' approach to mission which became the hallmark of the conference's influence thereafter. It was Oldham, too, who secured Harold Grimshaw of the International Labour Office in Geneva.[29] Of other notable Europeans, William Temple, an usher at the Edinburgh Conference, was present as Archbishop-designate of York eighteen years later and shared with R. E. Speer the responsibility for drafting the statement on the Christian message. Hendrik Kraemer, the Dutch layman and theologian, Karl Hartenstein, the German missiologist and mission administrator and Karl Heim, already noted, were allies against 'relativising' tendencies;[30] and, among the Americans, in addition to Mott and Speer, W. E. Hocking, professor of philosophy at Harvard, made a notable contribution to proceedings, as did the rural and agricultural expert, Kenyon Butterfield, and the

[27] W. Paton, *Jerusalem 1928* (London, 1928), p. 6.
[28] Edinburgh had an attendance total of 1,200, of whom 17 were nationals from younger churches: W. R. Hogg, *Ecumenical Foundations*, p. 135.
[29] *Ibid.*, p. 245; E. Jackson, *Red Tape and the Gospel: a Study of the Significance of the Ecumenical Struggle of William Paton (1886–1943)* (Birmingham, 1980), p. 251.
[30] J. Verkuyl, *Contemporary Missiology*, p. 48.

Methodist Bishop McConnell, who added his voice to Tawney's in commending a Christian social ethic.

The conference report, containing preliminary papers circulated before the meeting and the record of discussions at it, runs to eight volumes. The first, *The Christian Life and Message in Relation to Non-Christian Systems*, will be discussed in chapter 4. Here, the volume *The Relations between the Younger and Older Churches*, which underlined the change of perspective needed for the missionary movement of 1928 described by critics like Allen and Fleming, showed that the nationals, especially the Chinese leadership, were determined to drive home, courteously but firmly, the new relationship with the missions and the older churches. So, S. C. Leung, a leading figure in the Church of Christ in China (a uniting body formed in 1927), showed that the time for two parallel organisations, the mission and the indigenous church, was past. The Chinese church must be recognised as the 'chief centre of responsibility', missions must be content to function only through the church, and individual missionaries to act as officers of it rather than representatives of the mission boards. Property held in trust should be handed over to the 'complete control' of the Chinese church.[31]

Nevertheless, Leung was not calling on the missionaries to withdraw, but to work as members of the church, a view endorsed by David Yui: 'missionaries ought to have a permanent place in China, just as we hope Chinese missionaries must in future have a permanent place in America, if I am permitted to say so'.[32] Cheng Ching-Yi explained that by an indigenous church the Chinese meant 'a Christian church ... adapted to meet the religious needs of the Chinese people, most congenial to Chinese life and culture'.[33] He realised that there were deeper issues than simple indigenisation: 'the Christian church does not exist for the sake of becoming indigenous. When you have solved the problem of making the Chinese church indigenous in China you have not solved the main problem of the Church, which exists for the worship of God, for Christian fellowship, for training its members in spiritual and

[31] *IMC/J* vol. III, pp. 12–13.   [32] *Ibid.*, pp. 61–2.   [33] *Ibid.*, p. 171.

daily life for active service for the good of their fellow men and the propagation of the Christian message of love'.[34] The comments of the Japanese Christian, Kazeki Kudo, were cited in the volume: 'an assisted church is an absurd thing; it is like a sick church; a self-supporting church is the correct expression of the church's life'.[35]

A crucial theological concern at Jerusalem was the understanding of the kingdom of God. The Continentals remained as deeply suspicious of the prevailing social tendencies as in the pre-war period. Ideas of human beings 'building' the kingdom of God (of which there were many examples in the report and the discussions) ran counter to the theological recognition that it was and is *God*'s kingdom. To meet this disquiet the statement referred to working 'in preparation for the coming of His kingdom in its fullness'.[36] This phrase may be regarded as a typical piece of theological legerdemain by the arch-drafter of ecumenically irenic documents, William Temple: his statement, welcome as it was to the meeting, who acclaimed it with relief as something to which all could subscribe, was an example of his facility 'leading him at times to think he had found a solution, when he had found a phrase'.[37] Where the Continentals wanted still to emphasise the eschatological nature of the kingdom, contributors like Tawney, Paton and Grimshaw believed that, in Tawney's words, 'because God's kingdom is not of this world, it does not follow that this world is not part of his kingdom'.[38] The missionary movement and the Christian church must not only address individual life, but also the fabric of society to which individuals were exposed. So, it was an 'outrage on the image of God' to subordinate the welfare of human beings to economic interests and a 'naive illusion' that 'a society becomes more prosperous if its output of

[34] *Ibid.*, pp. 165–6.
[35] *Japan Christian Quarterly*, 2, no. 2 (April 1927), p. 151, quoted in *ibid.*, p. 17.
[36] *IMC/J* vol. i, p. 481; G. H. Anderson, 'The Theology of Missions 1928–58', unpublished Ph.D. thesis, Boston University (1960), p. 65; cf. J. D. Gort, 'Jerusalem 1928: Mission, Kingdom, Church', *IRM*, 67, no. 267 (July 1978), pp. 249–72.
[37] R. Craig, *Social Concern in the Thought of William Temple* (London, 1963), p. 13.
[38] *IMC/J* vol. v, p. 164.

commodities increases while the institutions which provide its moral stamina' were undermined. The Christian view, by contrast, was that 'national wealth is to be valued in so far as, and only in so far as, it assists and enriches the life of the spirit'.[39]

While some might have demurred, justifiably enough, at Bishop McConnell's assertion that saints could only flourish in a helpful environment (more ordinary citizens perhaps, but have not saints often flourished in very hostile and alien environments?),[40] Tawney's attack was well judged:

[for] drawing a sharp distinction between a change of heart and a change of social order and saying that the former must precede the latter there does not seem to be any foundation either in the teaching of the New Testament or in that of the church in its most vigorous periods ... the whole distinction between the life of the spirit and the fabric of society is a false antithesis which it should be the duty of a Christian community to overcome ...

'my purpose ... is to insist that the churches are neglecting an essential part of their mission unless they foster the zeal for social righteousness and disseminate the knowledge by which such zeal may be made effective'.[41] Some of Tawney's social passion found its way into the official statements, as also did William Paton's desire that the kingdom of God should mean something 'real and practical in the ordering of the world's industrial and political life', towards a better social order.[42] So, the council's statement on industrial problems included the words that 'the task of the Christian church ... is both to carry the message of Christ to the individual soul and to create a Christian civilisation within which all human beings can grow to their full spiritual stature';[43] and one result of the Jerusalem Conference was the setting up of the Bureau of Social and Economic Research under J. Merle Davis in 1930 as a branch of the work of the IMC, to fulfil the meeting's aspiration that the 'Christian churches ... may be less unworthy instruments

---

[39] *Ibid.*, p. 168.   [40] *Ibid.*, pp. 173–5.   [41] *Ibid.*, pp. 164, 169.
[42] *Ibid.*, pp. 27–8.
[43] *Ibid.*, p. 184.

in the advancement of His kingdom'.[44] Christ, said the statement, when he wept over Jerusalem, 'lamented the spiritual
ruin, not merely of an individual but of a whole society'.[45]

Here then was an attempt to hold together those who saw
their work in race relations,[46] in education[47] or rural development[48] as the building of God's kingdom and those who, while
accepting social concern and individual relief as legitimate
activities of the Christian church, drew back from theological
simplism. To some degree it was a question of the theological
status of the labels given to activities with which few would
disagree in terms of love of neighbour, so fundamental to the
gospel. With this, however, went a divide between the corporate and individual emphases in the social realm, which has
already been observed between the pietist emphasis on individual conversion and the corporate approach of figures like
Gutmann in the evangelistic realm: and also the reflection,
more obvious still in the LFMI, between the liberal and
conservative views of Christian obedience and the Bible. The
'comprehensive' ideal had been adopted by the IMC but not
necessarily by the missionary world, as Roland Allen's rather
carping little piece on Jerusalem indicated.[49]

THE LAYMEN'S FOREIGN MISSIONS INQUIRY 1932–3

Where some have seen the Jerusalem Conference as concentrating on the church, at least by comparison to the Edinburgh
Conference,[50] the sharply critical eye of a thinker like Roland
Allen discerned that the understanding of the kingdom was
central, even if, as a piece of writing, his comments were fairly
judged as a 'caricature' of what would 'seemingly be obvious to
scholars of much less standing than Mr Allen'.[51] The view of

44 *Ibid.*, pp. 191, 193.   45 *Ibid.*, p. 181.   46 *Ibid.*, vol. IV, p. 237.
47 *Ibid.*, vol. II, p. 242.
48 *Ibid.*, vol. VI, p. 276 see p. 288, 'kingdom building'.
49 R. Allen, *Jerusalem: a Critical Review of the World Mission of Christianity* (London,
1928), pp. 1–38.
50 W. Andersen, *Towards a Theology of Mission: a Study Encounter between the Missionary
Enterprise and the Church and Its Theology* (London, 1955), pp. 16, 20, 22.
51 G. H. Anderson, 'The Theology of Missions', p. 78.

mission as 'building the kingdom' was to be very apparent in the LFMI, to the point where the local church in rural contexts, for example, was made a secondary, even a supernumerary, consideration beside rural community development. It was a view of mission which hinged a good deal on 'personalities', outstanding leaders in specialist fields.[52] More than this, it contained effectively two views of Christian theology, present also at the Jerusalem Conference: one, a vision of Jesus the teacher and example (even 'personality'),[53] which received heavy emphasis in the literature of the Inquiry; and, secondly, as a backcloth, the heavily dogmatic preached Christ, encased in a certain rigid, even ossified, dogmatic clothing, biblically rooted enough but, as the inquirers were aware, failing to connect with the living concerns of the Chinese, Japanese and Indian peoples in their revolutionary ferment towards becoming modern: politically, industrially, socially and, as an unwelcome concomitant, militarily. The literature poses the question as to whether either of the versions of Jesus was adequately incarnational.

The Inquiry, which has deservedly received renewed attention recently,[54] was a notable piece of Christian self-criticism, whatever view is taken of the adequacy of its theological basis. It was financed by the wealthy Baptist layman, J. D. Rockefeller, a friend of John Mott, and it was mounted by eight mission boards in North America backed by their respective denominations.[55] The seven volumes of data, consisting of regional reports (volumes i–iii) and 'fact-finders'' reports (volumes iv–vii) contain an astonishingly full and extensive range of materials, not least in view of the short period of time in which the research was done (May 1930 – September 1931). They serve to give an invaluable portrait of Christian mission in the nations of the Orient in the 1920s and provided the

---

[52] *Laymen's Foreign Missions Inquiry* (hereafter *LFMI*) vol. i, p. 188 (India); vol. ii, pp. 74, 82, 161 (China); *Rethinking Missions*, pp. 82, 98, 292.
[53] *Rethinking Missions*, p. 49, 'the genius of Jesus'.
[54] W. Ustorf, *Mission to Mission? – Rethinking the Agenda* (Birmingham, 1991).
[55] *Ibid.*, pp. 13–14, note 16, for a full list of participating bodies.

essential information from which W. E. Hocking and others on the Commission of Appraisal compiled the book *Rethinking Missions* (1932), which was made available in 1933 in published form. *Rethinking Missions* caused furious debate in missionary circles, warmly espoused by some (among them Pearl Buck, prominent writer and daughter of a missionary and agricultural expert in China, and widely known for her book *The Good Earth* (1931)) but criticised and repudiated by a figure like R. E. Speer and other missionary leaders.

W. E. Hocking (1873–1966), who had been so prominent a contributor at Jerusalem,[56] was a professor of philosophy at Harvard and a Congregational layman. He had experienced conversion in his youth. As a philosopher he had occupied himself with questions relating to world community, the future co-existence of world religions and the search for a form of unity which would not surrender variety.[57] In one passage, which gives a hint of Hocking's ideas, he expressed at Jerusalem a vision of 'hospices', places of peace, tranquillity, study and openness to others, to be provided by religious traditions as oases of interchange.[58] Here Christian, Buddhist, Hindu and Confucianist could open to one another the treasures of their discoveries, so mutually advancing in truth and authenticity. In such a scheme, conceptions of Christian uniqueness, absoluteness or finality were likely to appear as barriers of interchange. In *Rethinking Missions*, which reflected Hocking's views, 'no variety of religious experience is to perish until it has yielded up to the rest of its own ingredient of religious truth': the Christian should be a co-worker with the 'forces within each such religious system ... making for righteousness'.[59] As will be seen, this was language which Rufus Jones had used at the Jerusalem Conference. Hocking was to write later *Living Religions and a World Faith* (1940) of which the *Dictionary of American Biography* commented, 'hopes for religious ecumenicity [were] expressed'. As Hocking had said at Jerusalem, 'I under-

56 *IMC/J*, vol. I, p. 369.
57 W. Ustorf, *Mission to Mission?*, pp. 6–7, 17–18, notes 44, 48.
58 *IMC/J*, vol. VIII, p. 161.   59 *Rethinking Missions*, p. 327.

stand to be the ultimate objective of all missionary enterprise the creation of a common spiritual life among men.'[60]

INDIA

The India confronted by the Inquiry was a sub-continent in transition in the 1920s. The era of the British Raj, which had dated from the event which the British referred to as the Indian Mutiny (after which the British Crown took over responsibility in 1858) had begun to wane, as indicated in the Montagu–Chelmsford reforms of 1917–19: by these, Indian self-government was conceded in principle, whatever the time-scale might be. Indian nationalism was a developing factor in the decade that followed, not least after the sense of outrage caused to the Indian National Congress by the shootings at Amritsar, when an English officer, General Dyer, had been responsible for the death of unarmed civilians at a time of civil disorder in 1919. For Indians, it rankled deeply that the English parliament, in particular the House of Lords, had been unwilling to censure Dyer. Acute missionary observers like Nicol Macnicol noted the change in India from quiescence to self-assertion, which, as he told the Jerusalem membership, affected the whole of the missionary situation.[61] One notable aspect of the nationalist movement was the participation by Indian women. A leader of the Arya Samaj, not always friendly to Christian mission, could say 'the best result of Christian Missions is the social emancipation of women',[62] and the educational uplift given to Indian women by Christian missions was generally admired by Indian leaders; but it was also true that comparatively few Christian Indian women took part, for example, in Mahatma Gandhi's campaigns of civil disobedience. Gandhi, who was widely admired by missionaries, exercised immense influence in India in the decade. The year 1920 proved to be a watershed in his relationship with the

---

[60] *Dictionary of American Biography*, Supplement 8 (1966–70), (New York, 1928–44), pp. 265–6; cf. W. R. Hutchison, *Errand to the World*, pp. 161–2; *IMC/J*, vol. VIII, p. 161.
[61] *IMC/J*, vol. I, p. 8.   [62] *LFMI*, vol. I, p. 223 note.

British government, a fact directly related to the exoneration of Dyer as he viewed it.

Among missionary figures in India, C. F. Andrews (1871–1940)[63] was in some respects pre-eminent. It could be argued that he and David Livingstone, neither ultimately a professional missionary in a conventional sense, were more influential as Christian 'icons' of mission than anyone else of their generation. K. T. Paul, the Indian Christian, expressed something of this at Jerusalem: 'I want to say in the clearest possible terms that the church in India does want missionaries, as many as you can send ... if you go to any Indian nationalist and ask whom among the foreigners he admires most, he will probably say "Mr C. F. Andrews".'[64] Like Roland Allen, Andrews had spent some years (1904–14) as a paid missionary with a mission of high church Anglican background, at that time teaching at St Stephen's, Delhi. In this consideration of missionary reassessment and scrutiny, Andrews represented a Western Christian made to feel increasingly uneasy by the close identification of the British government with the mission of the church. It caused Andrews to move from close friendship with S. K. Rudra, Indian Christian teacher at St Stephen's, to further deep friendships with the leading Indian figures, Gandhi and Rabindranath Tagore, poet and literary figure. He espoused the cause of Indians in Natal with Gandhi, where political concessions were won, and also the cause of the oppressed and exploited Indian indentured labourers in Fiji. Here, almost singlehandedly, Andrews brought about changed conditions, an achievement to which tribute was paid at Jerusalem by the Australian C. O. Lelean: 'the scandal was only righted as a result of the efforts of C. F. Andrews of India who said that they must stop. He was cursed by the government but in time the conscience of the community became stricken. In two years the scandal ceased.'[65] By becoming part of Tagore's ashram at Satiniketan, and through his deep friendship with

[63] H. Tinker, *The Ordeal of Love: C. F. Andrews and India* (Oxford, 1979); D. O'Connor, *Gospel, Raj and Swaraj: the Missionary Years of C. F. Andrews 1904–74* (Frankfurt-on-Main, 1990).
[64] *IMC/J*, vol. III, p. 184.   [65] *Ibid.*, vol. I, p. 405.

Gandhi, it seemed to some that he was guilty of syncretism and
had lost any Christian distinctiveness: but a reading of his
moving account of his Christian conversion (a reluctant testimony by one deeply inclined to personal religious reticence)
and subsequent discipleship in his *What I Owe to Christ* shows
that, however deep his admiration for Gandhi and Tagore
might have been, his own deep faith in Christ never wavered.
Andrews was one of those able to enthuse over the Inquiry.[66]

Before turning to the LFMI volumes on India in detail, two
other general factors may be noted: first, this was the period
when Gandhi and others with him were most critical of Christian conversion, often referred to as 'proselytising'. Gandhi
held that it was wholly inappropriate and improper that Christian humanitarian service in hospitals and schools should pose
as disinterested benevolence when in fact this was the 'bait' for
inducing Hindus and Muslims to change their faith: 'methods
of conversion', he said, 'like Caesar's wife should be above
suspicion'.[67] There is an interesting account of a conversation
on this question between Gandhi, Mott and Andrews in the
newspaper *Harijan*, which was also the name given by Gandhi
to the outcaste people, whose condition he tried so impressively
to improve. Mott agreed that there should be no inducements
and, as Gandhi urged, what mattered was to 'live the life'; but
Mott was unyielding on the Christian responsibility also to
bear witness by the spoken word on the basis of his own
experience with J. E. K. Studd: 'his life and splendid example
alone would not have answered ... my deepest need but I
listened to him and was converted'.[68]

Secondly, this was a period when, perhaps as part of a
reassessment of methods, alternative approaches to Christian
mission were adopted. There were a number of Christian
ashrams, communities of contemplation, discipline and
instruction, among them the Christa Seva Sangha initiated by
J. C. Winslow, an Anglican priest. The inquirers recognised

[66] *The Christian Century* no.3 (25 January 1933), pp. 115–17.
[67] *LFMI*, vol. IV, p. 28.
[68] *Harijan* 19 December 1936, p. 361.

these as valid for certain individuals, but not as a substitute for conventional methods.[69] E. Stanley Jones, who conducted a 'seasonal *ashram*',[70] adopted the role of student for much of the year, and became a travelling evangelist and lecturer for the rest of it. His book describing this pattern, *The Christ of the Indian Road*, was widely read and in *The Christ of the Round Table* he described early attempts at genuine inter-religious dialogue, mentioned at Jerusalem as a 'Hindu enquiry room'.[71] Apart from ashrams, Sundar Singh (1889–1929) gave hopes for the development of Christian *sadhus*, holy men, a form of religious expression familiar to Indians. Sundar Singh himself made a deep impression on many in East and West, but, despite the eremite tradition in earlier Christianity among the desert fathers and the hermits of the Middle Ages, it seemed unlikely that so individualist an approach to holiness would establish itself widely, even as a Christian form for India, where he has had, however, a number of imitators.[72]

Such missionary departures were of importance and much remarked upon, but easily detract from the main weight of the missionary effort and its examination by the Inquiry. Here was a country of 336.7 millions in 1931, of whom 71 per cent were Hindu, 22 per cent Muslim and a mere 1.5 per cent Christian, though this small percentage represented 4.4 million souls. The Inquiry found a force of 6,000 Protestant missionaries engaged in educational, evangelistic and medical work. There were 937 mission secondary schools.[73] It was an India of caste: Brahmin, Kshatriya, Vaisya and Sudra, beyond which were the outcastes, for whom Gandhi and the church had done much to alter perceptions.[74] The phenomenon of mass movements, soon to be covered in a work by J. W. Pickett, *Christian Mass Movements* (1933) (a book in which the kind of corporate approach described earlier was commended), was present, for example, among the Telugu people and their outcaste (Baptist)

[69] *LFMI*, vol. IV, p. 290.   [70] *Rethinking Missions*, p. 47 note.
[71] *IMC/J*, vol. I, p. 18; cf. vol. VIII, p. 135.
[72] *CDCWM*, p. 576; *RGG*, VI, pp. 526–7; cf. M. Nazir Ali, *From Everywhere to Everywhere* (London, 1990), pp. 155–6.
[73] *Rethinking Missions*, p. 119.   [74] *LFMI*, vol. IV, p. 324; cf. p. 18.

churches, many of which became self-supporting in the decade.[75] It was an India ridden with 'disease, drink and debt',[76] the last of which was met in part by 65,000 cooperative societies formed between 1925 and 1927.[77] The Christian emancipation of women was observed: one woman doctor in the Punjab described how she had prayed forty years earlier on her arrival in India that 'God would break down the walls and let the women free', but now that 'the walls are broken we did not have any idea what it would mean to India'.[78]

Considerable readjustment to surprise, even shock, was required by missionary personnel to the development. Yet an All India Women's Conference of India, formed in 1926, a powerful agency for change, had few Indian Christian women in it. There was a real danger of 'aloofness' on their part.[79] The inquirers accepted Gandhi's criticisms against proselytising, while noting that he had gone on record as saying he was not against conversion as such but against modern methods of securing it.[80] Here and elsewhere the inquirers came down against compulsory worship and compulsory religious instruction in schools, and they accepted that some of the practice of preaching in hospitals was offensive to Gandhi and others. Even some Christian practitioners in the hospitals would prefer its prohibition.[81] Tagore's invitation to missionaries to 'give themselves in love', rather than to seek to possess, was accepted[82] and they heard that Gandhi's spirituality inspired both Christian and non-Christian, giving some Indian Christians a new insight into 'our Christ', who was sometimes a 'narrowed Christ'. One Indian church leader went further: Gandhi had 'popularised Christ and ... done more to make him known to India than all the missions had done working for a hundred years combined'.[83]

To complete the picture given of mission in India, moves

[75] *Ibid.*, p. 214: 28 self-supporting churches in 1909 became 105 in 1929.
[76] S. C. Neill, *Out of Bondage* (London, 1930), p. 63, quoted in *LFMI*, vol. IV, p. 93.
[77] *LFMI*, vol. IV, p. 81.   [78] *Rethinking Missions*, p. 280; *LFMI*, vol. I, p. 235.
[79] *LFMI*, vol. IV, pp. 466, 484.   [80] *Ibid.*, pp. 28, 108–9.
[81] *Ibid.*, vol. I, pp. 69, 178–80; *Rethinking Missions*, p. 201.
[82] *LFMI*, vol. IV, p. 28.   [83] *Ibid.*, p. 538.

towards organic unity in what would become the Church of
South India were recorded;[84] an account was given of a special
category of works of mercy in the thirty-five houses run for
lepers, sixteen of them without financial support except that
supplied by the missions;[85] and, in an interesting aside, they
noticed the advent of broadcasting by the BBC in 1924,[86] a
form of mass communication which was to be employed in
missionary service widely, not least in the China of this period.

The Indian Inquiry also took in Burma, scene of Adoniram
Judson's epic labours, predominantly Buddhist but with a
minority Karen population almost exclusively Christian and
Baptist in affiliation (80 per cent of Karen Christians were
Baptist). There were 260,000 Karen Christians in the early
1930s and they were held up as an example in terms of
self-supporting churches.[87] The inquirers found that the 'comprehensive' approach of the Jerusalem Conference was here
rejected by a number of missionaries,[88] who laid overwhelming
emphasis on preaching and evangelism. They found that, to
Burmese Christians, religion meant evangelism and missionary
meant evangelist. Gospel teams of adolescents, though representing 'striking results,'[89] were regarded in certain respects as
'ill advised'.[90] Here, as elsewhere, the inquirers felt that the
excessive emphasis on preaching, referred to as 'talkies' by one
college professor who gave evidence, needed to be redressed by
attention to the social dimension of a Christianity which, in the
words of one YWCA worker, used 'the word "Christian" in the
larger sense': the YWCA, because of the social element in its
service, was not felt to have 'a strong Christian emphasis', as
the word 'Christian' was 'limited to evangelism'.[91] On the basis
of the Jerusalem report, the team urged the Burmese missions
to think out their aim again in relation to 'the total need' of the
people, an aim which would relate their activity to such pressing needs as nationalism, communalism and social welfare.
Nevertheless, the report makes clear that, as well as enabling

[84] *Ibid.*, p. 287.   [85] *Ibid.*, p. 433.   [86] *Ibid.*, p. 362.
[87] *Rethinking Missions*, pp. 88, 136, 142.
[88] *LFMI*, vol. IV, p. 592.   [89] *Ibid.*, p. 743.   [90] *Ibid.*, vol. I, p. 131.
[91] *Ibid.*, vol. IV, p. 709.

two evangelistic tours by E. Stanley Jones to take place in the 1920s, the Burmese Christian Council had mounted surveys on such important social issues as gambling, opium addiction and intoxicants.[92] Plainly, the social dimension was not entirely absent.

CHINA

In many respects it was in China that the issues raised by the LFMI were most clearly present. This was true especially in the realm of the liberal-conservative theological debate and spilled over into assessments of evangelism, preaching and its value, teaching in seminars and their organisation, the approach to rural life and other areas of discussion. China had made a major step into the modern world in 1905, when the old form of examinations, based on knowledge of the Chinese classics, and the only route into government and the civil service was abolished. In 1911 China had her own revolution, when the Manchu dynasty was replaced by a government led by the reformer Sun Yat Sen, a politican sympathetic to the Christian cause, but prepared to turn for help in the 1920s to communist Russia when rebuffed by the Western powers. In 1925 Sun died, by which time a Chinese Communist party had been formed and rival armies under Chiang Kai-shek of the Kuomintang party (KMT) and the Communist leader Mao Tse-tung struggled for supremacy. There was violence, unsettled political conditions and brigandage for missionaries to contend with. It came as a considerable encouragement to the Christians that, during the period of the Inquiry, Chiang Kai-shek became a baptised Christian.[93]

China was a country of 450 million in 1928, of whom 200 million were illiterate.[94] The Protestant missionary force was calculated as 6,346 in 1930, of whom 48 per cent were Americans.[95] This number had been still higher in 1927 (8,250) but the anti-foreign rioting and violence of that year

[92] *Ibid.*, pp. 601, 651.   [93] *Ibid.*, vol. v, p. 154.   [94] *Ibid.*, vol. ii, pp. 1, 102.
[95] *Ibid.*, p. 70.

reduced missionary personnel. As a percentage of the total
population the Christian church was very small: Roman
Catholics were calculated at 0.8 per cent and Protestants at
0.1 per cent; but, as Chiang Kai-shek's baptism indicated, the
period since 1842, when the treaty ports, and subsequently the
interior, had been opened up to missionary influence, had
given Christian mission a national influence. Chiang had
given as one of the reasons for his baptism: 'in the National
Government and among the men with whom he has had to
do, the most efficient and trustworthy are Christians'.[96] Evidence given to the Inquiry indicated areas of success in Christian terms in home life, among rural women, in the steady
advance against the ancient practice of foot-binding in girls,[97]
in education, especially among girls, and in active efforts
against illiteracy.[98] The work of the former YMCA worker
Y. C. J. 'Jimmie' Yen in this field was 'brilliantly successful'.[99]

China had formed its own National Christian Council in
1922, of which the Edinburgh participant Cheng Ching-Yi
was secretary, and a very able Christian thinker and leader.
At the time of the Inquiry the council was made up of thirty-
three Chinese nationals and twenty-seven missionaries;[100] and
the thrust, already noticed at the Jerusalem meeting, towards
an indigenous Chinese church, freed from the stigma of
appearing to be a foreign religion and accepting full responsibility for its own life, was strongly present. A typical expression was the letter of 18 July 1927 from the Congregational
church of Foochow to the American Board of Foreign Commissioners.

now that we are in the process of transfer of responsibility from the
mission to the Church, it is as if the mother eagle were suddenly
giving her fledgelings the opportunity to try their wings. For eighty
years the loving care of the mission for the Foochow churches has
never failed. On the day that they are being pushed out of the nest
and compelled to fly, it is hoped that the eaglets may diligently and

---

[96] *Ibid.*, vol. v, p. 158.   [97] *Ibid.*, pp. 157–160; vol. ii, p. 181.
[98] *Ibid.*, p. 158.
[99] *Ibid.*, vol. i, pp. 108, 128–9.   [100] *IMC/J*, vol. vii, pp. 118–21.

courageously exert themselves and that the mother eagle will give such help as is necessary when it is needed most.[101]

Cheng Ching-Yi, who had given an inspiring address at Jerusalem,[102] had himself been inspired by the meeting. Some of his own zeal as a Chinese Christian had been expressed there: 'we do long ... for men and women of God who possess such warmth and enthusiasm as was seen in the life of Jesus Christ and the Apostle Paul. Would that each one of us were "crazy" about the kingdom of God', though he qualified this by saying 'the Christian Church is [in no need] of more fanatics. We have too many of them already.'[103] On his return from Jerusalem, the NCC put into operation a Five Year Plan of church renewal and evangelism, which had the aims of combating illiteracy, promoting religious education, increasing the number of Christian homes and families, deepening the understanding of stewardship, tackling the social needs of the rural areas and strengthening the life of Christian communities generally. This had been launched in 1930: reports of its progress so far 'did not sound very encouraging to the listener' as far as the inquirers were concerned, though the energetic efforts of the leadership were recognised. The inquirers approved the aim, which spoke of a 'broader evangelism', and commented that 'though its objective aims at doubling the number of Christians in five years, it is qualitatively rather than quantitatively conceived'.[104] The preference for a 'broader evangelism' and the distaste for Christian understanding tied to winning numbers of individuals was a characteristic assessment. They commended the NCC for its broad social programme; and they noted also the important development that from 1929 no mission boards would be represented on the council as such, a policy decision in line with the more church-centred understandings of Jerusalem.[105]

Before turning to the liberal-conservative theological tensions

[101] *Ibid.*, vol. III, p. 265.
[102] W. R. Hogg, *Ecumenical Foundations*, p. 255; *IMC/J*, vol. VIII, pp. 46–60.
[103] *IMC/J*, vol. VIII, pp. 58–9.   [104] *LFMI*, vol. v, p. 11.
[105] *Ibid.*, vol. XI, p. 95; v, p. 79.

of the 1920s, one alternative approach to mission was observed in the work of Karl Ludwig Reichelt (1877–1952), who served with the Norwegian Missionary Society in China. In 1922 Reichelt had formed the 'Christian Mission to Buddhists', which sought in particular to set up Christian–Buddhist exchange with the monks in the Buddhist and Taoist traditions. Reichelt had been quoted at Jerusalem in the preliminary paper on Buddhism. He was one who sought 'points of contact' with the deeply religious in other traditions. His aim, based on what he found as parallel teachings, was to 'enter into partnership with the peoples of Asia in a great religious quest ... I feel the religious souls here must be led forward along these Johannine and Pauline lines and abundant "points of contact" can be utilized.'[106] The theological issues raised by this and other similar approaches will be handled later, but Reichelt, like C. F. Andrews and the initiators of ashrams in India, was especially significant in his attempt to open up dialogue with Chinese of alternative religious commitment.[107]

The liberal-fundamentalist debate

As early as 1921 the conservative theologian W. H. Griffith Thomas, well known to generations of Anglican seminarians through his commentary on the Thirty-Nine Articles of religion, *Principles of Christian Theology*, had visited the mission field in China when teaching at Wycliffe College, Toronto. Although more a conservative theologian than a fundamentalist, Griffith Thomas had been alarmed by what he had discovered, both among missionaries and among indigenous Chinese leaders. His visit confirmed his view, gained before leaving North America, that there were two Christian camps in China, those who 'favoured critical views' and those who 'were strongly conservative'. In an article in the *Princeton Theological Review* entitled 'Modernism in China' he voiced his

106 *IMC/J*, vol. I, pp. 165–6.
107 K. L. Reichelt, 'Buddhism in China', *IRM*, 26, no. 102 (1937), pp. 153–66; H. Eilert, *Boundlessness: Studies in Karl Reichelt's Missionary Thinking* (Aarhus, 1974); in *CDCWM*, p. 515; *LFMI*, vol. v, p. 36.

alarms, though in a measured, indeed statesmanlike, manner: he emphasised that he did not hold that liberalism could have no supernaturalism in it, but that it tended towards rationalism. The view that all was peace and harmony prior to his visit, and the assistance he gave leaders like D. E. Hoste of the conservative CIM in forming the conservative Bible Union, he believed misrepresented the facts: 'missionaries of long standing ... could tell a very different story'. He gave as evidence of this the burnings of copies of Hastings' *Dictionary of the Bible* on grounds of the 'higher critical' views it contained by conservatives and the remark of an English evangelist in China that 'German theology is no good in a revival'.[108]

It is important to remember that the CIM was the largest Protestant missionary body in China at the time of the Inquiry, with some 1,000 missionaries in the field. John Mott at Jerusalem had found it, rightly, an 'impressive example of a great international missionary society'.[109] It had given no reason for its withdrawal from the NCC in 1926,[110] but it was generally assumed to be on theological grounds. The inquirers found the mission, whose work they admired (as, among others, 'splendid examples of devotion and sacrifice in social service by fundamentalists'[111]), unwilling to cooperate with the Inquiry as a body, though help was given regionally. They found that the CIM operated under an 'autocratic system of foreign control'[112] and that, where questions of devolution to the Chinese were involved, the mission was only prepared to hand over under very strict conditions 'intended to safeguard the orthodoxy of the teaching permitted therein'.[113] Thus, deeds of lease stipulated that no one teaching 'doctrinal views contrary to the recognised standards of the Mission should be invited to speak on the property'.[114]

While it is easy to make merry at the expense of conservative

[108] *Princeton Theological Review*, 19 (1921), pp. 630–71.
[109] *IMC/J*, vol. VII, p. 19.
[110] *LFMI*, vol. II, p. 95; vol. V, pp. 39–40.   [111] *Ibid.*, vol. II, p. 95.
[112] *Ibid.*, vol. V, p. 72.
[113] *Ibid.*, p. 73.
[114] *Ibid.*, p. 41 and note 31 quoting CIM 'Statement of Policy' of 1928.

Christians and to deplore conservative attacks on the inquirers by the conservative organ *Bible for China*, which stated that 'there is no cooperation possible between the two groups',[115] it is necessary to look below the surface, as the inquirers did. Conservative Christians were aiming to *conserve*: and, in particular, they aimed to conserve missionary fervour and devotion, based on a ready acceptance of the Scriptures as the word of God written. In so far as the church historically has also sought to conserve, by creeds, forms of approved ministry, doctrinal formulations and other methods, because it has believed that by these means the vital life of God, with which it is charged, can be preserved and offered to the world, the phenomenon present here has been a constant theme of Christian history. So, the inquirers noticed that 'the conservatives deplore the lack of conviction and spirituality on the part of the liberals ... the liberals ... the obtuse conventionality of the fundamentalists'; one side failed to value and use intelligence while the other showed 'neglect of the devotional life'.[116] Where the editor of the *Christian Century* could deplore missionary work 'shackled' by the conservatives,[117] when a conservative body like the Sunday School Union refused to change, its more liberal parent body, the World Sunday School Association, refused it funding.[118] Behind the refusal to change lay a threat by the CIM to withdraw in 1929, so frustrating change.[119]

When the inquirers looked at theological training and preaching they found the largest theological institution firmly in the hands of the conservatives. Watson Hayes, the scholarly polymath in charge here, was referred to as the J. G. Machen of China,[120] Machen being the learned conservative theologian who had caused R. E. Speer problems in his criticism of mission policy in Speer's denomination. The inquirers judged that 60 per cent of missionaries and church members in China were fundamentalists, although their use of this label for the

---

[115] *LFMI*, vol. v, p. 41.   [116] *Ibid.*, p. 353.
[117] *The Christian Century* 47, no. 11 (12 March 1930); *LFMI*, vol. v, p. 41.
[118] *LFMI*, vol. v, p. 40.   [119] *Ibid.*, p. 324.   [120] *Ibid.*, p. 281.

two able Scottish theologians, James Denney and James Orr, conservative but not fundamentalist, raises questions against their theological percipience in the use of the category.[121] As in India, the inquirers found preaching which tended to doctrinal rigidity made for a static church.[122] They complained again of too much talk, and bring to mind E. M. Forster's gibe in *A Passage to India* about 'poor, talkative little Christianity': 'far too often one gets the impression that Christianity is a religion of talk ... within an ingrown system of doctrines':[123] the church is talked to death and there is too much emphasis on verbal transmission, so that the church becomes a 'preaching and listening institution': they complain, too, of the 'talkie-talkies' of the Christian educators.

Against this alienating background, they called for a greater emphasis on the kingdom of God, away from an exclusively 'preaching-based' strategy and its dogmatic rigidities.[124] The need was for a comprehensive ideal, a programme based on economic and social information and which embraced the Chinese nation's total needs; and this not as a substitute for 'religious and spiritual activities' but rather as 'an expression of a comprehensive Christian program ... to the deepest and most urgent needs of China'.[125]

Perhaps it is appropriate to conclude this often sombre analysis of the Chinese mission field with the story told to the inquirers of a Chinese grandson, refused education by his grandfather and made to work in the fields in clothing so verminous that his brother had to take a stick to scrape off the lice. When he was aged 15, however, his grandfather met a Christian missionary, Arthur H. Smith, and became a Christian. The missionary asked to teach the illiterate boy to read. This led on to Christian faith, ordination and a family which provided a daughter who became secretary of the NCC. The evidence concluded: '[he said] had his grandfather not become a Christian, Kuan Yu-Chen would be an ignorant farmer.

---

[121] *Ibid.*, p. 282.   [122] *Ibid.*, vol. II, p. 74.   [123] *Ibid.*, p. 77.
[124] *Ibid.*, vol. v, pp. 352, 408.
[125] *Ibid.*, vol. II, pp. 51, 74–5.

Such lives as Kuan Yu-Chen are the best arguments for Christian missions that I know of.'[126]

JAPAN

Whereas modern Japan has a population of around 100 million people, in 1930 it numbered 64.5 million. In the period of the inquirers' visit, the population was increasing at around 900,000 a year. This placed great pressure on the resources of the country. Immigration had been attempted in Brazil and there was a large Japanese population in Korea, which was under Japanese government at the time. There had been Japanese immigration in North America, especially on the Pacific coast, where by 1920 there were some 111,000,[127] but in 1924 the United States debarred Japanese from further entry, as Australia had done and Canada effectively also. This legislation was a handicap for those American citizens who preached a universal gospel of love in Japan.[128] A Japanese minister of religion in California was quoted at the Jerusalem Conference as saying 'I have watched Christian America break almost every ideal I possess.'[129]

Politically, the 1920s were an unsettled period, with a number of political assassinations, including an attempt on the life of Emperor Hirohito in 1923. Japanese militarism and expansionism were present, not future, realities. The Japanese had intervened in Manchuria in 1928, a move resented by China and ultimately leading to full-scale Sino-Japanese war in 1937 which included the bombing of Shanghai, at a time when Europe was largely distracted by the civil war in Spain. The inquirers were plainly disturbed by the presence of militarist instructors in the boys' schools in Japan, inculcating the kind of unthinking discipline which was highly alien to their liberal humanist views of education.

The Protestant church in Japan was younger than those in

---

[126] *Ibid.*, vol. v, p. 157.   [127] *IMC/J*, vol. iv, pp. 142–3.
[128] *LFMI*, vol. vi, p. 106.
[129] *IMC/J*, vol. iv, p. 148.

India or China but, although only sixty years old, advancing towards independence. There were 1,198 Protestant missionaries,[130] a figure which could be compared to the 25,000 professional religious workers in the service of the Shinto religion.[131] The desire for an independent church was stronger even than in China, and the inquirers were told that 'the feeling against missionaries is almost universal'[132] by a highly placed pastor. A. K. Reischauer, the greatly respected missionary and authority on Buddhism, had spoken at Jerusalem of Japan's openness, since the First World War, to consider that Christianity could help her 'to her rightful place in the fellowship of nations'.[133] Reischauer told the inquirers how unacceptable it was to the Japanese, in view of these aspirations, to be linked with undeveloped nations in Asia and Africa as a 'mission field'. This, rather than objections to individual missionaries, comprised much of the wish for their removal as a class.[134]

Leading Japanese figures gave evidence of the strong influence of Christianity in the nation, so that, in the words of Professor Itagaki, 'most people respect Christianity' and, in the view of Baron Sato, 'the government will gradually accept Christian views'.[135] Leaders like Dr Neesima, Dr Nitobe and Baron Sato himself were felt by fellow Japanese to be effective in the spread of Christian influence.

The pre-eminent Christian Japanese leader was Toyohiko Kagawa (1888–1960). Kagawa had experienced tragedy as a child, losing both his wealthy father and a beloved geisha mother when aged 6. After a loveless upbringing, he came into contact with two American Presbyterian missionaries, Dr Myers and Dr Logan. The story of the crucifixion, interpreted as an act of love, led to Kagawa's conversion from a strongly Buddhist background. Decision for ordination training caused Kagawa to be rejected by his family, disinherited and

---

[130] *LFMI*, vol. VI, p. 24.   [131] *Ibid.*, pp. 295–6.
[132] *Ibid.*, p. 200; cf. pp. 198–203.
[133] *IMC/J*, vol. I, p. 233.   [134] *LFMI*, vol. VI, pp. 44–5.
[135] *Ibid.*, pp. 153–4.

disgraced.[136] At this point, showing a Franciscan attitude to Christ's love for the poor, in 1909 Kagawa went to live in the slums of Kobe in a district called Shikawa. Here, amongst ex-convicts, prostitutes and alcoholics he lived in a small, one-room shack, preaching love and living a life modelled on the Sermon on the Mount. He contracted trachoma, which badly affected his eyesight for life, from one of his diseased lodgers.

Kagawa was supremely an evangelist, who had decided to mount a campaign for a 'million souls' and Kingdom of God Movement before the arrival of the inquiry: but he combined evangelism with far-reaching social involvement and wide intellectual awareness. He was among the pioneers of labour movements in Japan and suffered arrest as an industrial agitator. He was aware of the needs of the rural population and started rural cooperatives and peasant schools. He knew the power of the pen and wrote a number of best-selling books, which included a semi-autobiographical novel, *Across the Death Line* (1920), which sold in very large numbers: at the rate of 100,000 copies a year for some years.[137] He also launched his own newspaper, 'The Kingdom of God Weekly'. This combination of evangelism and social involvement, for which he was widely renowned in the Christian world[138] had been noticed as absent among the evangelistically inclined in China: 'at the moment there is no Chinese worker [who] is leading in the amalgamation of the social with the evangelistic message as, for instance, Dr Kagawa is doing in Japan'.[139]

Kagawa, whose international standing was of the same level as Mahatma Gandhi's, has suffered something of an eclipse. A thorough and helpful modern study of his life concluded that, from this high standing, he has been reduced 'to relative obscurity'.[140] This may have resulted from his pacifist stand in

---

[136] C. J. Davey, *Kagawa of Japan* (London, 1960), pp. 1–13, 18, 22; W. Axling, *Kagawa* (London, 1932), pp. 11–39.

[137] Davey, *Kagawa of Japan*, p. 64; *Rethinking Missions* paid tribute to Kagawa as a writer (p. 188).

[138] *IMC/J*, vol. v, pp. 63–5.   [139] *LFMI*, vol. v, p. 353.

[140] R. Schildgren, *Toyohiko Kagawa: Apostle of Love and Social Justice* (Berkeley, 1988), p. 290: there is an extensive Japanese literature on Kagawa on catalogue at the Yale Divinity School library.

the Second World War, which caused him to oppose equally Japanese militarism and American bombing, some of his anti-American statements being used by the Japanese government as useful propaganda to the American nation. He was investigated by General MacArthur's government in Japan for anti-American activities during the war, but cleared.[141] As far as the inquirers were concerned, Kagawa was 'a rare evangelistic preacher, a flame of fire, a passionate and devoted follower of Jesus',[142] echoing the admiration expressed at Jerusalem.[143] They felt, however, that he needed others to supply the economic gifts for his schemes for reform,[144] they disliked the quantitative emphasis on a 'million souls' in the Kingdom of God Movement[145] and noted its high drop-out rate; but they approved of his Peasant Gospel Schools[146] as an attempt to grapple with the problems of rural Christianity; and the influence of his 'Friends of Jesus' groups in China, as a stimulus to Christian living, caused them to judge that he, more than any other Christian leader, had drawn the attention of the church to rural needs, rural reconstruction and rural evangelism.[147]

Overall, the Inquiry recognised the need for increasing indigenisation, for example in the leadership of the high schools, which the Jerusalem Conference had judged should be handed over to Japanese men and women of high ability and 'speedily'.[148] The high quality of generally-provided Japanese education, which meant that Japanese Christian parents often preferred the state's provision to Christian schools on educational grounds, meant that they called broadly for withdrawal from education by the missions.[149] Inquirers did not think, either, that the time was ripe for a 'Christian' university. They noted the decaying appeal of what they called the 'fundamentalist epic', with its emphasis on saving the 'heathen'[150]

---

[141] Schildgren, *Toyohiko Kagawa*, pp. 229, cf. 267–8; Davey, *Kagawa of Japan*, pp. 116, 136.
[142] *LFMI*, vol. III, p. 45, cf. p. 61.
[143] *IMC/J*, vol. V, pp. 63, 64–9; cf. vol. I, pp. 150–7.
[144] *LFMI*, vol. III, p. 45.[145] *Ibid.*, pp. 61–2.[146] *Ibid.*, p. 66.
[147] *Ibid.*, vol. V, p. 337; VI, p. 42 and note 17, pp. 61, 88, 92, 228.
[148] *IMC/J*, vol. II, p. 182.[149] *Rethinking Missions*, pp. 172–6.
[150] *LFMI*, vol. VI, p. 100.

and its appearance of Christian superiority and patronage to
an advanced nation.[151] They observed a renaissance of
Buddhism,[152] Japanese distaste for Christian denominationalism[153] and desire to see holy lives.[154] They appear to have
been somewhat disturbed by the appearance of Barthian theology, especially in Tokyo, which they considered to be linked to
the pessimism of the Japanese character expressed in Shinto
religion.[155] Japanese Christians pondered whether such a theological attitude would lead to a lack of activism,[156] issuing from
a theology which they viewed as 'defeatist' and 'pietistic'. The
inquirers deplored the lack of study of, and interest in,
economic and social conditions by missionaries:[157] it could be
for this reason, that is, the church's neglect of such matters,
that many Japanese followed the Christian ethic and way of
life but did not attend churches: 'most Christians do not go to
church ... many Christians have no church affiliations'.[158] It
was an aspect of Japanese life that Emil Brunner, who taught
in Tokyo twenty years later, was to make the basis for an
alternative ecclesiology in the 1950s.[159]

REACTIONS TO THE LAYMEN'S FOREIGN MISSION INQUIRY

In the early 1930s, when the findings of the LFMI were
published, the result was that 'it was the Commission of
Appraisal that found itself on trial, not the missionary enterprise'.[160] Pearl Buck might say that *Rethinking Missions* was 'the
only book I have ever read which seemed to me literally true in
its every observation and right in its every conclusion',[161] but a

---

[151] *Ibid.*, p. 151.   [152] *Ibid.*, p. 19.   [153] *Ibid.*, vol. III, p. 60.
[154] *Ibid.*, p. 47.
[155] *Ibid.*, p. 63.   [156] *Ibid.*, vol. VI, pp. 148–9.   [157] *Ibid.*, vol. III, pp. 53–4.
[158] *Ibid.*, vol. VI, p. 157.
[159] E. Brunner, *Dogmatics* 3 vols. (Eng. tr. London, 1949–62), vol. III, *The Christian Doctrine of the Church, Faith and the Consummation*, pp. 106–33.
[160] P. Varg, *Missionaries, Diplomats and Chinese: the American Protestant Missionary Movement in China 1890–1952* (Princeton, 1958), p. 169.
[161] *The Christian Century* 49, no. 47 (23 November 1932); W. R. Hutchison, *Errand to the World*, p. 167.

missionary leader like R. E. Speer, confronted by heavyweight
conservative critics like J. G. Machen, who accused the Presbyterian Board of theological relativism, saw it differently. But
Speer's reaction in his *Rethinking Missions Examined* (1933) must
be viewed as more than simple expediency, how to hold
together the conservative and liberal supporters of the mission.
He and others, like J. A. Mackay and K. S. Latourette, discerned a shift, not simply in a greater emphasis on the social
implications of Christian mission away from individualistic
evangelism,[162] but in the central issue of the person of Christ.
In a passage of great importance at this range, *Rethinking
Missions* laid out effectively two forms of Christology:[163] Jesus,
the supreme religious teacher and exemplar of a life lived in
union with God, whose example provides support for those
who 'subsequently desire to carry out the same venture';[164] and
the Christ who 'to many Christians' (significantly not all)
offered a life of fellowship in union with himself and with other
Christians in the fellowship of his Church, and for whom he is
'in a unique sense "Son of God"'. This view is not shared by
all. There are 'differences of conception' which exist. Beneath
them, however, 'are underlying agreements belonging to the
essence of Christianity'.[165]

Speer's paper at Jerusalem, as Söderblom's and Temple's,
had shown how important historic understandings of the
person of Christ were to him.[166] It was here that the deepest
issues lay. For to take the first view was not untrue to Christian
sources; but it was certainly less than adequate as a representation of historic Christian faith. So, J. A. Mackay, the learned
missionary in South America, who became President of Princeton Theological Seminary, referred to the report as 'the sun-
set glow of nineteenth century romanticism',[167] and K. S.
Latourette, great historian of missions, saw it as a product of

---

[162] *LFMI*, vol. vii, p. 169.   [163] *Rethinking Missions*, pp. 55–6.
[164] *Ibid.*, p. 55.
[165] *Ibid.*, p. 56.
[166] *IMC/J*, vol. i, pp. 417–40 (Speer); pp. 459–76 (Temple); vol. iii, pp. 133–54
(Söderblom).
[167] *IRM*, 22, no. 85 (April 1933), p. 178, cf. pp. 180–1.

'left-centre' American Protestantism; he found in it no emphasis on the doctrine of the Cross and Atonement, none on the
resurrection or on the Holy Spirit; nor, ecclesiologically, on
ministry, creeds, sacraments or the church as the body of
Christ. Certainly, the report was critically weak on the church,
which occasionally seemed an optional extra to the kingdom
and community development, though O. A. Petty could write
of the church as an 'essential agency' for the kingdom;[168] but
he was a notable exception.

Among other responses, A. G. Baker, who will appear in the
next chapter as a writer on mission in relation to other faiths,
wrote with appreciation and discernment of the different positions which the report disclosed in the contemporary scene;[169]
J. H. Oldham welcomed the report but 'profoundly disagreed'
with it;[170] while William Paton shared J. A. Mackay's critical
theological response but still remained proud of his own
involvement in the Indian section, because the report would be
a stepping-stone towards the independence of the Indian
church.[171]

It would be a tragic mistake, however, to shelve the volumes
of the Inquiry on the grounds of such criticisms or the less-
than-adequate Christian theology, what Hendrik Kraemer
was to call 'a very weak sense of apostolic consciousness'.[172]
The report provided a wealth of information on Christian
mission in China, India and Japan; many of its judgements
have to be taken extremely seriously, then as now, not least by
any form of Christian mission which, under the guise of
'proclamation', allows itself to become the voluble reiteration
of an ossified theology, failing to relate to the context, national
and local, in which it is set. In its attempt to follow through a
'comprehensive' view of mission, as expressed at Jerusalem
(what today would be called 'holistic' mission) the *Inquiry*
served the missions well with its critique and attempt to apply

---

[168] *LFMI*, vol. IV, p. 156.
[169] *Journal of Religion* 13, no. 4 (October 1933), pp. 379–98.
[170] Oldham quoted in E. Jackson, *Red Tape and the Gospel*, p. 121.
[171] Paton quoted in *ibid.*
[172] H. Kraemer, *The Christian Message in a Non-Christian World* (London, 1938), p. 36.

correctives to existing programmes: and, as part of this, it supplied a searching appraisal of the missions' educational, medical and agricultural responses to human need which was of considerable value, as was the firm support and backing given to the younger churches in their search for independence and indigenisation.

CHAPTER 4

Mission appraised (2): 1920–1940

The period from 1928 to 1938, between the Jerusalem and Tambaram, Madras, Conferences of the IMC, with the short period that followed before the Second World War engulfed missionary thinking, were years when missiology focussed particularly upon the relationship of Christian faith to other religious traditions. The first volume of the Jerusalem report was entitled *The Christian Life and Message in Relation to Non-Christian Systems of Thought and Life* and included papers on Christianity and Hinduism (Nicol Macnicol), Christianity and Islam (Temple Gairdner and the American W. A. Eddy), Christianity and Buddhism (A. K. Reischauer and K. J. Saunders) and Christianity and Confucianism (J. L. Stuart and D. W. Lyon). The paper which probably caused the most stir was by the American Quaker Rufus Jones, 'Secular Civilisation and the Christian Task', which has been noted before as the product of Oldham's awareness of secular issues and Mott's choice of speaker. Between the Jerusalem Conference of 1928 and the Tambaram Conference of 1938, and as a direct result of the continuing debate on these questions, the IMC commissioned Hendrik Kraemer's preparatory volume for Tambaram, *The Christian Message in a Non-Christian World* (1938), the most substantial piece of theological work to emerge from the IMC's life. Again, the first volume of the Tambaram report was on the same theme: *The Authority of the Faith*, and the reverberations of Kraemer's book and the responses to it by theologians, previously noted, of the calibre of A. G. Hogg and

94

D. S. Cairns, continued at the conference and in the pages of
the *IRM* after it up to the outbreak of war in 1939.

From the opening issue of his editorship of the *IRM*, Oldham
had indicated that he intended to give an important place to
thinking about the relationship of Christianity with the other
living faiths and also the manner in which he hoped to see it
approached. So, it was not enough to do an exercise in comparative religion. What was required was to find 'in actual
experience [what is] . . . really living . . . as distinct from that
which is merely traditional and formal' in the other tradition:
what, also, are the 'vital forces of the gospel as it comes in
contact with non-Christian peoples' and 'what aspects of it
possess the greatest power of appeal'.[1] He encouraged experts
in the field, often but not always serving missionaries, to handle
this theme; for example, in a series of articles later published as
a composite pamphlet, *The Vital Forces of Islam.*[2]

On the whole these articles can be characterised as welcom-
ing and inclusive in general approach. So, Nicol Macnicol
could write of Hinduism, 'we see [Hindu seekers] seeking not
only God's gifts but God Himself . . . dare we say there are no
finders? "I have tasted sweetness at his feet" says Tukaram'.[3] A
Japanese national like Tasuku Harada, president of Doshisha
College, wrote that to him 'it is inconceivable that anyone who
has impartially studied the history of religion can fail to admit
the universality of the activity of the Spirit of God and the
consequent embodiment of a degree of truth in all faiths'.[4]
Contributors looked back to the days of the melting-pot of
religions in the Mediterranean world of the early church and
the inclusive responses of the early fathers: Henri Junod, missionary and religious anthropologist of renown, reflecting on
the Bantu religion he knew so well, recalled Justin Martyr's
emphasis on paganism as not simply 'a mixture of gloom and
vice' but also as containing 'discernible streaks of light'.[5]
Clement of Alexandria's view of the Logos, present in other

[1] *IRM*, 1, no. 1 (1912), p. 3.   [2] *Ibid.*, pp. 44–61; 2, no. 6 (1913).
[3] *Ibid.*, 5, no. 18 (1916), p. 219.
[4] *Ibid.*, 1, no. 1 (1912), p. 91.   [5] *Ibid.*, 3, no. 9 (1914), pp. 105–6.

traditions, was invoked by Professor K. Mackichan, principal of Wilson College, Bombay, in relation to Indian philosophical and religious literature, as Clement had developed it, to include pre-Christian philosophy: 'gleams of truth which the Christian church ought to be ready to accept as an evidence of the diffused energy of the divine Logos', and as 'thoughts which have sustained the philosophies of India through ages of profound spiritual seeking after God'.[6] The Anglican bishop of Calcutta, G. A. Lefroy, who reviewed the composite volume of the articles on Islam, was glad to find even in the Muslim world the signs of Tertullian's famous description *'anima naturaliter Christiana* [a spirit naturally Christian]'.[7]

There had been, however, another strand of opinion present in the *IRM*, as also among the Continental theologians who showed such anxiety before the Jerusalem Conference. One example of this was the only article in the early years of the journal's life to deal specifically with the subject of the Christian message. Julius Richter, when taking up his appointment as Professor of Missions in Berlin, had given his inaugural lecture on the subject of 'Methods of Missionary Apologetic'. This was translated and printed by Oldham later. By contrast to the views already noted, Richter was frankly exclusivist: 'Christianity is an exclusive religion. Wherever Christian missionary enterprise comes into contact with the non-Christian religions it sets itself to oust them . . . in the conviction that this is necessary to the salvation of their adherents.' For Richter, as the bacilli of unbelief spread even to the remote hamlets of Europe, the missionary needed to be made spiritually immune 'through the theological clarification of his Christian consciousness' on the vital matter of 'the superiority of his religion to all others', a conviction all the more necessary in view of the prevailing 'history of religions' school of the day which 'threatens to level down the religious conception of humanity to an unrelieved relativism'.[8] This emphasis was taken up prior to the Jerusalem Conference by Professor Frick

[6] *Ibid.*, no. 10 (1914), pp. 247–8, 253.   [7] *Ibid.*, 4, no. 14 (1915), pp. 319–20.
[8] *Ibid.*, 3, no. 7 (1913), pp. 521, 523, 525, 528.

of the University of Geissen. He took D. J. Fleming to task for 'eradicating a sense of superiority' in Fleming's *Whither Bound in Missions?* (1925). While wishing to distinguish carefully between the gospel and any civilisation to which it might give rise, Frick insisted that 'fragile and treacherous' as the Christianity offered might be, 'Christian missions must be based upon a conviction of the superiority of their message if they are to remain sound and honest'; and so missionaries and Christians generally 'may not surrender the conviction of superiority'.[9] A. K. Reischauer, a serving missionary in a Buddhist setting, regretted this emphasis on superiority by a kind of a priori appeal: what was needed was the empirical data of superiority in life and practice.[10]

There was, therefore, a background of divided opinions in missionary circles after the Edinburgh Conference of 1910. The generally sympathetic approach, which had been represented in the responses sent to D. S. Cairns by, for example, J. N. Farquhar, with his stress on fulfilment, was evident in the *IRM* of 1912–28: but if the 'yes' was present, however qualified by sympathetic contributors, the 'no' was also present, though A. G. Hogg, whose criticism of Farquhar was used as an example of an unqualified 'no' to this approach earlier,[11] was to join hands with Nicol Macnicol in affirming aspects of Hindu religion as not only seeking, but finding, in the debate which followed Kraemer's epoch-making contribution between the two conferences.

APPROACHES TO OTHER RELIGIONS: JERUSALEM CONFERENCE 1928 AND AFTER

In his preliminary paper at the Jerusalem Conference, Nicol Macnicol struck the note of sympathetic appreciation of the good in Hinduism: 'we have to see that . . . [with whatever is destroyed] is not destroyed the spirit of religion itself . . . the Indian spirit [has] much . . . that is precious and beautiful.

[9] *Ibid.*, 15, no. 60 (1926), pp. 625–6.   [10] *Ibid.*, 17, no. 65 (1928), pp. 122–3.
[11] See chapter 1 above.

[They] belong to the Indian heritage and it is our part and
endeavour so to bring Christ to the Indian people . . . that He
shall preserve and strengthen all that is noble and destroy only
the unworthy and evil'.[12] Faced with criticism, as from the
philosopher Bertrand Russell, who had recently visited China
and made adverse comment on missions, it was necessary to
make it clear that 'the Christ whom we preach does not destroy
any gracious and beautiful trait in the character of the Hindu
. . . He came not to destroy but to fulfil.' Christ, as He enters
the Hindu milieu, 'will make what he finds there that is fair
more fair, taking away only what is unworthy. He will not
quench the smoking flax.'[13] Macnicol was alive to the evils of
caste, which he believed must be wholly demolished as an
unjust and cruel edifice. He was also aware of the kind of
impersonal pantheism to which even fervent forms of Hindu
religious theism seemed to tend: monism, with its 'absolute
unity of *advaita* [non-duality]' 'leaves no room for the spirit of
man to breathe'.[14] Despite its virtues, for example, its emphasis
on home life, to Macnicol Hindu life was 'drab, dull, spiritless'
and its chief virtue was submission. Even so, he disliked talk of
Christian superiority. Any superiority lay in the vision of
Christ, which should humble Western Christians, often 'poor
in our lack of insight into religious truth compared with many
Hindus' and should induce humility.[15]

One may compare Macnicol's approach of sympathy with
one of the most able and theologically informed papers in the
whole report, not printed in volume I but germane to it.
Archbishop Söderblom, first met in these pages with Moody
and Mott as a young man at Northfield, Massachusetts, but
after 1914 Archbishop of Uppsala, was unable to deliver his
paper in person; but it was printed in volume III of the report.
He wrote as one who by then had spent thirty-seven years in
the study of comparative religion and was an acknowledged
authority in the field. At first, the study of religions revealed
similarities, but then came the recognition of sharp diver-

---

[12] *IMC/J*, vol. I, p. 4.   [13] *Ibid.*, p. 13.   [14] *Ibid.*, pp. 21–2, 42.
[15] *Ibid.*, pp. 50–2.

gences; for example, Buddha, Muhammad and Christ 'are quite different': 'unique and absolute truth has in Christianity the shape not of a rule, a law (*Dharma*) . . . ideas, theologies but Christian revelation has the shape of a man: God reveals himself in a human life. As Glover [this is T. R. Glover, a layman, Baptist and classical scholar at Cambridge, England] has expressed it, God cannot do better than to resemble Jesus Christ. Christ is no *avatar*, not a divine messenger among others: he is, according to the whole New Testament, the unique Son (John 1:18; Rom. 1:4).' This, to the Roman Empire, was a scandal: 'the uniqueness of this new *Kurios* [Lord] amongst all the different *Kurioi* worshipped at that epoch . . . further, the uniqueness, the supernatural claims and character of that Lord and of his message, in comparison with all the current conceptions of the Divine . . . was a new and scandalous thing in the antique world'. This claim of

uniqueness, of absolute truth itself belongs to the originality of the biblical revelation. The claim was inherited from Judaism . . . we do not find anywhere in the great religions that claim of being unique which characterises authentic Christianity from the very beginning. The other great religions are not only tolerant, they are eclectic, in principle if not in fact . . . Christianity puts up against all such ideas its own absolute truth.[16]

Particularly, how is one to explain that Christianity, generally reckoned as the highest of religions, obtrudes 'the hideous spectacle of the cross, abhorrent to every civilized taste? . . . The cross is the strongest testimony that God has been seeking man. God's way is as unhuman as possible. But it is no idea: it is an historic fact.'[17]

As a statement of his position Söderblom's paper was of a quality observed earlier in R. H. Tawney's submission. For someone who had been immersed in the 'history of religions' school, suspect for its religious relativism to many Continental theologians, he struck some remarkably Barthian notes, though his sources were plainly his own and direct influence uncertain. An equivalently profound student of other religions, Rudolf

[16] *Ibid.*, vol. III, pp. 144, 146, 148   [17] *Ibid.*, p. 149.

Otto, also contributed to the discussions, reminding the
members that F. D. E. Schleiermacher had always insisted
that 'coming to Christ is never a prolongation but always a
break'; and that, though there were similarities between Hindu
bhakti religion and Christian faith, as also between the teaching
of the *Bhagavad-Gita* and justification by faith, he would still
hold that there was a great gulf fixed between the two: a Hindu
convert, like Pandita Ramabai, showed that 'when Christ finds
a Hindu it means a complete break'. Not all, however, including the Indian woman participant, Miss Tilak, agreed: 'Christ
to some comes as fulfilment, to others he comes as a break with
the past'.[18]

Before turning to Rufus Jones' paper, certain other participants in the discussions deserve to be mentioned: of the Continentals, Julius Richter recognised the presence of spiritual
values in other religions but felt that 'as a method of missionary
approach this way seems to us [i.e. the Continental partici-
pants] of doubtful value' for they were aware of the 'great . . .
wave of syncretism which is approaching all the world over',[19]
a view endorsed by Karl Heim who, while accepting that it was
'remarkable progress . . . that they did not make any longer
the distinction between the one true religion and all the other
religions which were called false' still asked whether a 'free
discussion between all the leading spirits of all the religions of
the earth' was a fit replacement; if all religions were just
different expressions of the 'same mystic feelings' 'missionary
work was finished'.[20] Judge Chenchiah, a learned Indian
Christian from Madras, reminded the meeting that the non-
Christian religions could no longer be regarded as opponents of
Christianity but had now become its competitors, in his view
the chief change since the Edinburgh Conference of 1910.[21] Of
English contributors, Oliver Quick, whose article following
Jerusalem will be discussed later, identified the tension
between the universality of the Christian message and its
uniqueness, a uniqueness not sufficiently stressed in the prelim-

[18] *Ibid.*, vol 1, p. 383 cf. p. 51.   [19] *Ibid.*, p. 353.   [20] *Ibid.*, p. 351.
[21] *Ibid.*, p. 361.

inary papers in his view,[22] while William Temple stated that 'if the gospel was true, it has to be true everywhere', a note struck in the final statement that he drafted.[23] E. Stanley Jones asked himself if Gandhi's conversion to Christianity would make a difference to him and, on the basis of Christ's universality and uniqueness, held that it would 'satisfy the depth of his heart about God'.[24] J. A. Mackay, R. E. Speer, W. E. Hocking and S. M. Zwemer all contributed, Speer holding that to say Christianity was 'better' was but to use the language of the epistle to the Hebrews in its assessment of Judaism; and Mackay that 'in the fact of the incarnation one found the objectivity in religion which our whole personality craves'.[25]

Rufus Jones was not alone in laying emphasis on secular values: Quick, for one, drew attention to the scientist's disinterested search for truth with its moral discipline and willingness to face the facts.[26] Rufus Jones gave an extremely able paper, 'Secular Civilisation and the Christian Task', which recognised 'extra church values' as often strong. He compared the sacrificial consecration of the scientist to that of a saint. Nevertheless, the 'greatest rival of Christianity in the world to-day' was not Islam, Buddhism or Hinduism but 'a world-wide secular way of life and interpretation of the nature of things'. Faced with such a universal phenomenon, the response of Christians must be to view other religions 'which secularism attacks' as 'witnesses of man's need for God and allies in our quest for perfection ... gladly recognising the good they contain, we bring to them the best that our religion has brought to us that they may test it for themselves'. He concluded with a sentence which W. E. Hocking at least among his hearers must have approved: 'we ask them to judge us, not by what we have as yet made of our Christianity, but by that better and more perfect religion to which in the providence of God we believe our Master is leading us'.[27]

Despite his appreciative review of mission history, a know-

[22] *Ibid.*, p. 378.   [23] *Ibid.*, p. 356, 483.   [24] *Ibid.*, p. 356.
[25] *Ibid.*, pp. 431, 451.
[26] *Ibid.*, pp. 412, 451.   [27] *Ibid.*, pp. 284, 298, 338.

ledgeable and instructive survey, it was plain that Rufus Jones
was felt to have gone a great deal too far in the direction of
accommodation to other traditions. Temple's and Speer's final
statement tried to redress this by the stress given to the centrality of Christ. The existence of a 'new relativism' was recognised, 'which seeks to enthrone itself in human thought'. In
such a context 'our message is Jesus Christ' in whom 'we come
face to face with the ultimate reality of the universe'. The
gospel 'announces glorious Truth. Its very nature forbids us to
say that it may be right belief for some but not for others.
Either it is true for all or it is not true at all.' But Christ, with
St John's prologue, is the light which enlightens every man and
in the other religions this light, which shone in full splendour in
Christ, is also present, so that 'we welcome every noble quality
in non-Christian persons or systems' as proof that (again in
New Testament words) God 'has nowhere left Himself without
witness'. The gospel has the power to speak to the human heart
about the love of God, not as to a Muslim or Buddhist or an
adherent of any system, but as to a human being. What was
needed for Christian people was a 'more heroic practice of the
Gospel'.[28]

THE CONTINUING DEBATE

The Jerusalem statement was a fine attempt to hold together
positions which were certainly in danger of flying apart into
opposing camps. It could not, however, be expected to provide
finality. Various pieces of writing showed that the debate was
still very much alive. D. J. Fleming's two books of 1928 and
1929, *Attitudes toward Other Faiths* (1928) and *Ways of Sharing
with Other Faiths* (1929) pressed traditionalists gently but firmly
to go as far as possible in common understanding, though
Fleming made no secret of his own Christian commitment and
evangelistic purpose.[29] In the pages of the *IRM*, Oliver Quick
expanded on his contribution at Jerusalem in a particularly
fine article, which bears reading and re-reading on the subject:

[28] *Ibid.*, pp. 480, 483, 490–1, 495.
[29] D. J. Fleming, *Ways of Sharing with Other Faiths* (New York, 1929), p. 147.

faced with 'scientific relativism' it was necessary, not only on theological but also on practical grounds, for the Christian protagonist to avoid a false humility about the gospel, appropriate to the messenger but not to a message which is not his but God's. The old view of exclusivism, which successfully maintained the uniqueness of the gospel, did so at a certain cost and needed to be re-expressed: instead of a view of 'solids' displacing fluid, the kind of matter-based thinking which was unhelpful to theology, there needed to be a view of the gospel as the action of light, giving reflections of itself on surfaces, which in turn highlight its own brightness 'by the variety of tints which it makes visible'. As other religions are seen in their best and truest colours by the light of the gospel, so the gospel itself is enriched by its contact with all that is best in what it illuminates. This is not a relativist or syncretistic proposal but (as Quick had also said at Jerusalem) to find Christ unexpectedly at *Nazareth*, in Galilee of the Gentiles, despised for so being by the orthodox. Quick hoped to combine the two strands of the uniqueness and universality of the gospel by this means.[30]

In 1933, another English theologian of some eminence, Edwyn Bevan, Fellow of New College, Oxford, and author of a masterly small volume, *Christianity*, returned to themes touched on by Söderblom at Jerusalem in the *IRM*. He faced the perpetual question of the sheer intransigence of Christian faith, in both the early days of the church and again in the pluralist situation of his own century. In that fateful year for Jewry, he wrote on 'Christian Propaganda among Jews'.[31] He deplored equally Christian wrongs done to Jews in the past and Nazi persecution of them as non-Aryans in the present. Like Glover and Söderblom, however, he pointed to the 'intransigence' which both Jew and Christian had shown in the ancient world. In relation to Mithraism, Isis-worship and other religious manifestations, 'alone of the religions then in the world the two intransigent ones have survived. Such intransigence is essential

[30] *IRM*, 17, no. 67 (1928), pp. 445–54.
[31] *Ibid.*, 22, no. 88 (1933), pp. 481–99; Edwyn Bevan, *Christianity* (London, 1932).

to Jewish and Christian belief.' For the Christian, belief in Jesus was not a variable, which, as requested by one rabbi (arguing in the *IRM* for a shared biblical theism), could be set aside, it was essential and distinctive and the Christian was necessarily as intransigent over it as Jewish believers over the unity of God. Christians, Bevan held, because of their world-view, 'could not possibly renounce propaganda among Jews – or indeed among any people – without giving up their Christian faith'.[32] The case was argued with logic, clarity and learning and with realisation of the pain it might cause his Jewish readers.

In 1934 A. G. Baker, a Professor of Missions in the University of Chicago, published his *Christian Missions and a New World Culture*. For Baker, there was now no more reason for the Christian to claim 'special miraculous origin for his religion than for the Japanese to boast that they are the chosen children of heaven'; but to admit this 'does not for a moment require us to hold that one religion is as good as another'. There were differences, 'yet none can claim absolute finality and infallibility. Each religion – theistic, pantheistic, polytheistic, monistic or pluralistic – may be described as experimenting in its own peculiar manner with the problems of life.' For Baker, what seemed to matter most was the sense of values to be embraced by the developing world culture; it seemed a secondary matter whether these were given a Christian or a Buddhist label.[33] Jesus was seen to contain certain aspects which were universal and which could be offered to others beyond Christendom, but only as a unique collection in the sense that any other personality or set of physical combinations in the universe could be said to be unique. Jesus became ultimately a relative figure.[34]

Hendrik Kraemer's work may be regarded as the counter-blast to the kind of theology of missions propounded by Baker and underlying the LFMI report of 1933, but Kraemer was not alone. J. A. Mackay's article in the *IRM* of 1933 as a response to *Rethinking Missions* has already been noted. Another figure of

[32] *Ibid.*, pp. 487, 497.

[33] A. C. Baker, *Christian Missions and a New World Culture* (Chicago, 1934), pp. 291–2, 308.

[34] *Ibid.*, pp. 312–13.

stature, influenced by Karl Barth and himself both theologian and mission administrator, was Karl Hartenstein (1894–1952). Hartenstein was a considerable figure in German missionary circles. He was born into a banking family, Lutheran in tradition. He was educated in theology at the University of Tübingen and served with distinction in the German army during the First World War. He was decorated twice with the Iron Cross, the second of these awards being of the highest class for his bravery in the battle of the Somme in 1916. He was given a still higher award by the Kaiser in 1918. In 1926 Hartenstein became director of the Basel Mission. He was already a student of Barth's *Römerbrief* and other writings, under the friendly direction of Karl Heim. In 1927 he gave a lecture in Stuttgart, 'What Has the Theology of Karl Barth to Say to Mission?'.[35] In the *IRM* of 1931 he criticised equally talk of 'fulfilment' and of 'superiority', particularly in relation to Western civilisation. The cross of Christ indicated that human beings were mutineers, even the good ones, rebels against God and his revelation of himself in Jesus Christ. 'Fulfilment' must therefore be reserved strictly for Christ in his fulfilment of the Old Testament prophecies: and any so-called 'Christian culture', far from claiming any 'superiority', should recognise that it was palpably under the sentence of death, which Western culture plainly was. Here was the emphasis on the life of faith as struggle, the destruction of Western illusions and the need for radical decisions, which adopted the 'either-or' theology of Barth in the service of mission, even if, according to his friends, Hartenstein later came to side with Emil Brunner's views and version of the 'crisis' theology.[36]

HENDRIK KRAEMER (1888–1965)

Two remarkable Dutchmen contributed ably and extensively to the life of the IMC and the WCC, Hendrik Kraemer and

---

[35] W. Metzger, *Karl Hartenstein: ein leben für Kirche und Mission* (Stuttgart, 1954), pp. 9–44, 162–3; *Zwischen den Zeiten*, 6 (1928), pp. 59ff.

[36] *IRM*, 20, no. 78 (1931), pp. 223, 225; Metzger, *Hartenstein*, pp. 162–3; *IBMR*, 8, no. 3 (1984), pp. 128–30.

W. A. Visser 't Hooft. The importance of their fellow country-
man J. C. Hoekendijk in modern missiological development
has already been noted. Kraemer, a lay missionary in Java
from 1922, is a reminder of the importance of Dutch colonial
possessions in the East Indies from the days of the seventeenth-
century search for trade by English, French and Dutch mer-
chants in the East. The Dutch had acquired a substantial
empire in what became Indonesia, in Java and other possessions.[37] Dutch Protestant ministry had a long history in the
East, as did the Netherlands Missionary Society founded in
1797. It had a famous director in our period, J. W. Gunning
(1897–1923), who attended the Edinburgh Conference of 1910
and served on Commission IV on 'The Missionary Message'. In
the nineteenth century this society had seen substantial
numbers of conversions in central and eastern Java among
Muslims; and in the twentieth century, between the two world
wars, had benefited from the work of some outstanding missionary figures in Central Celebes (Central Sulawesi) from the
Netherlands Bible Society, Kraemer among them. This had
resulted in the kind of group and mass movements, by way of
the delay of individual baptisms, which has been described
among the Papuans. The Dutch had developed a view of their
colonial possessions not dissimilar to British ideas of
'trusteeship': such ideas, the so-called 'political-ethical'
approach, were espoused by the Dutch Reformed leader,
Abraham Kuyper. An interesting feature of the Dutch administration of missions was the establishment of a 'mission-
consulate' in Batavia, a government appointee who took
responsibility for the relationship between the government and
the missions. For some of our period, Baron van Boetzelaer was
consul. He and his wife were both active in IMC circles and the
baroness became one of two female vice-chairmen to Mott at
the Tambaram Conference of 1938.[38]

Hendrik Kraemer had lost both his parents in childhood and
was brought up in an orphanage. As a young man he was

[37] S. C. Neill, *Colonialism and Christian Missions* (London, 1966), pp. 170–202.
[38] Minutes of the IMC, Tambaram, Madras, p. 39; *CDCWM*, pp. 279–81.

introduced to the work of the Netherlands Bible Society by the Dutch missionary and Bible translator, Nicolaus Adriani (1865–1926). Adriani and his wife had worked with another great Dutch missionary figure, A. C. Kruyt, among the Toradjan people of Central Celebes. They were committed to the kind of structural approach towards a whole people in mission, and towards the building of an indigenous church, already noted. Kraemer had been impressed by John Mott, who had addressed the Dutch SCM in 1913 and urged the needs of an emerging Javanese student élite on Dutch members of the WSCF. Kraemer had also met and helped J. H. Oldham during a visit to Holland prior to the Edinburgh Conference, at a time when Oldham was finding J. W. Gunning a useful bridge between the Anglo-Saxon and Continental strands of missionary thinking. After his studies at Leiden, Kraemer suggested to the Netherlands Bible Society that he should be allowed to study Javanese development: through prompting from Adriani, this resulted in a thesis on Javanese mysticism, with the intention of equipping its author to reach Muslim intellectuals with the Christian message.

In terms of his intellectual background Kraemer had been exposed to a number of influences, missionary and theological, which could have been expected to cause him to emphasise a 'continuity' view of the relationship between Christianity and the non-Christian religions. Thus, both J. W. Gunning and Adriani saw mission as the injection into the existing society of a kind of Christian 'vitalism' not dissimilar to Bruno Gutmann's views, though Adriani considered that this 'divine life power' would entail a radical reorientation of traditional religion. Kraemer had also learned from the professor of the 'history of religions' school, P. A. Chantepie de la Saussaye, who saw Christianity as the summit of religious development and wanted to emphasise that there was no discontinuity in the divinely directed process, even if there was a qualitative difference in the revelation given in Christ. Kraemer did not study Karl Barth until the mid-1920s.[39]

[39] C. F. Hallencreutz, *Kraemer towards Tambaram* (Lund, 1966), pp. 21–53, 70, 85–93.

Between 1922 and 1928 Kraemer had done his first term of missionary service in central Java, where he met with the equally well-known missionary to Muslims, S. M. Zwemer, of Dutch extraction though from an immigrant North American family. The two did not always agree on the missionary approach to Muslims, Zwemer tending towards controversy and aggression, where Kraemer favoured dialogue rather than a controversial method, although he realised that dialogue could lead to dispute nevertheless. In 1927, Mott had invited Kraemer to give the leading paper on Islam at the Jerusalem Conference: Kraemer refused but had agreed to chair the section on Islam when Temple Gairdner, who was critically ill, was unable to do so. Kraemer's contribution at the conference and the general impression that he had created through his knowledge of Islam and other religions had led people like J. H. Oldham and others, among them Wilson Cash (the general secretary of the CMS) and William Paton to believe that, if the question of the Christian message was to be addressed at Tambaram, in Oldham's words, 'I do not think anyone better could be found to tackle the question.' A final invitation to contribute such a book was extended to Kraemer at the Old Jordans meeting of the IMC in 1936: it was to 'state the fundamental position of the Christian church as a witness-bearing body in the modern world, relating this to conflicting views of the attitude to be taken by Christians towards other faiths and dealing in detail with the evangelistic approach to the great non-Christian faiths'.[40] Kraemer realised that in accepting the invitation, he had accepted 'an impossible task'. Evangelism or the witness of the church had to be the 'main concern of this book'.[41]

Before embarking on his manuscript Kraemer wrote to some of the leading missionary interpreters of the Christian message among the other religions, A. G. Hogg (Hinduism), K. L. Reichelt and A. K. Reischauer (Buddhism) and the Chinese

[40] IMC Ad Interim Committee Minutes, Old Jordans 1936; C. F. Hallencreutz, *Kraemer*, pp. 141, 159–60, 181–2.
[41] H. Kraemer, *The Christian Message in a Non-Christian World*, p. v.

national, T. C. Chao, among others. He expressed the technical difficulties of his task to William Paton: to address a
varied readership of the missionary movement comprised of
English, Americans, Germans and Orientals on such a theme
with their differing expectations, although he held that the
IMC had been wise to give the task to one mind rather than
entrust it to a committee of multiple authorship. Despite his
hesitations and the range and profundity of a deeply theological work, with its world-wide perspective, he wrote the
book in seven weeks in the autumn of 1937.[42] By then he had
been appointed Professor of the History of Religions in the
University of Leiden.

In his preface Kraemer struck the kind of note which was to
recur throughout: 'missionary . . . manifestations can only
legitimately be called Christian and missionary when they
issue directly from the apostolic urgency of gladly witnessing to
God and his saving and redeeming Power through Christ'.[43]
This apostolic emphasis on witness, which he found absent in
the LFMI report, lay not so much in simply following the
apostles, but in the witness-bearing character of the church: it
is this which makes the Church apostolic and so to realise its
essential nature: 'to become conscious of its apostolic character
is for the church the surest way to take hold of its real essence
and substance'. So, true Christian identity is discovered by the
church when it bears witness and only so. From this understanding of the church and its essential nature, Kraemer
moved into a wide-ranging review of the world of his day, a
'single planetary world' inclining more and more to 'uniformity and conformity';[44] but not, in his view (*pace* A. G. Baker),
on the way to a single civilisation. The dawn of a 'great
cultural synthesis' was unlikely to be realised but cultural
change was everywhere apparent.

In the West, the outstanding characteristic was the 'complete disappearance of all absolutes' and the 'victorious but

[42] C. F. Hallencreutz, *Kraemer*, pp. 273–5; H. Kraemer, *Christian Messge*, p. vi.
[43] H. Kraemer, *Christian Message*, pp. vi–vii.
[44] *Ibid.*, pp. 2–3.

dreadful dominion of the spirit and attitude of relativism'. Mankind was 'literally wallowing in false absolutes', but, despite these spurious attempts at substitution, 'the problem of religious certainty is *the* ultimate problem of modern man'. This is the 'mortal but hidden wound' in the life of 'hosts of . . . people', this 'wholehearted surrender . . . to . . . relativism'.[45] While he had to recognise the great gains given through the Enlightenment in Europe, which had provided the kind of intellectual and cultural dynamite to blow apart previously stifling structures of thought and life and releasing enormous funds of energy, the accompanying belief in the autonomy of the human intellect was something with which the Christian church could have no truce. As those who were rooted in God, human beings had set about destroying themselves by erecting humanity in His place.[46] Kraemer drew attention to the sheer irony of the fact that as Western civilisation, so abhorred by a missionary like Gutmann in a tribal setting, was eroding tribal structures across the world, the West itself was creating new tribalisms by way of ideological pseudo-absolutes in fascism, National Socialism and communism, where total allegiance was demanded, and all the 'paraphernalia of a fully fledged religion' was present. So, state and nation assume absolute proportions. Turning to the East, the 'aristocratic relativism' of its religious traditions might at one level be better able to accommodate the cultural and intellectual climate: but here, too, there was the pseudo-absolute of Japanese deification of the emperor, while the nationalism associated with Gandhi in India and in China with Sun Yat Sen were tending to be both nationalist and (for example in Nehru's case) secularist.[47]

At various points of the book, Kraemer showed himself remarkably prophetic. Such 'militant world conceptions' would 'certainly disappear': they represented 'the result of a spasmodic crisis of the mass mind', which, looking into the abyss of spiritual dissolution, wants 'the strong old foundations

[45] *Ibid.*, pp. 6–7.   [46] *Ibid.*, p. 10.   [47] *Ibid.*, pp. 15, 22–4.

for life'.[48] Facing this moral and spiritual wilderness, the Christian church had become for the first time in its history a world-wide community, universal in every continent. The Edinburgh Conference of 1910 had surveyed this world, not only with the eye of faith but also with the eye of the Westerner. The Jerusalem Conference of 1928 was more introspective in mood. The LFMI report reflected a reaction from the earlier days of the century, 'a reflex of the rapidly declining fervour of missionary interest at the home base' into a reformulation of the aims of mission as 'the expression of the responsibility of the West [for] the emergence of a new Eastern world by making its spiritual contribution in the shape of Christian service'. It showed a 'remarkable mixture of sincere devotion to the missionary cause as a Christian obligation with a very weak sense of apostolic consciousness'.[49]

Kraemer grasped the nettle of the different understandings of the kingdom of God, manifested at the Jerusalem Conference and present in the LFMI report. The kingdom cannot be 'subverted' into a 'this worldly idealism'. The kingdom of God is a latent reality, always present and developing in the community of Christ, but 'it can never be the direct object and achievement of our labours, because it is in the hand of the Father'.[50] Here was a firm statement of the unease of the Continental theologians with the American and Anglo-Saxon talk of 'kingdom-building' in a thought-out theological critique based on an understanding of New Testament eschatology, where the kingdom is both present and yet to come in the purpose of God. American missionary thinking, with its emphasis on quick results and achievement, needed to take account of the Christian missions in early Europe, when to christianise Frisia took three centuries and Belgium four, not to mention the lessons of the East, where after ten centuries Islam had failed to replace Hinduism, or Buddhism the high religions of China and Japan.[51]

Over against these essentially human-centred ideas about mission, Kraemer wanted to put the radically theocentric

[48] *Ibid.*, p. 31.   [49] *Ibid.*, p. 36.   [50] *Ibid.*, p. 48.   [51] *Ibid.*, p. 50.

character of the Bible, what he called 'Biblical realism'. The apostle Paul was an example of this theocentricity, so that whether as 'apostle, missionary, pastor of souls and theological thinker' he presented 'an indissoluble unity', because each aspect of his life has a God-ward motive and witness.[52] When it came to the place of Christ in the early mission of the church, A. D. Nock's *Conversion*, the work of an erudite classical scholar, had shown conclusively that it was the exalted, divine Christ to whom the ancient world was converted, not the uniquely attractive figure of the Jesus of the Synoptic Gospels as expounded by modern theology.[53] Again, the modern dominance of social and political questions was by-passed by the early first-century missionaries, because of the overwhelming concentration on the proclamation of the kingdom of God and of Christ, a 'pristine enthusiasm for evangelism' to which the Japanese Kagawa had recalled missions in the 'present complicated world'.[54] In approaching other religions, the question was not one of values or their superiority but of the kind of claims for truth expressed in such texts as John 14:6 and Acts 4:12: only such a claim of truth could keep a missionary movement alive; that is, that God has 'revealed *the* Way and *the* Life and *the* Truth in Jesus Christ and wills this to be known through all the world'.[55] This should not, however, result in any sense of 'superiority', which is a denial of what God has done in the gospel and which, in a missionary, immediately obscures his message.

To propose a line of continuity between other religions and Christian faith, to propose 'fulfilment' in this form, is to ground one's view in the kind of false position of Thomas Aquinas, that 'grace does not abrogate but perfects nature' (*gratia non tollit sed perficit naturam*). Aquinas had destroyed the insuperable barrier between nature and grace, which Barth's theology was endeavouring to re-establish. Enlightenment thinkers like Lessing would not allow for God's ability to work something altogether

---

[52] *Ibid.*, pp. 65–6.
[53] *Ibid.*, p. 71; A. D. Nock, *Conversion: the Old and the New in Religion from Alexander the Great to Augustine of Hippo* (London, 1933).
[54] *Ibid.*, pp. 60, 97.   [55] *Ibid.*, p. 107.

new. Barth, by contrast, asserted the discontinuity between nature and grace.[56] Kraemer wanted to leave room for the experience of God and His revelation of Himself in the non-Christian world and, as in the example of Jesus with the Roman centurion who showed great faith, did not despair of other religions; but to use the term 'fulfilment' was to encourage 'the erroneous conception that the lines of the so-called higher developments point naturally in the direction of Christ'. Against this view, the cross was 'antagonistic to all human religious aspirations' because the 'tendency of all human religious striving is to possess or conquer God. Christ is not the fulfilment of this but the uncovering of its self-assertive nature.' Conversion and regeneration were better terms to express the unexpectedness of God's fulfilment of human aspiration.[57]

When it came to 'points of contact', the celebrated cause of dispute between Barth and Brunner in the 1930s, Kraemer followed Brunner in holding that human beings can respond to the gospel and are responsible for doing so: but the true 'point of contact' was not some supposed parallel in the non-Christian system but the essentially human *locus* of the missionary and his or her disposition and attitude to the other. Kraemer emphasised, from a wealth of knowledge, that every religion was an entity, a totality, an indivisible whole: to take some piece of the jigsaw and make it a 'point of contact' was to ignore its setting and context, so that the Chinese high god, Shang-ti, was not comparable to the personal God of Christian faith; and Buddhist emphasis on the transiency of human life, with its setting in a god-less monism, was not comparable to the biblical emphasis on 'all flesh is grass', set in a framework of time and eternity in God.[58] The missionary's task is to stand in dialectical relation to other religious traditions, saying both 'yes' and 'no', seeking to discern where God is at work and what is a corrupt response, in the style of Paul and Barnabas at Lystra (Acts 14), Paul at Athens (Acts 17) and Peter's response to the Roman centurion, Cornelius (Acts 10).

In turning to the other great religious traditions, Kraemer

---

[56] *Ibid.*, pp. 109, 115–17.   [57] *Ibid.*, pp. 123–4.   [58] *Ibid.*, p. 138.

wanted first, like Barth, to underline that the empirical religion, Christianity was as much under judgement and as far
away from a 'rash and erroneous identification . . . with the
revelation in Christ' as any other religion. The issue was not
about tolerance or lack of it but about truth; and recognition of
the truth in Jesus Christ involved an act of intellectual and
moral obedience.[59] Hinduism regarded belief in a personal god
as (in Max Weber's words) 'a second rate and absurd apprehension of existence',[60] not worthy of ascetic thinking. The
issue of truth was at stake in Gandhi's approach to 'prosely-
tism', which was a 'lamentable misunderstanding'. His stress
on Hinduism in its social and national character had brought a
'biological conception of religion', so 'benumbing' the search
for truth.[61] Westerners had been made sensitive to the criticisms made by Gandhi and others that to preach conversion
was to fail to respect personality: but conversion was God's way
of respecting personality.[62] Figures in the East like Gandhi
would give honour to Christ; but this was a very different thing
to acknowledging his Lordship over life as one to whom
supreme loyalty was due. Gandhi, Tagore and Radhakrishnan
were not rightly described as 'unbaptised Christians' but better
as 'invigorated Hindus': to 'decide for Christ' implied a break
with one's religious past and was radically different from
taking a sympathetic attitude to his personality and teaching.[63]
Even *bhakti* religion, with its emphasis on grace, had been set
aside as a kind of bridge to Christian faith by so notable an
Indian Christian convert from it as Pandita Ramabai.[64] In the
face of Hindu relativism, Christianity can 'never give up its
much criticised exclusiveness because if it did it would deny its
prophetic core . . . its life and essence'.[65] The real task with
Indian religion was not to relate Christianity to it but to
express it in Indian forms. Kraemer endorsed E. Stanley Jones'
dictum, 'we must become more Christian and more Indian'.[66]

Islam, which Kraemer knew so well, he described as

[59] *Ibid.*, pp. 145–6.   [60] *Ibid.*, p. 167.   [61] *Ibid.*, pp. 238–9.
[62] *Ibid.*, p. 45.
[63] *Ibid.*, p. 291.   [64] *Ibid.*, p. 300.   [65] *Ibid.*, p. 367; cf. p. 301.
[66] *Ibid.*, p. 374.

'theocentric in a super-heated state', leading to what he called 'white-hot Omnipotence' and 'white-hot Uniqueness'. This gave Islam a quality of absolute ruthlessness in its total surrender to Allah and to 'august divine arbitrariness'. This resulted in a 'hyperbolic religiousness', which exerts an 'intense grip' on the minds of its adherents.[67] Kraemer quoted Pascal: 'Mohammed chose the way of human success, Jesus Christ that of human defeat.' Islam had become a 'thoroughly secularised theocracy', which, with its fanaticism, devotion and 'creed of group solidarity' was comparable to the 'medieval and radically religious form' of European National Socialism with its totality of demand on its adherents, a 'group solidarity conceived with passionate religious directness'.[68] Those, like Wilson Cash, who sought to approach Islam by way of its mysticism were, in Kraemer's view, understandable but understandably mistaken, because mysticism was insufficiently central to what makes Islam the formidable collective that it is.[69] Of Judaism, Kraemer admitted that his knowledge of missions to the Jews was slight and that his lack of opportunity to study them in the time allotted must mean he could write little; but the 'obligation of the Christian church to carry out its apostolic privilege and duty towards Judaism is . . . as stringent as it is towards the rest of the non-Christian world'. This was the more true because of the anti-Semitism of the day, when a clear manifestation of what was really Christian was required. Nothing could justify a policy of hatred or indifference on the part of the Christian church.[70]

When he turned to African religion and the approaches made to it, it was predictable that Bruno Gutmann's ideas were accorded the same severe theological critique as they had been given by Barth. While Gutmann was commended for taking up an attitude of Continental scepticism towards Anglo-Saxon ideas, which emphasised the 'medium of the Christ-like personality' as the correct method, he himself was as guilty as the Anglo-Saxons, in their 'more genially humanistic way'. His

---

[67] *Ibid.*, pp. 221–2. [68] *Ibid.*, p. 353. [69] *Ibid.*, pp. 357–9.
[70] *Ibid.*, pp. 227–8

approach through the admirable pagan structure as an apprehension of life was mistaken, equally, in 'combining incompat-
ibles' and in destroying the 'whole idea of revelation'. Both sets
of approach were putting their trust in a kind of lofty ethic and,
in Gutmann's case, it was allied with a romantic view of the
primal ties and African life. Gutmann had erred in seeing these
ties as 'divinely sanctioned structures': they were, in fact, the
usual human combination of the angelic and the demonic and
should be treated as social and relative realities rather than
being invested with poetic and metaphysical glamour. Such
romanticism was no basis for any lasting work. As has been
shown in the treatment above Gutmann's work was particularly
effective and outlasted his and Kraemer's life-time. It is possible that the heavy emphasis on discontinuity between the
gospel and the created order as expressed in institutional and
social life led Kraemer astray: and it is interesting to observe
that he himself made room, despite his criticism of Gutmann,
for employing a people's 'social means of indigenous expression' 'in accordance with the gifts and means that God has
given to those peoples'.[71] This suggests that God's working
could be discerned in certain of the inherited forms of life and
that it was the missionary's task to discern which these were,
'not on the ground that we like or dislike it for some reason
extraneous to this particular situation'.[72] He could also commend
Gutmann, Adriani, Kruyt and Keysser for their 'intelligent
insight into the structure and functioning of the group life' and
for their encouragement of a group response.[73]

To sum up Kraemer's message: he was as eager to escape the
liberalism of the LFMI report as he was the dogmatic and
credal orthodoxies of fundamentalism. He had felt, at the
preparatory meeting in Cairo in 1927, that the Americans were
caught in this polarity and that there had been need at the
Jerusalem Conference and after to move beyond this debate.[74]
Such battles were irrelevant, he discerned, to people like T. C.
Chao in China.[75] It was possible to assert the apostolic message

[71] *Ibid.*, p. 344.   [72] *Ibid.*   [73] *Ibid.*, pp. 340–2.
[74] C. F. Hallencreutz, *Kraemer*, p. 183; and see p. 65.
[75] H. Kraemer, *Christian Message*, p. 383.

and the witness to it without falling into a sterile, dogmatic, intellectualist orthodoxy. Jesus himself had begun his ministry by calling for conversion, 'for the kingdom of God cannot be grasped except through conversion'.[76] Proposals (like Hocking's at Jerusalem) from some quarters were about to 'convert mission . . . the apostolic obligation of the Church, into an experiment for practical comparative religion'. Unless one held to the central truth that Jesus was *the* Way, *the* Truth and *the* Life (Kraemer's emphasis) 'what other reason than the inner conviction that He is *the* Truth will induce anyone to risk the painful experience of abandoning his ancestral religion with its many precious social and emotional bonds?'[77] It was a question to ask not least to Western 'cradle' Christians, who had never suffered the extremes of rejection and persecution which Jewish, Hindu and Muslim converts, let alone those of other religious backgrounds, had experienced in conversion.

TAMBARAM CONFERENCE 1938

It would be interesting to know how many of the more than 450 persons at the Tambaram Conference had read Kraemer's volume on arrival, surely as demanding a piece of intellectual preparation as ever offered prior to a conference. Immediate responses had varied between William Temple's preface, commending it as a book 'likely to remain for many years to come the classical treatment of its theme'[78] to C. F. Andrews' response which, according to a recent study, was to drop it 'unceremoniously' into the waste-paper basket.[79] Tambaram's composition was larger than Jerusalem but smaller than at Edinburgh. Two hundred of its members came from Asia, a very high proportion. There was also a high proportion of nationals from the younger churches. Europe's thirty-eight and North America's forty-three were not permitted to preponderate, though Africa with thirty-four was surprisingly small in representation, as also Latin America with thirty-three. Some

---

[76] *Ibid.*, p. 296.   [77] *Ibid.*, p. 290.   [78] *Ibid.*, p. ix.
[79] D. O'Connor, *Gospel, Raj and Swaraj*, p. 4.

of the most significant figures were among the list of 'coopted' participants: this category included C. F. Andrews, Kagawa, H. H. Farmer, Kenneth Grubb (representing the World Dominion Press), A. G. Hogg, E. Stanley Jones, Stephen Neill, K. L. Reichelt, K. S. Latourette and the future of Archbishop of York, C. F. Garbett. A small list of 'fraternal delegates' included V. S. Azariah and Baron van Boetzelaer, both representing the Faith and Order movement, R. C. Mackie representing the World Student Christian Federation and W. A. Visser't Hooft, representing the provisional committee of the World Council of Churches, ten years before the first meeting of the WCC at Amsterdam in 1948.[80]

Of the seven volumes of the report, here the concentration will be for the most part on the first, *The Authority of the Faith* and the third, *Evangelism*. Kraemer himself provided the first paper in volume I, *Continuity and Discontinuity*, taking one of the central themes of his book. The issue remained whether faith in Jesus Christ was 'absolutely *sui generis*': it could be presented as a debate between the approaches of Clement of Alexandria, holding together a theology of incarnation and of general revelation, and of Karl Barth. Kraemer admitted that, drawn as he was to Barth's discontinuity as well as his 'fundamentally religious position', it did not 'finally and totally satisfy'. The question remained: 'were those who live under the sway of the non-Christian religions entirely left to their own devices or has God also somehow worked in them? . . . if it is true that there is much that is true, good and beautiful in the non-Christian religions, what is their relation to God . . . for "God does not abandon the work of his hands"?'[81] To this central question, William Paton believed that the responses overall gave a clearly affirmative answer[82] to the point of near-unanimity. This was true for T. C. Chao, in his paper on revelation[83] and, very significantly in view of the rigour of his mind and the earlier criticism of J. N. Farquahar's 'fulfilment' ideas, also

---

[80] *IMC/Tambaram Report* (hereafter *IMC/T*) vol. VII, pp. 181–202.
[81] *Ibid.*, vol. I, p. 22.
[82] *Ibid.*, p. xii.   [83] *Ibid.*, p. 47.

true for A. G. Hogg: 'for my own part I am convinced that the answer to these questions must be in the affirmative', posed in his case in the form: 'in non-Christian faith may we meet with something that is not merely a seeking but in real measure a finding?'; and, further, 'by contact with which a Christian may be helped to make fresh discoveries in his own finding of God *in Christ*?' For Hogg, then, after many years of teaching in India (he had by this time been principal of the Madras Christian College, in whose new buildings the conference was taking place) the proper approach to a religious faith which was in 'quality and texture . . . definitely not Christian' was to 'put the shoes off the feet recognising that one is on the holy ground of a two-sided commerce between God and man'.[84] Hogg believed that there were many missionaries who could testify of persons of Hindu faith, that they were 'manifestly . . . no strangers to the life "hid in God"'.[85] He held that it was not the *occurrence* of revelation which was particular to Christianity but its *content* as seen in Christ.[86] Hogg, like the Canadian scholar Wilfred Cantwell Smith later, was at pains to emphasise the importance of faith, Christian or non-Christian, and also (with William Temple in *Nature, Man and God*) that in revelation God reveals Himself, not 'ready made truths about Himself'.[87]

W. M. Horton must have spoken for many present when he used the title 'Between Hocking and Kraemer' for his paper. Many will have found themselves wanting to affirm much of the critique of traditionalists in *Rethinking Missions* and the LFMI report and yet also drawn to Kraemer's powerful Christo-centric missionary vision. As Karl Hartenstein put it, 'the life of a missionary is a perilous life. He is always in danger of losing his way on the right hand by getting a superiority feeling towards the others and to lose his way on the left hand by getting an inferiority complex in regard to his message.' It was all too possible, as Horton pointed out from personal experience, to find that non-Christian persons could have 'the

[84] *Ibid.*, p. 103.   [85] *Ibid.*, p. 110.   [86] *Ibid.*, p. 125.
[87] *Ibid.*, pp. 102–8; W. Temple, *Nature, Man and God* (London, 1934), pp. 321–5.

Spirit without the Name' and Christians the 'Name without the Spirit'; to identify, as a Christian, with the patience displayed by a Buddhist under criticism rather than with the heavy-handed orthodoxy of the critic who was proclaiming 'no other name'.[88]

Not unexpectedly, the findings of the Tambaram report reflected both strands: in regard to the non-Christian religions, there was a clear recognition that there were to be found among them deep religious experience and great moral achievements. Nevertheless, the missionary movement called all to the feet of Christ and 'turning to Christ does not mean an evolutionary fulfilment but a radical breaking with the bonds of one's religious past'.[89] As to whether the religions as total systems were to be regarded as 'manifesting God's revelation, Christians are not agreed', but 'Christ is revolutionary' and, they concluded, 'it is He . . . alone whom we have to offer to a lost world'.[90]

The title of the report's other volumes indicated, as E. Stanley Jones was to complain later, that Tambaram concentrated on the church, its growth (II), its life (III), its economic basis (V), its relation to the state (VI). John Mott had said in an opening address, 'it is the church which is to be at the centre of our thinking . . . the Divine Society founded by Christ and His apostles to accomplish His will in the world'.[91] For Jones this was to neglect the other great reality, important at Jerusalem, the kingdom; but, whatever validity this may have had as a criticism, debated in print later with H. P. van Dusen after the conference, it underlined the growing recognition, which will be reflected in this book, that mission had become increasingly the realm of the indigenous churches and their life and development was therefore central towards its understanding.[92]

This was recognised in the volume on evangelism (III). Hopes were expressed that Tambaram would mark a 'still

---

[88] *Ibid.*, pp. 146, 150.   [89] *Ibid.*, pp. 200–1.   [90] *Ibid.*, pp. 211, 216.
[91] *Ibid.*, VII, p. 4.
[92] *Christian Century*, 56, no. 13 (29 March 1939), p. 410; 56, no. 22, (31 May 1939), p. 704.

further advance in making the Church in each country the primary factor in accomplishing the task of evangelism in that country' a task which can 'ultimately be accomplished by that church and that church alone'.[93] In this volume many of the themes already noted occur again. It contained also a very fine essay on German missions by Missions-Direktor Siegfried Knak, Director of the Berlin Missionary Society. Merle Davis had described the common ground he had discovered between the Batak mission in northern Sumatra and other believers in group conversion: Nommensen and other pioneer missionaries had taken the decision to use non-Christian social institutions within a Christian structure in the form of Batak *adat* (customary law), and Davis judged that their decision had been both 'brave and blessed'.[94] Knak defended Gutmann vigorously against Kraemer's strictures in the *Christian Message*. Gutmann was far from 'romantic' as there described; nor was he a friend to simple continuity either.[95] Indeed, Keysser and Gutmann were following a line of German missionary innovators, from David Zeisberger among American Indians and Peter Braun in Antigua and other Moravian missionaries, upon whom it had been 'borne in . . . time and again that missions to pagans were up against a collectivity'.[96] Knak used Keysser's experiences with tribal activities and festivals to good effect in illustrating his theme, including the story noted above of his use of the Papuans' fire and blazing logs as an acted parable.[97] The whole *Volkskirche* approach on the need to make forms of church life relative to the context, rather than imposed as 'absolute historical forms' by the Westerner, was ably set out.[98] On the broader missiological issues raised by Kraemer, Knak quoted Hartenstein to the effect that the gospel of Christ stands against all 'primitive religions', including Christianity itself in its 'historical manifestation': the tendency of the human heart to rebellion is the same wherever it is found; and

[93] *IMC/T*, vol. III, p. 41.   [94] *Ibid.*, vol. V, pp. 440, 454–5.
[95] *Ibid.*, vol. III, pp. 345–6.
[96] *Ibid.*, pp. 329, 316–18.   [97] *Ibid.*, pp. 337–8.
[98] *Ibid.*, pp. 312–65, especially p. 351.

yet 'the seeking for God in the non-Christian religions is a proof that man is designed for communion with God'.[99]

The Tambaram Conference gave evidence of some of the variegated factors of the Christian mission: the Anglican Bishop Pakenham Walsh and his wife were leading an ashram of young Syrian Orthodox men in India, and the work of a remarkable young Syrian Orthodox priest, Father Petros, and his 'Servants of the Cross' among the poor deserved notice;[100] accounts of revival movements in South Shantung between 1925–30 in China and an act of mercy by a firing squad of Japanese in the face of Christian worship and resolution;[101] continuing study projects following *Christian Mass Movements in India* by J. W. Pickett, compiled with the assistance of Donald McGavran, a name which will recur later;[102] the so-called 'faith missions' and their failure to found strong churches despite their zeal for evangelism; the vitality and fellowship of the Oxford groups, established by the American Frank Buchman, in China;[103] fervent appeals from George Sloan in the wake of anti-Semitism that Christians show Jewry 'what God's Church really means'[104] combined with his heart-rending accounts of Jewish family experiences in Austria and Prague, personally experienced in the summer of 1937,[105] which can be coupled with C. F. Andrews' exposé of racism towards both Jews and Africans: J. E. K. Aggrey had given him an unforgettable example of Christian forgiveness under racist provocation.[106] Of future intense debates, both the scheme for a united Church of South India and the relationship of the IMC to the incipient WCC were adumbrated here.[107]

Perhaps as moving a comment as any on the overall effect of the Tambaram Conference as an experience of Christian fellowship was Karl Hartenstein's, faced immediately with conscription to fight for a régime which he abhorred on his return to Germany. He wrote to William Paton:

[99] *Ibid.*, pp. 372–3. [100] *Ibid.*, vol. II, pp. 229–30.
[101] *Ibid.*, pp. 255–7, 262–3.
[102] *Ibid.*, vol. III, p. 82. [103] *Ibid.*, p. 187. [104] *Ibid.*, vol. VII, p. 108.
[105] *Ibid.*, pp. 103–5.
[106] *Ibid.*, pp. 92, 98–9. [107] *Ibid.*, vol. I, pp. 400, 408–22.

Tambaram . . . a bright star of God's promise . . . the communion and fellowship by all Christian churches of the world. But now darkness has come upon us and nobody knows when the holy but terrible will of God will be changed again to mercy and love . . . We are not alone on this way, Jesus Christ is being with us . . . remember my dear friend, if I am still alive, that there is a friend of yours in whose heart all the spiritual heritage of thirteen years of missionary work does not fade away.[108]

Hartenstein did survive but Paton died in 1943.

Finally, before closing this section with the outbreak of the Second World War, it remains to notice two articles in the *IRM* by distinguished theologians, struggling again with Kraemer's book and its effects. H. H. Farmer, a participant at the Tambaram Conference and contributor of a paper to volume I, *The Authority of the Faith*, demonstrated how deeply Kraemer had influenced the gathering, not least in driving home the truth that all religions were to be viewed as totalities: as totalities they were, in relation to the approach to God, 'in a very real sense all wrong . . . despite . . . incidental and isolated rightnesses for the reason that they leave (and must leave, being without Christ) the basic problem of a man's existence unsolved: the problem, namely, of his alienation from God through sin. Built upon another foundation, organised around another centre, they are radically and totally different; to say that is not in the first instance to make a judgement of value, it is merely to make a statement of plain fact.'[109]

Secondly, D. S. Cairns, veteran observer of missionary approaches to other religions from the pre-Edinburgh Conference days, while generally supportive of Kraemer's approach and expressing admiration for the quality of his book, asked again (as Kraemer himself had asked at Tambaram), 'can we regard "all religions" as merely products of the human mind? Must there not be in them something from that which is above nature, "bright shoots of everlastingness"?' Despite Kraemer's qualified support for Barth, Cairns saw 'the Barthian element

[108] E. Jackson, *Red Tape and the Gospel* (Birmingham, 1980), pp. 198, 355 note 20.
[109] *IRM*, 28, no. 110 (1939), p. 179.

in his thought . . . not only in conflict with the more "generous judgement" of the non-Christian religions . . . but in plain conflict with many of the facts of the non-Christian religions themselves'. He instanced tabu and, especially, Zoroastrian religious expression as pointing beyond Kraemer's 'monist naturism' towards what Söderblom had described (with reference to Zoroastrian religion) as 'true, if imperfect, theism', where 'not only is God one and moral but history is not cyclical' as in so much religion in the East. Cairns suggested that God had found in Zoroaster a servant who understood his spirit; and he also pointed to *bhakti* religion in India, Shin-Shu Buddhism in Japan (whose writings had an 'extraordinary resemblance to Christian preaching') and to the sages of Greece and Rome (Aeschylus, Socrates, Plato and Virgil) to argue again that 'in every nation he that feareth God and worketh righteousness is accepted of Him' (Acts 10:35).

Kraemer's work, whether agreed with or disputed, was the missiological monument to the Tambaram Conference and not less so because of its context, what Cairns alluded to as 'the hour of danger', the National-Socialist state and its attempted dominance of Europe and beyond. Cairns wrote of heathen practices which could easily return like a 'roaring flood' into 'hardly won clearings', a lesson of the Reformation period.[110] Neo-pagan darkness was indeed about to descend on Europe: it was a context of sharp polarities, when shades of grey were of little value to embattled Christians. Rather, the need was for the ringing tones of the Barmen Declaration of 1934, for Barth's outright rejection of nationalist religion rooted in nature and for Kraemer's concentration on Christ as the Light shining with absolute clarity in a world of darkness, darkness made all the more profound by way of the calls for total allegiance by fascist and communist to the state and its purposes, those pseudo-absolutes Kraemer had condemned with such great effect.

[110] *Ibid.*, no. 109 (1939), pp. 124–7, 129, 130–1.

PART II

1940–1990

Preface to part II

In his Bampton Lectures at Oxford, published as *The Church and Christian Union*, Bishop Stephen Neill made a judgement which has particular implications for the second half of this book: 'the problem of mission cannot be discussed *in abstracto*; it becomes intelligible only as the mission of the Church. Given a satisfactory ecclesiology, a satisfactory definition of the Church, the answer to all the main problems arising out of the Christian mission should lie ready to hand.'[1] In earlier chapters, the study of concepts of mission and their influence on missionary practice has shown also how the gospel comes in certain forms, which relate to their historical context. Much as many missionaries may have tried to avoid it in India, China, Japan and Africa in the nineteenth and twentieth centuries, these were also often Western forms, so that even those who laid most emphasis on the indigenous culture, like Gutmann and Keysser, brought with them aspects of Lutheranism, a form of the gospel hammered out in the sixteenth century in an essentially Western debate between Roman Catholic and Protestant understandings. What this means, in relation to Neill's words, is that it is impossible to avoid ecclesiology in the communication of the gospel, for the gospel does not come as pure message but issues from, and gives rise to, specific communities; and such communities will adopt certain characteristics which they believe express the gospel in churchly form.

In the period following the Tambaram Conference of 1938, the emphasis on the church, which had been stressed at the

---

[1] S. C. Neill, *The Church and Christian Union* (London, 1968), p. 319.

Christian mission

Jerusalem Conference and criticised by E. Stanley Jones as
ecclesiocentric to the point of absolutising the church to the
detriment of the greater reality of the kingdom of God,[2] nevertheless assumed greater and greater importance as the century
progressed. The formation of the WCC, which in 1938 had
been 'in process of formation' at Utrecht but became established in 1948 at Amsterdam, meant in itself that the church
(and its unity) became a major preoccupation in the years
following. A major breakthrough had been achieved in 1947 in
South India, where, for the first time, a church (Anglican)
holding to the historic succession of bishops (sometimes called
the 'apostolic succession') had entered into organic union with
Christians of Congregational, Methodist and Presbyterian
backgrounds: to many, not least among the 'younger
churches', this was a sign of hope that at last the so-called
fissiparousness of Protestantism, its tendency to split and divide,
had been reversed. The vision of one church in one geographical area, to which all Christians would belong and
which, by its unity, would be a powerful symbol and demonstration of the Christian gospel of reconciliation, continued to
fire the imaginations of many in the ecumenical movement as a
realisable ideal.[3] Stanley Jones himself, in a series of lectures in
the US in the 1940s, urged North American Christians to take
organic, or even 'federal', unity seriously, as he knew that the
younger churches already did.[4] At the IMC Conference at
Whitby, Ontario, in 1947 (next in line to Tambaram), and
again at Willingen in 1952, national Christians spoke eloquen-
tly of this: what might be a matter of little moment to Western
churches was, in their eyes, a matter of absolute necessity in
their countries: 'we believe that unity of the churches is an
essential condition of effective witness and advance. In the
lands of the younger churches divided witness is a crippling
handicap. We of the younger churches feel this very keenly.

[2] *Christian Century*, 56, no. 3 (15 March 1939), pp. 351–2.
[3] B. G. M. Sundkler, *The Church of South India: the Movement towards Union 1900–1947* (London, 1954).
[4] *Christian Century*, 64, no. 2 (15 October 1947), pp. 1231–2.

While unity may be desirable in the lands of the older churches, it is *imperative* in those of the younger churches.'[5]

As the century progresses, however, there was a paradoxical dynamic at work, on the one hand a drive to unity, on the other towards multiplicity and diversity. As an illustration, two churches can be referred to here, however inadequately, to make this contrast. The ancient churches of the East, in some cases, had been represented at Amsterdam, but it was at New Delhi in 1961 that Orthodoxy can be said to have added its great historic presence to the ecumenical movement. Here was a church which believed itself to stand in direct succession to the apostolic church, viewing itself not as one church among many but (not least as bearer of its own unity of life) as the uniquely endowed bearer of the divine life. It recognised the Roman Catholic communion as a sister church in error, from whose misunderstandings it had separated with reluctance, including over its estimation of the universal primacy of the Bishop of Rome: but at no point did it regard itself, even in membership of the WCC, as less than the bearer of that unity which, if mission was to progress, was an essential prerequisite, even as it had been in Christ's prayer (John 17), so central to the ecumenical movement as an inspiration. In Orthodox understanding, unity would not come about by missionary activity and mutual participation in it by Christians of different allegiances, but, first and foremost, by recapturing the unity of the church, of which Orthodoxy was the symbol, from which effective mission would issue.[6]

Such an approach has a powerful appeal. In Orthodox writing on mission in recent years it has been combined with a strong emphasis on the church as a eucharistic community,

---

[5] Willingen report: *The Missionary Obligation of the Church* (London, 1952), p. 40; 'a statement by younger church delegates' (pp. 39–41); R. K. Orchard, *Missions under the Cross* (London, 1953), pp. 233–6.

[6] Metropolitan James of Melita 'The Orthodox Concept of Mission and Missions' in J. Hermelink and H. Margull (eds.), *Basileia* (Stuttgart, 1959), pp. 76–80; G. Khodr in *St Vladimir's Seminary Quarterly*, 6, no. 1 (1962), pp. 16–25, 'Church and Mission'; N. Nissiotis in *Porefthendes*, 5, no. 17/18 (1963), pp. 4–7, 'The Ecclesial Foundation of Mission'; A. Yannoulatos in *Porefthendes* 4, no. 13 (1962), pp. 4–5,

with each local body of Christians fully catholic, in the sense
that the wholeness of church life is present in every local
church, and where every celebration of the eucharist is an
essentially missionary event. Here the divine life is discovered
which makes the participants share the divine nature (*theōsis*:
II Peter 1:4); and the divine energy is experienced to extend
the *missio Dei*, the extension of God's love, compassion and grace
to a needy world. Such understandings may not be confined to
Orthodoxy, but they are strongly present in it, a church which
can point to a missionary tradition which stretches honourably
from Methodius and Cyril, sent from Constantinople to be
'apostles to the Slavs' to pagan tribes of eighth-century Europe,
through centuries of confrontation with Islam in the Balkans
and in what became the USSR; churchly forms which have
showed an extraordinary ability to root themselves in national
life, so that, to give one example, after decades of communist
rule in Rumania in the 1980s, some 80 per cent of the population regarded themselves still as members of the Orthodox
church. If mission has to do with identifying the church's life
and message with a nation's life, few churches can compare
with the Orthodox, whatever risks may have been run, to some
observers, of becoming the handmaid of the state, something
which even fellow Orthodox feared of their Russian brethren
at the New Delhi meeting of 1961.

As a contrast to this view, where mission is understood to
arise out of unity, there is the empirical reality of the development of Christianity in Africa. According to statistics published
in the early 1980s, Africa began the century with rather less
than 10 million Christians in 1900. By 1980 this had become
230 million or more.[7] This represents one of the most extraordinary phenomena of human history and will attract a
growing number of interpreters, though a cluster of studies
already exists.[8] In a post-war world after 1945, which became

'Orthodox Spirituality and External Mission'; J. Meyendorff in *St Vladimir's Quarterly*, 6, no. 1 (1962), pp. 59–71, 'The Orthodox Concept of the Church'.
[7] D. B. Barrett (ed.), *World Christian Encyclopaedia* (Nairobi, 1982), p. 4.
[8] E. Fasholé Luke, R. Gray, A. C. Hastings, G. Tasie (eds.), *Christianity in Independent
Africa* (London, 1978); B. G. M. Sundkler, *Bantu Prophets in South Africa* (London,

also increasingly post-colonial, it was to be expected that the desire for an African and indigenous Christianity, present earlier in the century in 'Ethiopian' movements and in 'Zionism'[9] would gather momentum once freed from Western controls and cultural accretions. What could hardly have been foreseen was the explosion of indigenous independent movements, which resulted in Nigeria, for example, in one indigenous expression (the Church of the Cherubim and Seraphim), giving rise to some 200 additional denominations, one of which alone (the Church of the Eternal Sacred Order of Cherubim and Seraphim) had 300,000 affiliated members in 1980.[10]

Early in the century, a 'prophet' like William Wade Harris (1865–1929) on the Ivory Coast in 1913–1915 had shown the impact that 'prophetism' could make, though in his case the call to repentance and faith led to many entering, or returning to, the historic denominations. In the case of Simon Kimbangu in the Belgian Congo (Zaire), whose ministry of healing as a Baptist catechist led to a collusion of missionary and state power against him and a thirty-year imprisonment by the Belgian colonial government between 1921 and 1951, a massive new denomination was founded, L'Eglise de Jésus Christ sur la terre par le prophète Simon Kimbangu (The Church of Jesus Christ on earth through the prophet Simon Kimbangu). This church, referred to often as EJCSK, like the Orthodox, joined the WCC in 1969 and became one of only four denominations recognised by the government of Zaire, two of the others being the Roman Catholic and the Orthodox. If, as a later chapter will consider, Christian mission is about church growth, a church which grew to embrace 3

1948) and *Zulu Zion and some Swazi Zionists* (London, 1976); C. G. Baeta, *Prophetism in Ghana* (London, 1962); Robin Horton, 'African Conversion', *Africa*, 41, no. 2 (1971), pp. 85–108; D. B. Barrett, *Schism and Renewal in Africa* (Nairobi, 1968); F. B. Welbourn and B. A. Ogot, *A Place to Feel at Home: a Study of Two Independent Churches in Western Kenya* (London, 1966); H. W. Turner, *African Independent Church*, 2 vols. (Oxford, 1967); J. D. Y. Peel, *Aladura: a Religious Movement among the Yoruba* (London, 1968); V. E. W. Hayward (ed.), *African Independent Church Movements* (London, 1963).

9 Cf. C. P. Groves, *The Planting of Christianity in Africa* 4 vols. (London, 1948–58), vol. III, pp. 149, 179; vol. IV, pp. 63, 128–9.

10 D. B. Barrett (ed.) *World Christian Encyclopaedia*, p. 529.

million Christians in fifty years, with extensive social and medical expressions of the gospel and its own agricultural centre and theological seminary, has deserved the study it has received and will receive.[11] Here is a church which, like many others in Africa, seems to reflect something of tribal patterns in its church forms, with Joseph Dagienda, son of Simon Kimbangu, at its head and the kind of worked-out system of councils and consultative patterns which Gutmann, for instance, found amongst the Chagga and turned to use in the service of the gospel.[12]

What follows cannot be an essay in ecclesiology, but the second half of the twentieth century presented striking illustrations of the link between understandings of the church and its mission. In a period when mission was seen to be the responsibility of the indigenous church rather than of 'missions', the forms in which the gospel was commended became inescapable. The re-examination of its ecclesiology by the Roman Catholic church at Vatican II in the 1960s, when a static and hierarchical understanding was revised in the direction of a dynamic view of the church as the people of God, released fresh energies, which were expressed in such manifestations as the 'base communities' (*communidades de base*) in Latin America, providing new ecclesial forms for the gospel. For the missionary movement in the 1950s, the question presented itself as to what the relationship should be of the International Missionary Council and the new World Council of Churches: should not mission become integrated into the most representative church body available to non-Roman churches? The 1950s were to see that question debated and a decision reached.

---

[11] M.-L. Martin, *Kimbangu: an African Prophet and his Church* (Oxford, 1975) and *Prophetic Christianity in the Congo: the Church of Jesus Christ on Earth through the Prophet Kimbangu* (Johannesburg, 1968); W. Ustorf, *Afrikanische Initiative: das aktive Leiden des Propheten Simon Kimbangu* (Frankfurt, 1975); W. Ustorf and Wolfmann Weisse (eds.), *Radiokolleg: Kirchen in Afrika* (Erlangen, 1979), pp. 42–51, 'Der Kimbanguismus in Zaire'.

[12] M.-L. Martin, *Prophetic Christianity in the Congo*, pp. 29–31, for the constitution of June 1968.

CHAPTER 5

Mission as presence and dialogue 1950–1960

As the title implies, this chapter will concentrate in the main on the decade from 1950 to 1960, though not without backward and forward glances. It was a period characterised not least by post-colonialism, the steady devolution of power upon Asian and African peoples by the nineteenth-century colonisers. A figure who provided a prototype of others, and who was to appear in person at the Ghana Assembly of the IMC in 1958, was Kwame Nkrumah, who became leader of the government of Ghana (hitherto the Gold Coast of British rule) in 1952.[1] African leaders like Jomo Kenyatta (Kenya), Hastings Banda (Malawi), Kenneth Kaunda (Zambia) and Julius Nyerere (Tanzania, earlier Tanganyika in these pages) and, in Indonesia, President Sukarno, provided examples of post-colonial political leadership. A number of these men had been educated in mission schools.

The decade which followed the Tambaram Conference of 1938 had shown the world Christian community the virtue of its new internationalism. During the 1914–18 war, the embryonic IMC had lost the confidence of the German missionary leadership to the point where Mott's identification with the allied war effort had caused Germans to call for his resignation, but a very different spirit prevailed in the 1939–45 war. Great efforts were made by the IMC leadership to provide international financial support for German missions, starved of funds by their government's strict limits on currency outflow.

---

[1] R. K. Orchard (ed.), *The Ghana Assembly of the IMC* (London, 1958), pp. 148–50 (Nkrumah's speech).

Men like Karl Hartenstein and Walter Freytag, both directors
of missionary societies as well as theologians of mission, were
aware of, and grateful for, the support given. Relationships
which had been so close at Tambaram were quickly restored
after 1945 and there was no period of estrangement as there
had been in the immediate aftermath of the Treaty of Versailles after 1918.[2]

Of the leading figures up to 1940, C. F. Andrews had died in
that year. Two devastating losses to the IMC and the developing WCC were William Paton and William Temple in 1943
and 1944. Paton, who died aged 57, was by then joint secretary
of the IMC and editor of the *IRM* while in addition acting as
joint general secretary of the provisional committee of the
WCC. No one had done more than Paton to ensure that the
'orphaned missions' should receive support after 1939.[3]
William Temple, ecumenical leader *par excellence*, died aged 63.
John Mott had resigned his chairmanship of the IMC in 1942,
to be succeeded first by another American Methodist, Bishop
James Baker, and then by J. A. Mackay (1889–1983) Scottish-
born missionary, who had served in Latin America from
1916–32 and written a widely read book *The Other Spanish
Christ*. His response to *Rethinking Missions* and its theology was
noted earlier. He was president of Princeton Theological Seminary when he took office. Three major international meetings
of the IMC took place in succession to the Jerusalem Conference of 1928 and that at Tambaram in 1938: those at Whitby,
Ontario (1947), Willingen in Germany (1952) and Accra,
Ghana (1958).

In the wider political field developments of profound significance to the whole world order were the use of atomic
weapons to end the war with Japan in 1945, the partition of

---

[2] W. R. Hogg, *Ecumenical Foundations* (New York, 1952), pp. 306, 315, 427–8; K. S.
Latourette and W. R. Hogg, *World Community in Action: the Story of World War II and
Orphaned Missions* (New York, 1949); A. L. Warnshuis, 'The Story of the Orphaned
Missions', *Student World*, 37, no. 1 (1944), pp. 23–31.

[3] E. Jackson, *Red Tape and the Gospel* (Birmingham, 1980), pp. 196–208; *CDCWM*,
p. 474; *IRM*, 32, no. 128 (October 1943), pp. 462–3 (J. H. Oldham's tribute to
William Paton).

India and Pakistan in 1947 and the communist ascendancy in China in 1949. Of the first, Ronald Williams, a colleague of William Paton in the war years and past home secretary of the CMS, who was to become an English church leader, wrote: 'the reverberations of the first atomic explosions have shown us in grim clarity the end of human discovery unmatched by an adequate moral purpose';[4] the second was a sign to the world that Indian Muslims were determined to follow through the theocratic logic of their faith in the creation of a separate Islamic state in Pakistan, despite the large numbers of their fellow religionists whose domicile remained in the avowedly secular state of India among a Hindu majority after independence; and the third involved, ultimately, the expulsion of all expatriate missionaries and perhaps the most intensive indoctrination of a population in history, with Chinese workers reporting for two hours of communist instruction before beginning their working day. The church in China, object of much heroic and sacrificial labour for the previous hundred years, was pressed to renounce its 'imperialist' connections.

The literature of the period up to the Willingen Conference of 1952 included W. E. Hocking's *Living Religions and a World Faith* (1940), already mentioned and to be noted again; A. G. Hogg's final book *The Christian Message to the Hindu* (1947) and a fine but overlooked book by the American E. D. Soper, *The Philosophy of the Christian Mission* (1943), a fluent and persuasive piece of missiology. Neither the Whitby Conference of 1947 nor the Willingen Conference of 1952 produced the body of material of the kind that the Jerusalem and Tambaram Conferences had done, although some of the presentations were notable, not least that of Bishop Stephen Neill at Whitby, 'The Church in a Revolutionary World', a profound reflection by a powerful Christian mind on the confrontation between the gospel and the world of the Brahman, the Muslim, the Marxist and religionless moderns. Other contributors included John Baillie, the Scottish theologian and philosopher, Walter Freytag from Germany, H. P. van Dusen the American and two prominent

---

[4] *Durham Johnian*, 1, no. 1 (January 1947), p. 13.

Asian leaders, T. C. Chao and the Indian D. G. Moses. The
Willingen 1952 Conference was notable, among other aspects,
for a submission by the Pentecostal churches, a growing world-
wide phenomenon not least in South America, by their representative and official observer, David du Plessis.[5]

FRANCE AS A MISSION FIELD

As significant a piece of writing as any of these for mission in
the 1940s was a small paperback book published in France in
1943, *La France: pays de mission?*. In this abbés Godin and
Daniel reflected on religionless paganism in France, the gulf
between the church and not only the artisan population but
also many of the *bourgeoisie*; and the need for the church to find
new ways of identifying with, and being present among, the
alienated masses. French attempts to build bridges included
the Jeunesse Ouvriers Chrétiennes (Jocists), with their cells
based on the three principles of 'observe, judge, act'; Catholic
Action; and the experiment of worker priests, who might work
in the docks of Marseilles by day to return in the evening to a
simple community house to say mass, as Stephen Neill told the
Amsterdam assembly of the WCC in 1948. Behind this way of
approaching mission as Christian presence among the alienated loomed the figure of Charles de Foucauld (1858–1916), a
very powerful missionary *ikon* in the France of the time.[6]

Charles de Foucauld had been born into an aristocratic
family and became in turn soldier, explorer in North Africa
and priest. He had spent the last years of his life at a lonely
outpost among the Touareg people of North Africa at his
mission compound at Tamanrasset in the Sahara. His devotion

---

[5] C. W. Ranson, *Renewal and Advance: Christian Witness in a Revolutionary World*
(London, 1948), pp. 62–84; *IRM*, 36, no. 144 (October 1947), pp. 434–51;
N. Goodall (ed.), *Missions under the Cross* (London, 1953), pp. 249–50 (Willingen
statement and addresses).

[6] R. Bazin, *Charles de Foucauld, Hermit and Explorer*, Eng. trans. (London, 1923);
A. Fremantle, *Desert Calling* (New York, 1949) (see conclusion for de Foucauld's
importance in the France of the 1940s); M. M. Preminger, *The Sands of Tamanrasset*
(New York, 1961); E. Hamilton, *The Desert My Dwelling: a Study of Charles de Foucauld*
(London, 1968).

to an ideal of Christian service by immersion in an alien environment, sealed as it was by a violent death (he was bound and then shot by raiders), became an inspiration to many; among them, long after his death, were the orders known as the Little Brothers and Little Sisters of Jesus, who applied his understandings to industrial and secular settings in, for example, cities of the industrialised world, by establishing small houses in urban 'wilderness' settings, where they sought to create a Christian presence.[7]

WARREN, NEILL AND CRAGG

In the first chapter three Americans, Mott, Speer and Eddy, were shown to be of importance in the early years of the century. Here an equivalent importance has to be accorded to three Englishmen. In so far as ecclesiology, the understanding of the church, has been introduced as of increasing importance after 1940 in the shape of the missionary response, all three were Anglicans, a church which has understood itself to be a bridge between such major communions as Roman Catholicism and Orthodoxy, with their emphasis on an ordered ministry and sacraments guaranteed by an episcopal succession from the apostles, and the churches of the Reformation, which, like the Church of England itself, broke with Rome in the sixteenth century. Certainly both strands, Catholic and Reformed, were present in the Church of England, leading one eighteenth-century prime minister (William Pitt the Elder) to say that the church had a Catholic liturgy and Calvinist articles of religion. In this decade, however, it had shown itself unable to accommodate to the Church of South India, whose advent in 1947 was a sign of hope to those who believed that the historic episcopate could be accepted by the Protestant churches and so organic union could be achieved. In the eyes of the Church of England, the CSI was still suspect on church order and full communion between the churches was deemed inadmissible.

---

[7] R. Voillaume, *Au cœur des masses: la vie religieuse des Petits Frères du Père de Foucauld* (Paris, 1952) and *Seeds of the Desert: the Legacy of Charles de Foucauld* (London, 1955).

Max Warren and Christian Presence

This was a position vigorously disputed by the first two of our missionary leaders and thinkers, coming as they did from the evangelical wing of Anglicanism, though both had a high doctrine of the church and an appreciation of the importance of church order. M. A. C. (Max) Warren (1904–77) became general secretary of the Church Missionary Society in 1942. An important source for twentieth-century missiology in the period 1942–63, the years of his general secretaryship, as also after, was the CMS *Newsletter* of the time. Warren did not begin this monthly series (they were begun by his predecessor, W. W. Cash, noted previously here at the IMC conferences and as a writer on Islam) but Warren developed them. In his hand, they became a means of engaging with many aspects of the post-colonial world which he confronted, resurgent world religions often linked to nationalist aspirations in Islam (October 1950), Buddhism (June 1956), Hinduism (November 1956 and January 1957) and communism (March 1953). Could the last be seen in biblical terms, he asked, as a kind of Cyrus, depicted in the Old Testament as 'the rod of God's anger'? And was there not both a right and wrong to imperialism: if God had used Constantine in his purposes could he not also have used the *pax Brittanica* and, if he had, was the use of the British Empire 'derogatory to God'?[8] These and other topics were handled in what Warren himself referred to as a 'theology of attention'. He expressed his aim in the first of his *Newsletters* in July 1942: he wanted to 'consider the meaning of some of the things that are happening', which was 'no small part of what the Bible means by a prophet'.[9] He wrote later, 'if the interpreter of missionary history' was to achieve the distinction between legend and fact 'he should insist that Christian missions must always be studied in their political, social and

---

[8] M. A. C. Warren, CMS *Newsletter* no. 139 (May 1952), p. 3.

[9] CMS *Newsletter* no. 31 (July 1942), p. 1; see F. E. Furey, 'The Theology of Mission in the Writings of Max Warren', unpublished Lic. S.T. thesis, University of Louvain, 1974; F. W. Dillistone in *IBMR*, 5, no. 3 (July 1981), pp. 114–17.

economic context'.[10] This he did in the letters, so that, for example, US tariff barriers and their effect on the Japanese economy could be assessed quite as much as the missionary confrontation with Shinto. He reached some 14,000 readers with these *Newsletters*.[11]

Warren himself had been the son of missionary parents who served in British India. After securing first class degrees at Cambridge, where he was also Lightfoot Scholar in Ecclesiastical History, he volunteered to CMS for what became known as the 'Hausa band', a group of volunteers who offered themselves for the northern, Muslim, areas of Nigeria. Here a great CMS missionary and doctor, W. R. S. Miller, was stationed, having reached Kano in 1900 but by now living in Zaria.[12] Warren arrived in Zaria in December 1927 but he spent only ten months as a serving missionary before being invalided home in a critical condition: it was the same year that his brother Jack, also a missionary in Africa but serving in Uganda, came home to England because dying of tuberculosis. In his autobiography Max Warren, like C. F. Andrews before him, was courageous enough to draw back the veil on a decisive encounter during his convalescence, not in his case a conversion but an experience of God which in his view proved determinative of his later life.[13]

In his *Newsletter* and his numerous other writings, Warren approached missiological issues both as a historian and as a biblical interpreter of history. He saw God as in control of the development of history: and this meant the whole historical process, without any division into sacred and secular. God was to be thought of as in the whole. Like another contemporary theologian and Anglican thinker, Alan Richardson, Warren was deeply suspicious of any retreat, as for example by some

---

[10] M. A. C. Warren, *Social History and Christian Mission* (London, 1967), p. 11.

[11] CMS *Newsletter*, no. 156 (double number) (December 1953), p. 3; number of readers cited in CMS *Newsletter*, no. 194 (May 1957).

[12] F. W. Dillistone, *Into all the World: a Biography of Max Warren*, (London, 1980), pp. 35–6.

[13] Warren, *Crowded Canvas* (London, 1974), pp. 65–9, 76; Dillistone, *Into all the World*, pp. 45–50.

Continental theologians, into 'sacred history' (*Heilsgeschichte*), if this meant abstracting the history of the people of God from the general historical continuum.[14] He disliked the title 'church history' and what it stood for: rather the subject to be studied was 'the church in history'. By some, he was held to have laid a welcome stress on eschatology, so providing a bridge between the Continentals and the Anglo-Saxons, in, for example, his book *The Truth of Vision*. He was certainly aware of the importance of eschatology: 'history', he wrote, 'without eschatology is in the strictest sense without meaning',[15] but he disclaimed over-much emphasis on this. He preferred to judge that his general influence had been through the historical perspective that he had brought to bear.[16] 'For our storm tossed generation', he wrote, 'it is the prophetic outlook that we need, the profound conviction which we have to recover that history is not a tale full of sound and fury, signifying nothing, but a record of the activity of God – and all this at the institutional as well as at the personal level'.[17]

Warren favoured the small, the creative minority, the voluntary association, the particular and what he called the 'critical mind' over against the 'synthetic mind'. Where the philosopher Lessing dismissed the truths of history, with their particularity, as 'accidental' and so unworthy as vehicles for universal thinking, for Warren even the smallest particularities of history had some relation to Christian truth. How much more significant was Judaea, historically, than Babylon, for all the latter's contemporary size and importance.[18] No Christian should despise the day of small things: 'if God comes in the little things, then *a fortiori* he is to be discovered at work in the "high tumultuous lists of life"'. Like Jesus himself, the entrance of the Christian mission is always particular. We can only

---

[14] A. Richardson, *History Sacred and Profane* (London, 1964), pp. 138–9.
[15] Warren, *The Uniqueness of Jesus Christ* (London, 1969), p. 6 and *Strange Victory* (London, 1946), pp. 37–41; *IRM*, 41, no. 163 (July 1952), pp. 337–50.
[16] CMS Archives, Warren Papers, Box 24, Warren to P. G. C. Meiring, 23 May 1960.
[17] Warren, *The Christian Mission* (London, 1951), p. 12 and *Interpreting the Cross* (London, 1966), p. 51.
[18] CMS *Newsletter*, no. 128 (May 1951), p. 7.

generalise about salvation because it has been particularised in time and place.[19]

The voluntary principle was as badly needed in the welfare state as it was in missionary work: for it displayed spontaneity, flexibility and initiative.[20] He quoted Lord Beveridge, architect of the modern welfare state: 'initiative ... the abrupt contradiction of the secular world's practice of concentrating power at the centre'.[21] This insight goes far to explain Warren's opposition to the IMC's merger with the WCC, which will be discussed later. The 'synthetic' mind longed for tidiness and a bureaucratic order; but such tidiness can spell 'the creeping paralysis of death'.[22] 'Christian strategic thinking [must be] flexible ... and never, never, never trying [*sic*] to be tidy!'.[23] His horror of the urge to centralise and absorb was shown also in his expressed preference in the early centuries for the Celtic mission against that of Rome.[24]

In the later 1950s Warren became an advocate of the 'Christian presence' understanding of relationships with the other great religions. He had admired very greatly the approach of his friend and fellow Anglican, Kenneth Cragg, in *The Call of the Minaret*, to be examined shortly. Copies of Warren's *Newsletter* were studded with references to this book and appeals to his readers to acquire it.[25] The form of dialogue espoused by Cragg was the background for Warren's 'Christian Presence' series of which he was general editor and SCM the publisher. Here, missionary thinkers were encouraged to engage sympathetically with other religions. Warren's general introduction to the series encouraged an expectation of finding Christ

[19] Warren, *Interpreting the Cross*, p. 48; *The Christian Mission*, p. 37; *Gospel of Victory* (London, 1955), p. 33.

[20] Warren, *The Christian Mission*, pp. 47, 56–7.

[21] Warren, *The Truth of Vision* (London, 1948), p. 142.

[22] Warren, *The Christian Mission*, p. 76 (Warren is reflecting here on abbé Michonneau's book *Revolution in a City Parish* (London 1949) and the Mission de Paris's distrust of organisation).

[23] CMS *Newsletter*, no. 236 (March 1961), p. 2.

[24] CMS Archives, Warren Papers, *Iona and Rome* (1946), review pamphlet of J. McCleod Campbell, *Christian History in the Making* (London 1946).

[25] CMS *Newsletter*, no. 192 (March 1957); no. 195 (June 1957); no. 209 (October 1958); no. 213 (February 1959); no. 234 (January 1961); no. 258 (March 1963).

already present in the alternative traditions, where God has 'nowhere left himself without witness' (Acts 14:17), Christ present before he is proclaimed. He encouraged also a view of Christian witness which hinged on Christian presence: 'our first task in approaching another people, another culture, another religion is to take off our shoes for the place we are approaching is holy. Else we may find ourselves treading on men's dreams ... to be "present" with them'.[26] An array of thinkers of quality produced studies, among them Kenneth Cragg on Islam (*Sandals at the Mosque*), George Appleton on Buddhism (*On the Eightfold Path*), Peter Schneider on Judaism (*Sweeter than Honey*), J. V. Taylor on African religion (*The Primal Vision*) and William Stewart on Hinduism (*India's Religious Frontier*), all of whom had lived among the followers of these religions. The series also included a penetrating essay on the secular mind by Martin Jarrett-Kerr of the Community of the Resurrection, *The Secular Promise*. For Warren, the missionary task was to 'unveil the Lord who is already there'[27] 'not to take Christ to some place from which he is absent but to go into all the world and discover Christ there ... to uncover the unknown Christ'.[28] It was a view of the universal Christ, cosmic in range, awaiting discovery, as much by the Christian in his dialogue with the best in another's religious tradition as by the adherent of another faith.

Warren's genius, as it would appear to have been, as a director of missions has yet to be fully revealed, his correspondence mainly being held under the fifty-year rule operated by CMS. It is likely that he will be accorded a place with such figures as Karl Graul, Rufus Anderson and his great predecessor and nineteenth-century model, Henry Venn, whom he studied in his time at CMS and after, and on whom he wrote.[29] But in one area at least his flexibility of mind failed to

---

[26] Warren, editor's general introduction in A. K. Cragg, *Sandals at the Mosque: Christian Presence amid Islam* (London, 1959), pp. 9–10.

[27] Dillistone, *Into all the World*, pp. 196–7; Warren, *Perspective in Mission* (London, 1964), pp. 21, 41 and *Challenge & Response* (London, 1960), p. 66.

[28] Warren in *Modern Churchman*, 18, nos. 1 and 2 (Winter 1974), p. 64.

[29] Warren, *To Apply the Gospel: Selections from the Writings of Henry Venn* (Grand Rapids, Mich., 1971).

grasp the change of mood in missionary service from the nineteenth century. The day of the life-long vocation to missionary service was increasingly replaced in his period by the short-service volunteer. Warren in his *Newsletter* set himself against this contemporary trend. The reader is left with the impression of a Canute, standing for a noble ideal of service but unable to stem this new tide, for whom the ideal was unrealistic in a possibly more brittle and certainly more mobile generation.[30] His successor J. V. Taylor, general secretary 1963–75, adapted more easily to the development.[31] It was for Warren a rare blind spot in eyes which, in general, raked the horizons for signposts to the Christian future with great discernment.

Stephen Neill

Stephen Neill (1900–84) must be regarded as one of the intellectual giants of his generation. A scholar, and later Fellow, of Trinity College, Cambridge, he carried off most of the classical prizes of his day; and his facility for languages, displayed there in Latin and Greek, was to extend to many European and some Indian languages, including Tamil, of which he made himself a master. Like Warren, he offered himself for missionary service, so the brilliant young Cambridge don became a lay missionary and village evangelist, arriving in India in 1925. His early book, *Out of Bondage*, which arose out of his experience of rural India, was noticed by the Laymen's Foreign Mission Inquiry and used to build up their picture of mission in India.[32] During his stay in India, Neill spent time with E. Stanley Jones and admired the approach adopted by the evangelist to the Hindu intelligentsia.[33] Neill was ordained in 1926 and worked in theological education in South India at Tirunelveli, where he became bishop in 1939. He was involved in the Church of South India reunion scheme, the beginnings of which reached back to 1919; in the later stages his skill as a drafter of

[30] CMS *Newsletter*, no. 250 (June 1962), p. 6; no. 253 (October 1962), p. 7.
[31] CMS *Newsletter*, no. 289 (January 1966).
[32] See above, p. 77.   [33] S. C. Neill, *God's Apprentice* (London, 1991), pp. 101–2.

documents requiring theological acumen and literary skill was in demand. The circumstances of his departure from India after six years as bishop remain unclear: but by then he had left a considerable mark on Indian Christian life. Two golden books on the Christian creed, compiled from addresses given to missionaries in those days and both published in Madras, *Beliefs*, (1939) and *Foundation Beliefs* (1941), deserve to be reprinted.

After his return from India Neill spent time again in Cambridge, acting also as the Archbishop of Canterbury's assistant bishop before becoming, first, co-director of the Study Department and then assistant general secretary of the WCC in Geneva. Whether based in Geneva or as Professor of Missions in Hamburg (where he succeeded Walter Freytag) or as professor in the university of Nairobi, where he set up a new department of religion, or in his retirement in Oxford Neill remained an international missionary statesman. A particularly valuable initiative to help the younger churches was his launch of the series World Christian Books in 1955, when internationally known figures like himself, Bishop Azariah and Georg Vicedom presented students with simply written manuals on great questions. Neill himself wrote on *The Christian's God*, *Who Is Jesus Christ?*, *What Is Man?*, while Bishop Azariah wrote on *Christian Giving* and Georg Vicedom on *The Church in New Guinea*. Like Mott, Speer and Eddy, Neill was a notable student evangelist, who could hold audiences of 2,000 in the Sheldonian theatre at Oxford for an explanation of the Christian gospel.[34] In addition, he was a theologian of wide ranging erudition, at home equally in New Testament studies, as his book *The Interpretation of the New Testament 1861–1961* showed; in comparative religion, as his *Bhakti, Hindu and Christian* and his *Christian Faith and Other Faiths* demonstrated; and in historical study. In this last field, he wrote of his own communion in *Anglicanism*, of the ecumenical movement in his *History of the Ecumenical Movement 1517–1948* (which he edited with Ruth Rouse) and in *The Church and Christian Union*; and of the

[34] *IRM* 36, no. 144 (October 1947), p. 449.

missionary movement in his *History of Christian Missions* and his unfinished *History of Christianity in India* (1984–5).

Here there is only space to concentrate on certain aspects of Neill's large *corpus* as they bear on missiology. In relation to the other religions, Neill expressed himself as 'wholly committed to the method of dialogue' at a time when many were suspicious of it. With his background in the Greek classics, he reminded intending participants that the object of Socratic dialogue was that truth should emerge. Such dialogue must be rigorous and uncompromising and is only possible if 'all the interlocutors are committed, resolute and uncompromising'. The necessary pre-requisite was

to enter into this for us alien world, as far as may be to understand it as it is understood by those who live within it, not to score points off them or to criticize, but to go as far with them as it is possible to go – and only then to consider whether there may not be a whole dimension in Christian faith, of which the partner in the dialogue is unaware but to which perhaps he may be introduced ... nor is there any guarantee that it will lead to the conversion of the other party.[35]

Enrichment will follow, however, as the participants have to rethink their faith in terms familiar to others, while remaining faithful to their own body of truth. He commended the way of dialogue again in an article on the subject in the valuable reference work of which he was an editor, *The Concise Dictionary of the Christian World Mission* and pointed to the approaches of E. Stanley Jones and Kenneth Cragg. Christians need not fear that they were surrendering Christian conviction because they put themselves in the position of learning from others, though it was certainly true that to enter such dialogue could expose one to wounding criticism and attack. It was necessary to stand for one's own truth while refusing to exert pressure on the will of the other in the attempt to convince.[36]

Neill admired the work of Hendrik Kraemer and, like Kraemer, held that religions, like individual lives, must be seen

---

[35] Neill, *Christian Faith and Other Faiths* (London, 1961), p. vi and *The Church and Christian Union* (London, 1968), pp. 182–3.
[36] Neill, 'Dialogue', *CDCWM*, pp. 165–6.

as totalities. So, 'every religion exists as a totality: every particular article of faith is influenced by every other article ...
Consequently, in any attempt at fusion, each of the bodies
which is brought into the alleged unity is bound to suffer a
radical transformation and to become very different from what
it was before'.[37] When Christ confronts another religious
system, it is as if he confronts the totality of an individual's life.
Every individual brings with him or her an inheritance and
culture, family tradition and formation, for all of which Christ
is both Judge and Fulfiller. For some of this inheritance Christ
means death, for some a new and resurrection life. In a lecture
in which he applied this 'yes' and 'no' to Judaism, Neill gave
an originally expressed contribution to the debate, so important at the Tambaram Conference, which Neill himself had
attended, about continuity and discontinuity:

we believe in Christ as the fulfiller of all things. But [this] ... raises
the question whether he must not first come as the destroyer before he
can be the fulfiller, whether the only way in which he can fulfil
human aspirations is first to reduce them to ashes? ... Moses and
Elijah have died. And yet Moses and Elijah are still alive for us, they
are a continuing part of the inheritance that has come to us through
patriarchs, prophets, apostles and martyrs. But this is so only because
we can now look back on them Christologically; we see them as part
of that historical preparation which found its culmination in the
Christ. It is in his light that they are enlightened; they have died to
their own proper being; they are alive for us only because they have
died to their own proper being; they are alive for us only because they
have risen in the resurrection of the Christ ... should we perhaps
proceed [to the 'no' first] ... We have recognised this in our own
personal experience of passing from death to life. The judgement of
Christ has been passed on everything that we were before we knew
him: and yet the identity and continuity of our personal life has been
maintained. Every religious system is as much an articulated unity as
an individual human life. Each one in its autonomy, in its aim of
self-realization, is so far in rebellion against God and so far under
judgement. But this need not be the last word. As in the case of
Judaism, we can learn to read these other religions Christologically,
to look upon them from the vantage point of the gospel.[38]

---

[37] Neill, *Creative Tension*, pp. 16–17; *The Church and Christian Union*, pp. 171–2.
[38] Neill, *Creative Tension* (London, 1959), pp. 28–9.

As this quotation makes clear, Neill, like Kraemer, gave a central position to conversion in Christian life and experience. He himself, as a boy at Dean Close school, in Holy Week of 1914, had undergone a conversion experience, despite his background as the son of a clergyman, brought up in a devoutly evangelical Christian home. It was seen by him as the beginning of consciously Christian life. He described how, as he reflected on the truth of the atonement, Christ's death for sinners, he went to bed one day unconverted but the next day came into an overwhelming sense of God present in his life through Christ. In one of his World Christian Books, *What Is Man?*, he tried to express something of the mystery of Christian conversion as death and new life:

if there is a real death, what is it that has died? It is I myself. It is the self which, in its pride, has organised itself in independence of God and in rebellion against Him. And does it want to die? It clings to life with the fury of despair. It is prepared to go to any length to make any kind of compromise with God, if only it can be let off dying. That is why it is so hard to be converted; that is why we must never lightly use the expression 'faith in Jesus Christ'.[39]

One is reminded of Bonhoeffer's words that when Christ calls a man he bids him to come and die. Neill complained later in life that 'in some Christian circles the word "conversion" seems to be regarded almost as a dirty word'.[40] He believed that research was needed, work to complement, correct and update William James' *Varieties of Religious Experience* (1902), if only because, since James' day at the turn of the century, so many instances of conversion from other faiths had occurred. Enquirers needed to determine what the convert found in Jesus Christ which 'drives him to face exclusion, obloquy, peril, isolation, entrance into an alien world which he often finds cold and unwelcoming'. 'Why,' he asked, 'is it that [the convert] so rarely speaks of his former religion as a preparation for the gospel and much more often as a hindrance ... from which he has escaped with great joy? Many [converts] answer precisely

---

[39] Neill, *What Is Man?* (London, 1960), p. 41.
[40] Neill, *Expository Times*, 89, no. 7 (April 1978), p. 205.

that they have found here a *salvation* such as they have not found anywhere else and that therefore they must run to receive it, whatever may be the cost'.[41] He recalled that C. F. Andrews, with his deep regard for Gandhi, had differed openly when Gandhi expressed disapproval of the Christian appeal for conversion and had held that 'conversion is necessarily present in any religion which claims to be the truth'.[42]

Like Kraemer, Neill too found the relativism of the modern world a disturbing feature. Questions of truth were at issue and truth must be necessarily exclusive and intolerant of alternatives. Thus, for Arnold Toynbee to appeal to Christians to purge themselves of their exclusive-mindedness and claims to uniqueness as 'a sinful state of mind' was, in Neill's view, 'surely a very odd piece of argumentation'.

If Christianity is purged of something that is intrinsic to itself, it will be transformed into something wholly other than itself ... what underlies Professor Toynbee's argument appears to be a curious inability to distinguish between two quite different things, the human arrogance and intolerance which are unable to conceive the possibility that they may themselves be wrong and the awful and necessary intolerance of truth itself.[43]

Pluralism must not lead to a relative view of truth. It is interesting to find a classical scholar, from the same realm of learning as Edwyn Bevan, noted earlier, laying an equal stress on what Bevan called the intransigence of Christian truth. An example of this was Neill's reaction to Will Herberg's *Protestant-Catholic-Jew*, in which Herberg called for the end of talk of conversion as a stage of aggression now past, or again to Reinhold Niebuhr's plea that the Jew be left in his own tradition to find God. If the church adopted such a position

have we not yielded to the relativism which is so popular to-day? The Christian is a Christian because he believes that to have encountered God in Jesus Christ ... is an experience entirely different from any other kind of experience. This being so he cannot do otherwise than

[41] Neill in M. Green, ed., *The Truth of God Incarnate*, (London, 1977), pp. 84–6; William James, *Varieties of Religious Experience* (London, 1974; 1st edn New York, 1902).
[42] *Ibid.*, p. 84.   [43] Neill, *Creative Tension*, pp. 11–12.

desire, not to impose his conviction on others, but to share with all men, Jew and Gentile alike, the unique experience of his life.

It could be said that to deny the Jew the opportunity to respond to Christ was an act of anti-Semitism. The question of truth posed with Jews was: either Jesus is the Messiah of the Jews or he is not.[44]

The same basic issue of truth was at stake with the Hindu tradition. Tempting as it was to accept Christ as another figure in a syncretist pantheon, the Christian could not neglect that conversion involved joining a community:

if Christianity meant simply the adoption of good and new ideas about God and man, this would be a simple and acceptable solution [i.e. for the Hindu to remain in his own tradition] ... but this falls very far short of what a Christian understands by the word 'conversion' ... [which] involves commitment to a particular Person. On this follows self-dedication to a particular manner of life, in which every detail must be organised in relation to the central loyalty. Such a life can be lived fully only within a community of which every member is ideally inspired by equal loyalty to the divine Head. Thus we come to appreciate that the doctrine of the church is not an appendage to the Gospel but an integral part of it.[45]

In addition to this thinking, writing and speaking one other important service paid by Neill to the international missionary movement in this period was a visit to Africa, made at the suggestion of the IMC, to investigate and make recommendations for the improvement of theological training and education. The visit took place in 1950 and resulted in a written survey, supplementing the work of C. W. Ranson in *The Christian Ministry in India* and a step towards a later study by Bishop Sundkler, *The Christian Ministry in Africa*. When the benevolence of John D. Rockefeller endowed the Theological Education Fund with 2 million dollars, matched by 2 million from the Mission Boards, this initiative, launched at the Ghana Assembly of 1958, had been provided with an informed basis

---

[44] Neill, *Crises of Belief* (London, 1984), pp. 42–4 and note 9; Herberg, *Protestant-Catholic-Jew: an Essay in American Religious Sociology* (New York, Garden City, 1960).
[45] Neill, *Crises of belief*, p. 121.

for funding and developing strategic institutions with the tools of scholarship in libraries and literature.[46]

Kenneth Cragg and 'The Call of the Minaret'

The third of the Anglican figures to be considered is Kenneth (A. K.) Cragg (b. 1913). A life-long student of Islam, he has spent various spells of his life in the Middle East, that meeting-ground of faiths, in the Lebanon (1939–47) and in Jerusalem in the 1950s and 1970s. An Arabic scholar and student of the Qur'an in the original tongue (to Muslims, the only true text) he established a reputation as a sensitive, scholarly and sympathetic interpreter of the tradition, deeply committed to the way of dialogue to further understanding between Christian and Muslim. He has written widely on inter-faith matters since the 1950s, but here the concentration is on the book which made such a deep impression on Max Warren, both because of its content and because of its tone and method. Cragg (*O si sic omnes!*) has never been afraid to deploy his imagination in theological writing nor his wide knowledge of literature as an aid to imagination. In *The Call of the Minaret* he shaped the book round the daily call of the *muezzin* to the Muslim faithful, a call to prayer. As a Christian is made aware of this great religious tradition, with its emphasis on the unity of God and the call to worship Him, there was need, in words used by the guards in Shakespeare's *Hamlet*, to 'sit down awhile and let us once again assail your ears which are so fortified against our story'.[47] Only in such a posture will the Christian, aided by the Holy Spirit, be enabled to make an authentically Christian response to Islam or the Muslim set aside false versions inherited from the past and retrieve the truth.

Cragg will not allow Christians to escape the use of a shared referent to God: the Allah of Islam points to the same trans-

---

[46] Neill, 'Report of a survey of theological education in East and West Africa, with special reference to the training of the ordained ministry, undertaken in April to July 1950 under the auspices of the International Missionary Council' (1950).

[47] A. K. Cragg, *The Call of the Minaret*, 2nd edn (London, 1985), p. ix. In what follows, this edition of 1985 is used.

cedent reality as the God of Christian tradition: 'inasmuch as both Christian and Muslim faiths believe in one supreme sovereign Creator – God, they are obviously referring ... to the same Being ... Those who say that Allah is not "the God and Father of our Lord Jesus Christ" are right if they mean that God is not so described by Muslims. They are wrong if they mean that Allah is other than the God of Christian faith'.[48] At the heart of Muslim understanding is *islam*, surrender to God, leading to *falah*, which includes 'communal allegiance, a social order and a religious experience', together contributing to well-being, salvation, 'a state of spiritual and social "prosperity" brought about by pardon and obedience to God's revealed law in the state of "*islam*" submission'.[49]

Cragg sought to recapture for Christian readers some of Muhammad's greatness as a religious leader, not least in his vigorous repudiation of *shirk* (idolatry), still the object of Islam's greatest abhorrence and prevalent in Muhammad's Arabia. Muhammad was concerned essentially with what God demanded: hence the centrality of law in Islam: 'the crux of Islam was law not metaphysics'.[50] The revelation of the Qur'an to the prophet emphasised above all God's activity for Muslims. Some Muslims will claim that the prophet was illiterate, to heighten the miraculous nature of what was conveyed through him: 'the traditional view insists throughout on the instrumentality of the Prophet, not his initiative; on his being the agent, not the originator',[51] though Cragg himself cannot so easily dispose of Muhammad's historical influence, which he regarded as decisive. Cragg recognised that at a certain point, Muhammad 'elected for a religious authority armed with sinews of war and means of government ... externally it succeeded',[52] but, in this view, at a spiritual price. The Prophet's biography is, for Cragg, an example of a choice as crucial as that taken by Jesus in Gethsemane. For Muhammad this was a decision 'for community, for resistance, for external

---

[48] Cragg, *Minaret*, p. 30. [49] *Ibid.*, p. 27. [50] *Ibid.*, p. 42.
[51] *Ibid.*, p. 84.
[52] *Ibid.*, p. 85.

victory, for pacification and rule. The decision for the Cross –
no less conscious, no less formative, no less inclusive – was the
contrary decision'.[53]

Cragg reflected on the prayer and religious life of the different groupings of Islam, Sunni and Shiah, and the tradition of
mysticism in Sufism. Sufis 'have not seldom been [Islam's]
salvation' and 'among their humblest devotees one may still
find a rare quality of spiritual desire and a sensitivity of soul to
God, life and eternity'.[54] Like his Anglican predecessor,
Temple Gairdner (who, however, complained of its rarity)
Cragg found spirituality and depth of religion among Muslims.
Christians who penetrate into this world, however, will find 'an
exactingness to mind and spirit'[55] which they may wish that
they had never confronted. Nevertheless, 'once the measure of
the involvement of things Christian in things Islamic has been
taken, there is no evading its demands. Christians remain
haunted by the obligations to an interpreting fidelity and
patient expression'.[56] Cragg himself has exemplified these
characteristics even if, it would seem, at some cost. Christians,
he wrote, would find in Islam a harsh world, 'harsh to some of
their tenderest convictions, a world that disallows the Cross
and strips the Christian's Master of his most tremendous
meanings. Yet the harshness has to be transcended', for 'not to
care about Islam would not be to care [*sic*] about Christ. To
hold back from the fullest meeting with Muslims would be to
refrain from the fullest discipleship to Christ. Valid Christianity is interpretive Christianity.'[57]

Christianity and Islam needed to meet, not simply on
grounds of coexistence in one world, nor as mutual heirs of
Judaism, nor as prudence in the face of contemporary
pressures, but as an obligation built into their own structure.
Unlike Judaism they had transcended racial boundaries and
had become supra-national. In so far as they transcend already
'race, language and geography' it followed that 'their duty in
the total situation of to-day must ... hinge upon their duty to

[53] *Ibid.*, pp. 84–5.   [54] *Ibid.*, p. 125.   [55] *Ibid.*, p. 163.   [56] *Ibid.*
[57] *Ibid.*, p. 164.

each other'[58] and this implies mutual witness. When the *muezzin* calls from his minaret, he invites others to relationship to God and to responsible attitudes to human beings: he 'stands ideologically upon revelation. His concern is for a world in which the reign of God obtains. He acknowledges himself the trustee of what is greater than himself.' In all these respects there are comparisons to be made with Christian faith, even if 'contrasts there are, sharp and ineluctable'.[59]

What is to be the Christian response to the Muslim? Not, Cragg insisted, to fail to witness. That would be to 'betray the Christian's deepest trust and fail the world at a deeper point than its disease or poverty'.[60] The gospel of Christ does not 'belong' to Westerners nor can 'the eternal gospel of a world-inclusive love ... be treated as a piece of Anglo-Saxon privacy'.[61] To believe in Christ at all 'is to acknowledge Him a universal Christ ... requisite for all ... perquisite to none'. Christ 'belongs to us only because he belongs to all. He is ours only by virtue of his universality. To think otherwise would be unpardonable presumption'.[62] A key word for Cragg in commending Christ to Islam is 'retrieval'. If a proper form of coexistence is established, commendation can and will follow,[63] an opportunity for the Christian to 'undo the alienation ... by as full a restitution as they can achieve of the Christ to whom Islam is a stranger ... the restoration to Muslims of the Christ whom they have missed',[64] not least through the legacy of such historical enormities as the Crusades. To do this is to recover One who is relevant to Islam, enabling the Muslim to discover 'a divine revelation that is primarily personal, not oracular; that proceeds by enabling, not over-riding, the minds of its writers'.[65] Yet in such a valid dialogue and apologetic, it is fatally easy to commend the Christ to be retrieved by attitudes which, had they prevailed, would have ensured that Christ would never have gone to the Cross: 'if we say "in this sign conquer" it must only be the victory of meekness'.[66]

[58] *Ibid.*, pp. 166–7.   [59] *Ibid.*, p. 169.   [60] *Ibid.*, p. 199.
[61] *Ibid.*, p. 167.
[62] *Ibid.*, p. 168.   [63] *Ibid.*, p. 201.   [64] *Ibid.*, p. 220.   [65] *Ibid.*, p. 249.
[66] *Ibid.*, p. 265.

The last part of the book, entitled 'The Call to Interpretation', is a sustained and valuable handling of Muslim differences on the Scriptures, the person of Jesus, the Cross, the doctrine of God and the Christian society, the church. Cragg shows that the plea for a common 'theocentric' approach can compound difficulties for the Christian interpreter: for it is precisely the Muslim's insistence on God's unity and transcendence which baulks at incarnation; the suggestion of God manifest in the flesh is seen as unworthy,[67] in the same way that, to Muslims, the idea that God could allow his servant to suffer and to die by crucifixion is intolerable in one he would regard as a true prophet. Such a one cannot 'suffer ignominy', so some form of divine intervention has to be introduced. This re-writing of the crucifixion story in order to protect God's glory fails, however, to deal with 'the sure, if slow, processes of a moral order where love wins by suffering'. Instead, the God presented is 'in the arbitrary assertion of the inscrutable'.[68] Here, too, lies the contrast with Muhammad. Like Jesus, Muhammad faced opposition to religious truth based on 'prestige and pride'. He too was rejected as an upstart, 'disruptive of the *status quo* ... but there the similarity ends'.[69] When Muhammad rode 'into prostrate Mecca' he 'clinched the submission of the tribes' by victory. Jesus in Jerusalem 'chose to refuse external patterns of success. They were within his reach and to his hand. He rejected them for the way of the Cross'.[70] Any Christian speech about the resurrection to Muslims must not fall into the trap of making it an 'arbitrary finale', for this is to allow Muslims to by-pass the cross. Instead, retrieval here should interpret the resurrection in terms of the 'intrinsic victory of Christ as crucified' of the one who has 'proved himself the king of love'. If Muslims seek to avoid Christ in agony, in Gethsemane and on Calvary, the interpreter who retrieves the true Christ must lead them back 'to that interrupted pathway' that leads from his ministry to the empty tomb by way of the cross.[71]

[67] *Ibid.*, p. 258.   [68] *Ibid.*, p. 268.   [69] *Ibid.*, p. 274.   [70] *Ibid.*, p. 273.
[71] *Ibid.*, p. 275.

No digest will suffice to do justice to this richly suggestive book. It remains a significant text for Christians, challenged more than ever to coexistence with Islam, in the West as well as in the East. Cragg remained convinced that in regard to mission, the Church had no option: 'as long as Christ is Christ and the Church knows both itself and him, there will be a mission to Islam ... we present Christ for the sole sufficient reason that he deserves to be presented ... we cannot neglect that Christ claims discipleship and that his Gospel is something expecting a verdict'.[72] Nevertheless, he looked for many things in Muslim society which must be retained and preserved by any such disciples: hospitality, simplicity, discipline, dignity, family affection, sensitivity to the poor. Such 'Christian-Muslims', while retaining these qualities as disciples of Christ, would be able to point to how such living can be sustained, to the 'constraining love of Christ', that 'deepest well-spring of unselfish character and unwearied goodness'.[73]

IMC AND WCC: THE DEBATE ON INTEGRATION

As early as the 1940s and before the WCC Assembly at Amsterdam in 1948, the future relationship between the WCC and the IMC had provoked memoranda. A draft suggestion for a possible relationship was sent to various people, among them Max Warren, in 1947. While some welcomed the idea of some kind of structural relationship between the two bodies, others were cautious and in the case of two Swedish leaders, Archbishop Eidem and the respected professor of missions at Uppsala, K. B. Westman, opposed. The WCC needed first to prove itself. At this early stage, Max Warren welcomed ideas put forward by Norman Goodall as 'quite first class'. Even then, however he sounded warning notes. It was important for people who moved in WCC circles, he wrote, to realise how far away their estimate of the importance of the church was from

[72] *Ibid.*, p. 305.
[73] *Ibid.*, p. 323; see C. Lamb, 'The Call to Retrieval: Kenneth Cragg's Vocation to Islam', unpublished Ph.D. thesis, University of Birmingham 1987; J. R. W. Stott, *Christian Mission in the Modern World* (London, 1975), pp. 76–9.

many who were associated, for example, through constituent mission bodies, with the IMC. The risk was that those bodies, whose trust had been won for the IMC after initial suspicions, often among conservative mission boards of evangelical persuasion, might be lost if an untried body like the WCC began to have influence. S. C. Graaf van Randwijck, a contributor to IMC counsels from Holland, illustrated this very point in his return: certain Dutch Reformed bodies had accepted by implication membership of IMC but explicitly rejected relationship with the WCC. Warren, like Neill, was well qualified by his evangelical background to interpret certain minds to others: he wrote 'I confess to being not a little impressed by what seems to be a mounting tide of fundamentalism, and not only in America. I do not think that we ought to put it right beyond the region of possibility that the fundamentalist Churches and mission bodies may some time in the next few years try and constitute an international organisation of their own.' The gulf, he noted, between the theologically aware and others was very wide.[74]

In the years after the first meeting of the WCC at Amsterdam in 1948 Warren's attitude hardened against the idea of merger. As his autobiography shows he was, as ever, fearful of the effects of bureaucracy, the effect of the 'synthetic' mind here, as in general over proposals for organic union.[75] At a joint committee of the two bodies in 1956 he stated his case that 'whereas cooperation between the two bodies was eminently desirable, the proposal to unite them within a single structure was premature'.[76] His was the only vote against integration. The momentum towards merger continued. The overlapping areas of concern made some kind of close relationship necessary. The Dane, Erik Nielsen, was to put it pointedly

[74] YDS John Mott Archive: memoranda by J. W. Decker, 'Present and Future Relationships of the IMC and the WCC' (1 November 1946) and Norman Goodall (with responses), 'The International Missionary Council and the World Council of Churches' (February 1947): see N. Goodall, *Second Fiddle* (London, 1979), pp. 101–5; E. A. Payne and D. G. Moses, *Why Integration?* (1957); *New Delhi Report*, pp. 3–4, 6–7, 57–8, 259–60.

[75] Warren, *Crowded Canvas*, pp. 156–8.

[76] Dillistone, citing Warren, *Into All the World*, p. 118.

in a paper, 'The Role of the IMC': 'saying "No!" to integration with the WCC means saying "Yes!" to something else – to
what? We cannot escape this question.'[77] Warren had failed
to carry the WCC–IMC leadership in 1956 and had proposed to
remain silent on the issue at the Ghana Assembly of 1958: but a
combination of anxieties felt by those with little command of
the English language and a direct question from the platform
as to whether he felt his objections as keenly still, launched
Warren into a speech in which all his objections were restated
in public. It was, wrote his biographer, a dramatic scene,
where 'like a modern Luther' Warren had to stand against the
opinions of the leadership, including personal friends like
Walter Freytag and Lesslie Newbigin, to argue against centra-
lising tendencies in favour of freedom from potentially stifling
structures. Years later, despite voting for integration at Ghana
after this statement of deeply felt doubts, Warren still held to
his position of dissent with, if anything, greater strength, describing the merger to D. A. McGavran as 'disastrous'.[78]

Stephen Neill was able, at least, to put the integration
achieved at Ghana and formalised at the New Delhi meeting of
the WCC in 1961 into an optimistic theological framework,
after the new Division on World Mission and Evangelism of the
WCC had come into being as the successor of IMC: 'if the
theological significance of the action was realised', he wrote

this was indeed a revolutionary moment in Church history. More
than two hundred Church bodies in all parts of the world, assembled
in the persons of their official representatives, had solemnly declared
themselves in the presence of God to be responsible as Churches for
the evangelization of the whole world. Such an event had never taken
place in the history of the Church since Pentecost.[79]

It was the end of the forty-year life of the IMC, begun formally

[77] E. W. Nielsen, 'The Role of the IMC' in *The Ghana Assembly of the IMC* (ed. R. K.
Orchard), pp. 187–9; cf. Freytag, *Reden und Aufsätze*, 2 vols. (Munich, 1961), vol. II,
Integration, pp. 110–11.
[78] Warren essay in *Zending op weg naar de Toekomst*, pp. 190–202 (*Festschrift* for
J. Verkuyl); *Church Growth Bulletin*, 11 (1975), pp. 466ff.; cf. *IRM* 70, no. 280
(October 1981), pp. 240–6, 247–55; 62, no. 28 6 (April 1983), pp. 267–72.
[79] Neill, *The Church and Christian Union*, pp. 108–9.

at Lake Mohonk in 1921, years of remarkably creative activity
for the missionary movement and the international church.

What, finally, of Christian presence as an approach to those
of other faiths and none, warmly espoused by Warren and
others in the late 1950s and early 1960s? In the introduction to
the 'Christian Presence' series already quoted, in which
Warren called for a recognition that God preceded any missionary in alternative settings, he went on: 'we have to ask what is
the authentic religious content in the experience of the
Muslim, the Hindu, the Buddhist or whoever he may be ... to
try and sit where they sit, to enter sympathetically into the
pains and griefs and joys of their history ... the premises of
their argument ... in a word to be "present" with them'. This
was the meaning of the series title 'The Christian Presence
amid Islam' etc. This will 'not be an easy approach. But then
the love of God is not easy'.[80] It is significant that the first
words printed in the first of the studies, Kenneth Cragg's
Sandals at the Mosque, were a quotation about, and description
of, Charles de Foucauld; 'his vocation was one of being present
among people with a presence willed and intended as a witness
to the love of Christ'.[81] In the book the sandals of Cragg's title,
which needed to be removed both literally and metaphorically
by the Christian approaching the mosque, could also be seen,
as in the portrait of the Christian in Ephesians 6, as bringing
peace. The gospel and its representative should (in the title of
his third section) be 'present with the peace of God'. Both
Cragg and Warren faced the challenge of co-existence: both
wanted to set aside aggression and its methods,[82] but for
neither did co-existence imply limitation on the universal relevance of the gospel. The question for both was not whether,
but how, the gospel was to be commended: 'not in mere
assertion but by the mediation of the human presence ... is the
peace of God made known'.[83]

The idea of Christian presence continued to attract attention after 1960. Its popularity in the student world was

[80] Warren, Preface to Cragg, *Sandals at the Mosque*, pp. 9–10.   [81] *Ibid.*, p. 12.
[82] *Ibid.*, pp. 8–9 (Warren); p. 141 (Cragg).   [83] *Ibid.*, p. 140.

reflected by two whole numbers of the *Student World* being devoted to its examination. Members of the WSCF, faced with the strongly secular climate of the universities of the West, were drawn to this form of understanding, expressed in a WSCF statement, quoted in their journal, as 'being there in the name of Christ'. In an able editorial article, Philip Potter, then general secretary of WSCF but soon to hold that office for the WCC, rehearsed the biblical background. Here was an idea rooted in Old Testament passages like Exodus 3:1–14 (the story of the Burning Bush), where Yahweh is described as 'the one who is present'; or in Leviticus 19 where He is 'present beside the neighbour'. Potter rendered God's words to Abraham in Genesis 17:1–6 as a call to 'be present with me and before me in open integrity', rather than by the more familiar 'walk before me and be blameless'. The Jesus portrayed in the Gospel of John is one in whom God's presence (*Shekinah*) tabernacles (John 1:14), but he is also the one who fills others with his presence when he sends them out (John 20:19–23). Potter wrote, on the basis of this, that presence, witness and mission were inextricably linked in John's thinking.[84] Nor was God's presence a neutral idea: for the *Parousia*, which can be translated by both 'presence' and 'coming', was associated with acceptance or rejection: 'we cannot avoid the element of confrontation and decision about "presence"'.[85]

Potter had discerned that the student world he knew found words like witness and mission 'too big and too definite'. They suggested a certainty of faith which 'created difficulty for many people, not least those most committed to Christ and his gospel'. Such Christians trusted that 'while present' (in a curiously paradoxical phrase) they would be given 'new words in an authoritative silence'. Potter was aware of the danger of his readers and others latching on to a catch-phrase: hence his attempt to give the idea some biblical content. John Arthur, another contributor, was prepared to be more critical: such talk of 'listening before speaking' would have been acceptable enough from a body like the IVCF (the evangelical student

---

[84] *Student World*, 58, no. 3 (1965), pp. 211–13.   [85] *Ibid.*, p. 214.

body) with its zeal and emphasis on verbal witness, but it was less so from the WSCF: if words like 'evangelism' were 'suffering from "tired blood" then the word "presence",' he wrote, 'was born with it'.[86] Others were more sympathetic. Jean Diment, noting, as Potter had done, its origin in the 'absence' of the church in contemporary France, mentioned the French bishops' statement of April 1960 and detected an 'increasing accent on a presence involving both spirituality and solidarity'. Such presence should be active, an emphasis shared with Arthur. Service was 'active presence'.[87] Another contributor drew attention to the danger of a book like Jacques Ellul's *La Présence*, as a Christian re-working of the philosopher Gabriel Marcel and his philosophy of 'being'. Here 'presence' was detached from action ('what matters is to live and not to act' (Ellul)). In Marcel this led to an a-historical mysticism, a form of retreat; in Ellul, into what was called 'apocalyptic pietism'. There was a distaste for the industrialised, technological context of modern France in such escapism: what was needed was to discover God's presence in this context and this culture.[88] Here was Warren's view transposed.

Finally, D. A. McGavran, previously noted in these pages as a missionary in India and assistant to J. W. Pickett in his work on Indian mass movements, turned the full weight of a conservative evangelical critique on Warren and the whole notion. McGavran realised that Warren and others were searching for a middle way between aggression, which they disowned, and simple co-existence, equally disowned. Nevertheless, what was prudent policy for Charles de Foucauld in Muslim Algeria was not necessarily a blueprint for others in less life-threatening contexts: presence as defined at the beginning of Cragg's *Sandals at the Mosque* in relation to de Foucauld was 'a very good definition of mission ... where your throat will be cut in the morning if you preach effectively for conversion'.[89]

[86] *Ibid.*, pp. 237–9.   [87] *Ibid.*, pp. 229, 231.

[88] *Student World*, 59, no. 2 (1966), pp. 207, 208–13; J. Ellul, *La Présence au monde moderne: problème de la civilisation post-chrétienne* (Geneva, 1948); Eng. trans. Philadelphia, 1951.

[89] D. A. McGavran, *Evangelical Missions Quarterly* (Winter 1970), p. 100.

McGavran saw 'proclamation' as the traditional and received method, but he was not unaware that this too was open to abuse: he mentioned a missionary band who used loud-hailers in Japan and considered their end had been achieved once the message had been broadcast. Such a crude understanding ignored the true end of mission, which he defined as 'to bring ... into redemptive relationship to Jesus Christ'.[90]

The danger of both 'proclamation' and 'presence' was to mistake the means for the end. McGavran admitted a number of helpful aspects in Warren's approach to the other religious traditions, including respect for the other and a dialogue that promoted communication; but he demurred at Warren's stress on 'authentic religious content' in other faiths on the basis of his reading of such New Testament passages as Acts 14 and 17 and Romans 1:18–23.For McGavran, such a positive expectation of discovery was the beginning of a slippery slope by which an advocacy of Christian presence could lead to a pluralism which resulted in co-existence for mutual edification.[91] God might be present before the missionary arrived but McGavran disputed that he could be discerned, for example, in Hindu scriptures. Even Warren's friend and admirer Stephen Neill expressed caution over the approach: he preferred the use of the more general biblical term 'wisdom' for what was found in another tradition, on the grounds that the New Testament reserved terms like 'the Spirit of God' and 'the Spirit of Christ' exclusively for the operation of Christ in His Body, the church.[92]

The strength of the approach was well described in Thomas, *Attitudes to Other Religions*: 'the "Christian presence" view represents the openness of the missionary to the concrete reality of the other person's religion and an unwillingness to prejudge it by some framework which may distort it'.[93] In certain areas of the world and in certain life settings, being known as a Christian believer, expressing Christian faith by quality of life and service in the manner of Charles de Foucauld remains an

---

[90] *Ibid.*, p. 107.   [91] *Ibid.*, p. 107.
[92] Neill, *The Church and Christian Union*, pp. 292–4.
[93] O. C. Thomas (ed.), *Attitudes to Other Religions* (London, 1969), p. 221; see p. 26.

appropriate, sometimes the only appropriate, form for Christian mission. The elements of identification and engagement with the life of those far removed from Christian life and practice is surely applicable more broadly: and the willingness to listen and learn before earning the right to other, more overt, forms of witness is usually a priority. Poised on the Baluchistan frontier, between Afghanistan and Pakistan, on a visit to the Pathan people (who had been in turn Hindu, Buddhist and Muslim), Max Warren wrote in 1961 that he was less and less convinced by the polarising of 'influence' and 'conversion', the argument 'we are not sent to influence people but to convert them'. For him, that was to pose a contrast which was nonexistent. 'The Christian workers on the Frontier are not content with influence. They are creating commitment. But they refuse to despise influence'.[94] This was applicable to more frontiers than one. Again, if Jesus' words about the two or three gathered in his name being where he is to be discovered are applied to mission, small communities of the kind used by the Little Brothers and Little Sisters must find their place in alienated settings. As far as verbal witness is concerned, it must be the missionaries' longing that Christian presence expressed in being and action will provoke the question, in reply to which they can give 'a reason for the hope that is within them' (I Peter 3:15). Dialogue, such as that text presupposes, as a necessary partner to presence (recognised as such by Warren, Cragg, Neill and McGavran, among many others), will be pursued into the next chapter, not least in the thinking of Vatican II.

[94] CMS *Newsletter*, no. 238 (May 1961), p. 4.

CHAPTER 6

Mission as proclamation, dialogue and liberation 1960–1970

Although historians will contine to see 1945 as a convenient moment of transition in the twentieth century into a post-world war period, it is the decade of the 1960s, which displayed changes in society and showed a sharpness of discontinuity with what had gone before, that may prove to have been the greater transition. Here were breaks with much of what had been accepted norms of life, belief and behaviour which seemed to many to be revolutionary in character. Whether in the focus of a larger historical perspective the decade of the 1960s will be viewed as an aberration or as a period of forma-tive transition to a post-modern age, there can be no denying that it was a time of upheaval, especially in North American and European societies. It was marked in particular by a revolt of youth against accepted values and traditions, a revolt char-acterised in North America by protest against the Vietnam war, for example, in student riots in California in 1964, and in Europe in equivalent riots in Paris by students in 1968. In the Christian student world, the WSCF meeting in Strasbourg of 1960 has been interpreted as a sign of the times: here, accord-ing to recent interpreters, the voices of Karl Barth, Visser't Hooft, Lesslie Newbigin and D. T. Niles, Asian Christian leader, evangelist, scholar and ecumenist, were unable to hold their hearers with neo-orthodox presentations: rather, the missiologically radical views of J. C. (Hans) Hoekendijk, showing a certain impatience with the church and its institutional forms, while pointing to the *missio Dei*, God's activity in the world and its structures independently of the

163

church, caught the student mood.[1] The de-sacralising of
mission, including its de-clericalising, propounded by Hoekendijk, became part of a stream of changing attitudes which
converged at the Uppsala meeting of the WCC in 1968.[2]

In the wider context, the Cold War between the great
powers of the US and the then USSR came near to the kind of
confrontation which, in a nuclear age, could have resulted in
annihilation. J. F. Kennedy's ill-starred attempt at a Cuban
invasion soon after his succession to Eisenhower as president in
1961, the 'Bay of Pigs' episode, was followed by a deadly game
of bluff between himself and Nikita Khrushchev, the Cuban
missile crisis of October 1962. A less alarming form of competition led to the Russians putting the first astronaut (Yuri
Gagarin) into space in 1961, while by the end of the decade the
Americans were able to land the first man on the moon in 1969.
The Civil Rights Movement in the US, led by Martin Luther
King, alongside the anti-Vietnam war demonstrations, made
for social upheaval in the US up to and after Kennedy's Civil
Rights Bill, which was blocked, and his assassination in 1963.
Lyndon Johnson, his successor, proved unable to extricate the
Americans from the quagmire of Vietnam. The USSR, which
had suppressed a Hungarian uprising in the 1950s, proved
unwilling to relax its hold on its satellite, Czechoslovakia, in the
1960s, and a brief 'Prague spring' was ruthlessly crushed in
1968. This new-style imperialism contrasted with the acceler-
ating momentum towards devolution by the old-style imperial
governments like Britain. Harold Macmillan, the British prime
minister, made a famous 'winds of change' speech on this
theme in Pretoria in 1960; and, although this was followed
within weeks by the shootings at Sharpeville of many black
citizens by a South African government committed to the
widespread use of force to uphold the system of apartheid, in

---

[1] R. C. Bassham, *Mission Theology 1948–75: Years of Worldwide Creative Tension, Ecumenical, Evangelical and Roman Catholic* (Pasadena, 1979), pp. 47–8; D. J. Bosch, *Transforming Mission: Paradigm Shifts in Theology of Mission* (New York, 1991), p. 382;
W. R. Hutchison, *Errand to the World* (Chicago, 1987), pp. 183–6.
[2] J. C. Hoekendijk, *The Church Inside Out* (London, 1967); A. Th. van Leeuwen,
Christianity in World History: the Meeting of the Faiths of East and West, (London, 1964).

other parts of Africa black participation in government leading to independence of the colonial powers proceeded apace. In China, the theme of social upheaval common to the decade was given violent expression in the activities of the Red Guards, young Communist zealots urged on by their ageing leader, Mao Zedong (Tse-tung), in the Cultural Revolution of 1966.

CWME AT MEXICO CITY

It was to be expected that the world church, set in such a context, would reflect some of the pressure for change, even revolution. In the Protestant world of the WCC and IMC, a world shared by the Orthodox churches after the New Delhi meeting of the WCC in 1961, the integration of the two bodies under Lesslie Newbigin's leadership (secretary of the IMC 1959–61) led to a fresh series of international missionary conferences. These began at Mexico City in 1963, now sponsored by the Commission on World Mission and Evangelism of the WCC, the IMC's successor. Where the Whitby, Ontario Conference of 1947 had emphasised partnership between the older and younger churches in recognition of their developing equality of standing, Mexico went further in recognising that the old 'sending and receiving' model of mission was past. Instead, the emphasis had to be on God's mission in every part of the world, 'mission in six continents'.[3] Like the conferences at Willingen and Ghana, a comparatively small number of church leaders assembled at the Mexico City conference, around 200 in all three cases. Something of the same tension between God's work in the church and his activity in the secular structures and agencies, present at the WSCF meeting of 1960, was felt again here. The report handled issues of dialogue and has been judged to be at its strongest in this section.[4] The statement declared that 'true dialogue with a man of another faith requires a concern both for the Gospel

---

[3] R. K. Orchard (ed.), *Witness in Six Continents: Records of the CWME ... Mexico City 1963* (London, 1964).
[4] Bassham, *Mission Theology*, p. 66.

and for the other man. Without the first, dialogue becomes a pleasant conversation. Without the second, it becomes irrelevant, unconvincing or arrogant.'[5] The inauguration during the decade of regional meetings of church leaders and theologians from the younger churches, in Asia of the East Asia Christian Conference, whose first meeting was at Kuala Lumpur in 1959 and, in Africa, with the meeting of the All-Africa Conference of Churches in Kampala in 1963, was an important development. A small but significant change of title in the *IRM*, which changed from being a review of missions to a review of mission, while also becoming 'the organ of the Commission on World Mission and Evangelism of the WCC', illustrated a dictum of Stephen Neill's of 1964: 'the age of missions is at an end; the age of mission has begun'.[6]

VATICAN II

Such changes in the Protestant world were, however, dwarfed by the revolution set in motion in the early 1960s in the Roman Catholic church, when Pope John XXIII summoned the Second Vatican Council in 1962. The aim was stated to be *aggiornamento*, which can be rendered as 'updating'. It is important to remember, not least in reference to those ecclesiological forms already noticed, the sheer size of world-wide Roman Catholicism. Figures in the early 1980s indicated a Roman Catholic church of 802 millions, compared, for example, with 160 million Orthodox and a mere 49 million Anglicans. It was and is an overwhelmingly greater Christian presence than other churches, even when great communions like the world Lutheran (54 million), world Methodist (over 50 million), world Baptist (33 million) and other churches affiliated to the WCC are taken into account. A combination of all such non-Roman Christians is still heavily outnumbered by this great church. At the Vatican Council something of this size and

---

[5] Orchard, *Witness in Six Continents*, pp. 146–7.
[6] *IRM*, 58, no. 2 (1969), pp. 141–2; S. C. Neill, *A History of Christian Missions* (London, 1964), p. 572.

universality was represented by the attendance of 2,300 bishops, 800 of them from younger churches of Asia, Africa and Oceania. Pope John's ecumenical vision had also included Christians of other communions and expressed his wish for an 'ecumenical council of the whole church'.[7] He had created the Secretariat for Christian Unity before the council and, under the leadership of Cardinal Bea, this had done much preparatory work for it. At the council itself the Pope insisted that Orthodox and Protestant observers should sit in St Peter's across the aisle from the cardinals.[8] One eminent Protestant theologian, Oscar Cullmann, said of the document *De Ecumenismo* that 'no Catholic document has spoken of non-Catholic Christians in this way'.[9] The 'separated brethren' were made to feel welcome.

Of the other great documents of the council, *Gaudium et Spes* (the Constitution on the Church in the Modern World) opened up, with freshness of approach, a range of modern issues, in marked contrast to the legacy of the nineteenth century, the so-called 'Syllabus of Errors' of Pius IX, which had appeared to set the Roman Catholic church in opposition to modernity. It called for material assistance to the developing nations and for a 'profound change' in the priorities of the modern business world to help to provide it.[10] Nuclear war was seen as 'a crime against God'; and, although the traditional Roman Catholic view against artificial methods of birth control was maintained (to be reinforced in 1968 by the document *Humanae Vitae*) those advances which enabled natural methods to be more effective were commended to the faithful.[11] On the specifically missionary front, there was an endorsement of St Peter's words in Acts (4:12): 'Christ ... can through His Spirit offer man ... the strength to measure up to his supreme destiny. Nor has any other name under heaven

[7] W. M. Abbott (ed.), *Documents of Vatican II* (London, 1966), p. 336; *Dictionary of the Ecumenical Movement*, p. 1054; cf. D. Barrett, *World Christian Encyclopaedia* (Nairobi, 1982), A. J. van der Bent (ed.), *Handbook Member Churches WCC* (Geneva, 1985), pp. 19, 21, 23 for church statistics of 1980s.

[8] Abbott, *Documents*, p. 336.   [9] *Ibid.*, p. 338.   [10] *Ibid.*, p. 299.

[11] *Ibid.*, pp. 294, 302.

been given to man by which it is fitting for him to be saved'; in the church's Lord and Master can be found 'the focal point ... of all human history'; and the mission of the church, in uplifting Christ, will manifest both its religious and, 'by that very fact', its 'supremely human character'.[12]

Lumen Gentium

Before turning to the two great missionary documents, *Ad Gentes* and *Nostra Aetate*, it is important to dwell on *Lumen Gentium* (the Dogmatic Constitution of the Church), which provided the essential ecclesiological background and in which the revolutionary nature of Vatican II was focussed particularly. In the period after the council Adrian Hastings, then a missionary priest in Africa, was assigned the task of communicating the substance of the council's teaching in five East African countries, a duty which resulted in a helpful guide to the council's documents.[13] He has described the shift from a basically monarchical and hierarchical understanding of the church:

preconciliar Roman theology had described the Church as a 'Monarchy': it had been preoccupied with authority – conceived in very legal terms ... it had ... maintained that Christians not within the Roman communion were at best within the Church only 'by desire'. Such teachings and much else were abandoned either implicitly or explicitly in the council documents. The Church is seen primarily as 'the People of God' united by faith and the Holy Spirit, by baptism and Eucharist, rather than by government. The ministry within it is a 'collegial' one of the bishops as a group carrying on the collective ministry of the original apostles. 'Monarchy' is never once mentioned ... the Church is a communion and other Christians, whose baptism is recognised, are at least partially members of that communion.[14]

It was this dynamic view of the church as 'the people of God' in pilgrimage, over against static and over-hierarchical

---

[12] *Ibid.*, pp. 208, 210.
[13] *IBMR*, 16, no. 2 (April 1992), pp. 63–4; A. C. Hastings, *A Concise Guide to the Documents of the Second Vatican Council* 2 vols. (London, 1968–9).
[14] A. C. Hastings, *A History of English Christianity 1920–1990* 3rd edn (London, 1991), p. 527.

emphases, that led to fresh forms of the gospel in, for example, the 'base ecclesial communities' in Latin America. One Roman Catholic commentator referred to 1960–70 as the ecclesiological decade.[15] *Lumen Gentium* had important things to say, also, on other religious traditions and the approach to alternative cultures: on Jews and Muslims, the document described the Jews as 'most dear to God'; of Muslims, as those who, 'professing to hold the faith of Abraham along with us adore the one merciful God';[16] on other cultures, the church's missionary work should include taking what is good so that it becomes 'ennobled and perfected to the glory of God'.[17] At one point the document can be interpreted to open the door to extra-ecclesial salvation for Jews and Muslims and others who live according to the 'dictates of conscience', with the corollary that Judaism and Islam could be considered as 'salvific'. This has been adjudged, however, by both Roman and non-Roman interpreters as an over-interpretation: while salvation can be attained by those who live according to their conscience, *Lumen Gentium* is judged not to attach any 'specific salvatory significance to different human religions as such'.[18] If Jews and Muslims are saved it would be by living according to their consciences as individuals, rather than through their participation in their religious traditions as such.

Ad Gentes

In *Ad Gentes* (The Decree on the Church's Missionary Activity) many of the themes noted already in this book were covered and developed: mission understood as proclamation, as presence, as dialogue. The document begins by reference to *Lumen Gentium* and its emphasis on the church as the sacrament of salvation. This church is sent to the nations in obedience to the

[15] R. Michiels, 'The Self-Understanding of the Church after Vatican II', *Louvain Studies*, 14, no. 2 (1989), pp. 83–107.
[16] Abbott, *Documents*, pp. 34–5.   [17] *Ibid.*, p. 36.
[18] C. F. Hallencreutz, *Dialogue and Community: Ecumenical Issues in Inter-religious Relationships* (Geneva, 1977), p. 44; A. C. Hastings, *Concise Guide*, vol. I, p. 200; M. Ruokanen, *The Catholic Doctrine of the Non-Christian Religions* (Leiden, 1992).

command of her Founder and by virtue of her own universal
character to preach to all (*AG*, 1).[19] By its very nature the
church on earth is missionary, a nature which has its origin in
the plan of the Father and originates in the mission of the Son
and the Holy Spirit. The Son of God entered the world by
means of a true incarnation, through which he was made poor
for our sakes (II Cor. 8:9). He came as a servant and gave his
life for all (Mark 10:45). As the early fathers 'constantly proclaim', what was not assumed by Christ was not healed; so, full
human nature was assumed by him. It is this salvation which
must be 'proclaimed and spread to the ends of the earth' (Acts
1:8; *AG*, 2, 3).

The spread of the gospel was begun through preaching and,
as at Pentecost, the church 'speaks every language' and so
overcomes the dispersal of Babel towards union of all in a
universal, catholic faith. The Lord Jesus sent the twelve to
preach and founded his church as 'the sacrament of salvation',
which means that the church has an obligation to proclaim the
faith and salvation which come through him (*AG*, 4, 5). There
follows a strongly traditional ecclesiological stance: the order of
bishops are seen as the equivalent of the apostles, who, in
company with the order of priests, are charged 'with the
successor of St Peter' with the missionary task. The principal
means at their disposal for its fulfilment is seen to be preaching,
which serves for the planting of the church: the 'principal
instrument' towards 'implanting the church' is 'the preaching
of the Gospel of Jesus Christ'. Indigenous churches 'ought to
grow' from the 'seed of the word of God' and, in time, develop
their own hierarchy. These churches in turn have the same
obligation to preach the gospel, a responsibility which devolves
upon them (*AG*, 6).

Proclamation is therefore basic. There is, however, a clear
recognition that at times the way of Christian presence can be
the only way. Direct and immediate preaching of the gospel is
often not possible. In that case, the missionary 'patiently,

[19] References in the text to *Ad Gentes* (*AG*) and *Nostra Aetate* (*NA*) give the paragraph
numbers in the documents, as also later *Evangelii Nuntiandi* (*EN*).

prudently and with great faith can and ought ... [to] bear
witness to the love and kindness of Christ and thus prepare a
way for the Lord and in some way make him present' (*AG*, 6).
In a word, the witness of, say, Charles de Foucauld and many
like him was strongly affirmed. Presence alone, however, is not
enough: 'it is not sufficient for the Christian people to be
present ... in a particular nation, nor sufficient that it should
merely exercise the apostolate of good example ... it is present
so that it might by deed and word proclaim Christ to non-
Christian fellow countrymen and help them to a full reception
of Christ' (*AG*, 15).

There is recognition also of the need for united witness by all
baptised people. Division is injurious and 'unanimous witness'
before the nations is necessary. As proclamation, presence and
witness are given emphasis, so is conversion, for God wishes all
to be saved: 'everyone therefore ought to be converted to
Christ ... through the preaching of the Church' (*AG*, 7): faith
in Christ and baptism into the church are the way of salvation,
for Christ is 'the Truth and the Way' and 'the words of Christ
are at once words of judgement and grace, of life and death'
(*AG*, 8). Only by putting to death what is old can we come to
newness of life.

Like the Orthodox, the document lays heavy stress on the
eucharist as a missionary event, described here as the centre of
that missionary activity which 'makes Christ present', the one
who is 'author of salvation' (*AG*, 9). Before Donald McGavran
asked his famous question to the WCC prior to its meeting in
1968, 'Will Uppsala betray the two billion?', *Ad Gentes*
reminded readers of the 'two billion people ... increasing day
by day – who have never, or barely, heard the gospel message'
(*AG*, 10). The compilers drew attention to certain 'articles' to
address this great issue: (1) Christian witness; (2) preaching the
gospel and assembling the people of God; (3) forming the
Christian community. Space forbids extensive treatment
beyond that already given, but, under the first, a place is given
to dialogue where Christians are called to familiarise themselves with national and religious traditions in order to
'uncover with gladness and respect those seeds of the Word

which lie hidden among them'. Here is a view as old as Justin
Martyr. Christ himself used the method of 'human dialogue' to
lead to the 'divine light' and so Christians, too, should 'through
sincere and patient dialogue' converse with men of other faiths
and 'learn of the riches which a generous God has distributed
among the nations'. At the same time, however, they are to
'endeavour to illuminate these riches with the light of the
gospel', words which are reminiscent of the view of Oliver
Quick, noted earlier (*AG*, 10, 11).

Love is to animate the work done, especially among the poor
and afflicted, and Christians are to associate with all who work
for peace and fight famine, ignorance and disease. The church
disclaimed any desire to 'become involved in the government
of the temporal order': serving in charity was its true role (*AG*,
12). Ecumenical action was encouraged: while 'avoiding ...
indifferentism', Catholics can 'collaborate with their separated
brethren' in a 'common profession before the nations' (*AG*, 15).
In turning to the missionaries of the future, a high ideal of
missionary character was drawn, those who can bear loneliness
and exhaustion, can accommodate to different customs and
circumstances, living by faith and with 'inexhaustible hope',
spending themselves for souls (*AG*, 25). Specific missiological
study was commended in preparation for missionary work, so
that the missionary 'may be aware of the paths that have been
followed by the messengers of the gospel down through the
centuries' (*AG*, 26). The church which nurtured missionary
giants of the stature of Boniface, Francis Xavier, Bartholomew
de las Casas, Robert de Nobili, Ramon Lull and a host of other
missionary heroes deserved to point to the past as well as to 'the
present state of the missions and with the methods considered
most effective in the present time' (*AG*, 26). In the realm of
dialogue, this meant exposure to the work of 'scientific insti-
tutes which specialise in missiology' (*AG*, 34).

To sum up: in this, the third longest document of the
council, missionary activity had been made central to the life of
the Church. It is described as 'the greatest and holiest duty of
the church' and the bishops are urged to pay it special attention (*AG*, 29). While the main stress was on proclamation and

preaching, this was to serve the aim of *plantatio ecclesiae*, called here the implanting of the church. Place is made for 'presence' and dialogue, but they are subordinate to proclamation and the witness to the gospel involved in preaching. With this went a strong emphasis on service in love and the display of Christian life. This last was, for all Christians, 'the primary and most important contribution' they can make 'to the spread of the faith ... to lead a profound Christian life'. Such fervour and love for others 'will be like a new spiritual breeze throughout the whole church' (*AG*, 36).

Nostra Aetate

Compared to *Ad Gentes*, *Nostra Aetate* (the Declaration on the Relation of the Church to non-Christian Religions) is a very much shorter document. Its significance lay in the highly positive view of the non-Christian religions, a distinct change of approach: here 'for the first time ... non-Christian religions [were seen] as entities which the Church should respect and with which the Christian should enter into dialogue'.[20] Words like 'pagan', 'idolatry', 'error' are notably absent.[21] The document had originated in Pope John's wish to restore relationships with the Jewish people, badly damaged in the 1939–45 period by the Vatican's ambiguous record in relationship to the fascist governments at the time of Hitler's savagery. Pope John was aware of the need to build bridges between the church and the Jews and to undo some of the damage done by the outbursts of anti-Semitism which had sullied the church's history over many centuries. Having begun with the Jews, the compilers of the document's drafts brought into view members of other world faiths, Muslims, Hindus and Buddhists. In each case, the conciliar mind gave a positive account: in Hinduism, men were said to 'explore the divine mystery and express it both in ... myth and ... accurately defined insights of philosophy' (*NA*, 2). Ascetic practices and 'profound meditation'

[20] M. Ruokanen, *The Catholic Doctrine of Non-Christian Religions According to the Second Vatican Council* (Leiden, 1992), p. 7.
[21] *Ibid.*, pp. 7–8.

and 'recourse to God in confidence and love' were all practised. Buddhists sought a 'state of perfect liberation', the
experience of 'supreme illumination' either through 'their own
efforts' or 'by the aid of divine help' (the recognition is implied
that forms of Buddhism are atheistic). Such faiths 'often reflect
a ray of that truth which enlightens all men' (John 1:9).
Nevertheless, the church 'proclaims and is in duty bound to
proclaim without fail Christ who is the way, the truth and the
life (John 14:6)' for in him human beings 'find the fullness of
their religious life' (*NA*, 2).

Turning to Islam, Muslims are held in 'high regard', submitting themselves, as they do, to God 'without reserve', as
Abraham did 'to whose faith Muslims eagerly link their own'.
Although not acknowledging Jesus as God, yet 'they worship
[him] as a prophet' and honour his virgin Mother. Dissensions
of the past should be forgotten by both Christians and
Muslims: for this the 'sacred council now pleads'. Instead,
there should be cooperation to promote 'peace, liberty, social
justice and moral values' (*NA*, 3). Jews were recognised as the
origin of the church's life, the good olive tree, to paraphrase St
Paul, on to which the 'wild olive branches of the Gentiles have
been grafted (Rom. 11:17–24)' and they are inheritors of God's
covenants, the law, worship and the Christ (Rom. 9:4–5).
They remain still 'very dear to God'. Attempts to father guilt
for the death of Christ on Jews indiscriminately were as wrong
as speaking of the Jews as rejected by God. The church
deplored all hatreds and displays of anti-Semitism; and this,
not on grounds of political expediency, but as a breach of
Christian charity and so from a purely religious motivation.
The document, however, holds to a universal atonement and
therefore to the obligation of the church to preach the cross of
Christ as a sign of God's universal love: by implication this
includes its obligation to hold forth the love of God in Christ to
Jewish people. 'Conversion' as an idea, however, was removed
as 'not appropriate in a document striving to establish common
goals and interests first'.[22]

---

[22] Abbott, *Documents*, p. 665 and note 19.

Dialogue was urged, though less explicitly than in *Ad Gentes*: 'the church ... urges her sons to enter with prudence and charity into discussion and collaboration with members of other religions. Let Christians, while witnessing to their own faith and way of life, acknowledge, preserve and encourage the spiritual and moral truths found among non-Christians' (*NA*, 2).

Interpretation of these documents in relation to non-Christian faiths and the church's attitude to them has differed, as is likely in documents intended to be inclusive. Progressive and radical proponents have professed to see in them a wider acceptance of alternative religions than the actual wording of the text can bear.[23] Here, whatever arguments are adduced from silence on certain issues, the judgement of a recent and thorough study of the approaches of Vatican II to non-Christian religions is accepted: namely, that whereas the moral, cultural and social goods in non-Christian settings are affirmed as coming from God the Creator, this judgement is not made in the context of the *religions*, but, instead, in relation to human life and society as the creation of God.[24] Hence the call to acknowledge, pursue and promote the spiritual and moral goods 'found among non-Christians', as well as the values of 'their social life and culture' (*NA*, 2). Positive as the wording is, for example, on Hinduism, the emphasis is on the direction of the Hindu's search as *ad Deum*, directed towards God, rather than on discovery of Him.[25]

Anonymous Christianity

One of a number of theologians who contributed to the background thinking of Vatican II was Karl Rahner.[26] During the 1960s he was responsible for a theory of the relation to non-Christians which gained a good deal of currency. Not dissimilar ideas were propounded in a Hindu context by the Indian

---

[23] *IBMR*, 14, no. 2 (April 1990), pp. 56–64.
[24] Ruokanen, *Catholic Doctrine*, p. 113.
[25] *Ibid.*, p. 73.   [26] *Ibid.*, p. 29.

Roman Catholic theologian, Raimundo Panikkar, one of a growing number of Asian thinkers and theologians, Catholic and Protestant, who emerged after 1945, which included D. T. Niles, P. D. Devanandan, M. M. Thomas and R. B. Manikam. Where Panikkar explored these themes in *The Unknown Christ of Hinduism* (1964), Rahner took the same standpoint of Christ present already in the other religions a stage further in designating their adherents as 'anonymous Christians'. The alternative traditions were 'lawful religions'[27] which contained supernatural elements present through Christ. It was an affirmative position argued with great theological sophistication, but it ran the risk of Christian patronage: the question was well put as to how far the Christian would welcome being titled an anonymous Buddhist or Hindu. A further and pointed criticism related to the importance of the name in Christian faith and biblical writing. To know God, in the Old Testament, is essentially to know him by his name: and this is taken over into the New Testament, so that 'anyone who calls on the name of the Lord will be saved' (Rom. 10:13).[28] Naming has to do with identity, as with Jesus' naming of Peter. Anonymous Christianity ran the risk of being a contradiction in terms. It is not insignificant that naming and baptism are interrelated.

After Vatican II, which closed in 1965, the Roman Catholic Church began an immense process of adjustment. There were many outward signs of this ecclesiological revolution: in liturgy, where mass was practised in the midst of the congregation and the 'distancing' of priest from people removed: in the religious orders, where new attitudes found expression in a greater identification with the world leading, for example, to nuns forsaking their habits and becoming outwardly indistinguishable: in a greater attention to local context and indigenous forms of worship and Christian life, leading to the abandonment of the Latin mass, unchanged for more than 500

---

[27] K. Rahner, *Theological Investigations* 23 vols. (London, 1963–92), vol. V (1966), p. 121.
[28] J. W. Charley, *Mission – Some Contemporary Trends* (London, 1973), p. 39.

years, in favour of vernacular forms; experiments, too, in the realm of catechesis and ecclesial life in the *cursillo* movement and the base communities, groups of Catholic Christians which encouraged lay participation and leadership, sharing in the ministry of word and sacraments, sometimes radical in their social and political agenda, some well integrated into the church's institutional life, some (as the document *Evangelii Nuntiandi* was to complain in 1975) using their group life to set themselves over against the church as institution.

LATIN AMERICA AND THE LIBERATION THEOLOGIANS

Nowhere was influenced more decisively by these elements than Latin America. Here were countries whose Christianity dated from the period of the Spanish and Portuguese empires of the sixteenth century and after, where Roman Catholicism was dominant. This can be illustrated by some statistics. In Brazil, the population in 1900 was 17·9 million of whom 17·1 million professed Roman Catholicism. In the mid-1970s, despite an upsurge of Pentecostalism and Evangelicals[29] there were still 85·9 million Roman Catholics in a population of 95·2 million. Argentina presented, if anything, an even greater Roman Catholic dominance during the century: what had been 4 million Roman Catholic Christians out of 4·2 million in 1900 had become by the 1970s 22·7 out of 23·7 million. Countries like Colombia (21·3 out of 22 million in 1970), Chile (7·8 out of 9·3 million), Paraguay (2·1 out of 2·3 million), Peru (12·9 out of 13·2 million) and Uruguay (1·8 out of 2·9 million) confirmed the picture.[30]

In these countries great poverty existed alongside great wealth. The *favelas* (slums) of Rio de Janeiro contrasted sharply with the lifestyle of the urban rich. A small percentage of Brazilian landowners controlled a large proportion of Brazil's land. A United Nations' report of 1952 had found that

---

[29] Neill, *History of Christian Missions*, pp. 459–60.
[30] Barrett, *World Christian Encyclopaedia*, pp. 186 (Brazil), 147 (Argentina), 240 (Colombia), 226 (Chile), 556 (Paraguay), 569 (Peru), 733 (Uruguay).

two-thirds of the people of Latin America were undernourished, three-quarters were illiterate (a variation between 20 and 60 per cent in different countries) and that two-thirds of the land was owned either by large landholders or by foreign cooperatives. A decade of development was mounted by the United Nations. It was joined by President Kennedy's 'Alliance for Progress' in Latin America, launched in 1961, which aimed to regenerate the national economies: the huge sum of 91 billion dollars of aid was given in this development programme to South American countries. Nevertheless, according to observers like José Miguez Bonino, the gap between the rich and the poor widened further.[31] In addition, this was a period of oppressive régimes, often military governments, who were perceived to favour the wealthy, powerful and capitalist sectors of society. To the poor, figures like the Cuban revolutionary and friend of Fidel Castro, Che Guevara, active in Bolivia prior to his execution in 1967, or the Columbian priest, Camilo Torres, who forsook the priesthood to join with revolutionary guerrillas and was killed in an ambush in 1966, became symbols of hope. When some Uruguayan young people were asked, 'who then is Jesus Christ?' the reply came 'for us Jesus Christ is Che Guevara': which, wrote Miguez Bonino, was their way of saying 'liberation and revolution are a legitimate transcription of the gospel'.[32] Guevara himself had said: 'only when Christians will have the courage to give a wholehearted revolutionary testimony will the Latin American revolution become invincible ... up to the present they have allowed their doctrine to be instrumentalised by the reactionaries'. For Camilo Torres, his calling was to 'change the structures of society which create and multiply every day these conditions': this meant for him that 'I am a revolutionary because I am a priest'.[33]

[31] J. Miguez Bonino, *Revolutionary Theology Comes of Age* (London, 1975), pp. 22–5; this book appears in an American edn, *Doing Theology in a Revolutionary Situation* (Philadelphia, 1975).

[32] *Revolutionary Theology*, pp. 2–3.

[33] *Ibid.*, quoting Che Guevara, pp. 43–5; J. Gerrassi, *Camilo Torres: Revolutionary Priest* (London, 1971); M. Zeitlin, *Father Camilo Torres: Revolutionary Writings* (New York, 1972).

It was against this background that the Roman Catholic bishops gathered in Colombia for their Medellín meeting of 1968. They acknowledged that 'our nations are not masters of their own resources and economic decisions'. In Brazil, for example, 41·6 per cent of all industry was in foreign hands, including 71 per cent of the railways, 82 per cent of the rubber industry and 94 per cent of the chemical industry, making Brazil 'a factory of the multi-national corporations'. The bishops recognised that the basic issue was a situation of economic dependency rooted in structural injustice as the root problem.[34] They wanted to look beyond development or revolution to transformation. The need was to 'conscientize' (in the terminology of the Brazilian-born educator, Paulo Freire) and towards this the church was to commit itself to an 'instructional ministry'. The gap between this kind of pronouncement and the revolutionary groups of Catholic radicals was still great, but the hierarchy had shown its understanding of the need for structural change.

The theology of liberation which developed in the late 1960s and flowered in the 1970s represented a radical approach to Christian mission and theological method. Although Jesus' Messianic programme in Luke 4 was more frequently appealed to, as important a New Testament text as any for Christian appreciation of the stance adopted could be Jesus' words in the Fourth Gospel: 'if any one wills to do God's will, he will discover whether my doctrine comes from God' (John 7:17). Taken together with Marx's dictum that the object is not to understand society but to change it, this emphasis on action in relation to reflection is central to the theological programme. Liberation theology, along with much subsequent theology from Africa and Asia, has refused to accept the Western philosophical inheritance of a disjunction between reflection and action. At its best, it has sought an integration between the two and in this has believed that it had the support of the thinking of Vatican II.[35] Christian response needs to be integral. The

[34] CELAM documents of Medellín 1968, *Between Honesty & Hope* (New York, 1970), p. 203; Miguez Bonino, *Revolutionary Theology*, p. 57.
[35] G. Gutierrez, *A Theology of Liberation* (London, 1974), pp. 72, 76 and note 36.

starting-point for such a theology therefore is a specific context among, for example, the oppressed poor; and its origin would lie in action (*praxis*: lit. deed) leading to reflection. The traditional academic 'neutrality' of the Western universities was disowned. A typical statement read: 'we reject as irrelevant an academic type of theology which is divorced from action. We are prepared for a radical break in epistemology which ... engages in critical reflection on the *praxis* of the reality of the Third World.'[36]

The bishops at Medellín had called for a shift in theological method in 1968. The first stage must be analysis of the reality in which God acts, that is, the context: the second stage is reflection upon it, which included the traditional emphases on prayer and meditation; the third stage was response. The approach bears a strong similarity to the Jocist cells, noted earlier, with their method of observe, judge, act. Among those who reflected in this way was the Peruvian priest and theologian, Gustavo Gutierrez, whose context was the poor of Lima. In his *Theology of Liberation* he was eager to insist that theology was the 'second step', reflection arising out of pastoral activity.[37] Theology becomes a critical reflection on Christian *praxis*.[38] As for the bishops, so for Gutierrez: the way of development had proved a failure. By contrast, what was needed was liberation, by means of a 'profound transformation of the private property system, access to power of the exploited class and a social revolution'.[39] He gave explicit recognition to Marx, who linked knowing indissolubly to transformation.[40] Latin America's need was for liberation from the great capitalist countries, most of all from the US.[41] The aim must be to emancipate, and, in Christian terms, to create a new humanity. Gutierrez pointed to words of Che Guevara: 'the true revolutionary is guided by strong feelings of love ... a sense of

[36] S. Torres and V. Fabella, *The Emergent Gospel* (New York, 1978), p. 269; cf. P. Frostin, 'The Hermeneutics of the Poor – the Epistemological Break in Third World Theologies' *Studia Theologica*, 39 (1985), pp. 127–50.
[37] Gutierrez, *Theology of Liberation*, p. 11. [38] *Ibid.*, p. 13.
[39] *Ibid.*, pp. 26–7.
[40] *Ibid.*, p. 29. [41] *Ibid.*, p. 88.

justice and truth [which need] to avoid falling into dogmatic extremes, into cold scholasticism, into isolation from the masses. They must struggle every day so that their love of living humanity is transformed into concrete deeds.'[42] Fidel Castro's admiring tribute to Camilo Torres was also quoted.[43] Medellín had shown the contrast between institutionalised violence, practised by the ruling régimes and unjust in character, and the just violence of the oppressed.[44] Whatever else, however, Medellín had been rooted in the reality of Latin American life as 'deeply conflictual'. This was its greatest merit. It had given legitimation to movements for renewal.[45]

Gutierrez's *Theology of Liberation* was and is a fundamental text for liberation theology. For a description of the theological method proposed, J. L. Segundo's *Liberation of Theology* has been judged to be even more significant.[46] Segundo was based in Uruguay, though like Gutierrez he had studied in France and Belgium, a reminder that a number of those who criticised the European theological method had acquired their skills in its universities and seminaries. Segundo gave a clear and arresting description of the so-called 'hermeneutical circle', the 'continuing changes in our interpretation of the Bible which is dictated by the continuing changes in our present-day reality, both individual and societal'.[47] Four stages were described in the movement towards a new interpretation or hermeneutic: first, an experience of reality which leads to 'ideological suspicion'; next, this suspicion is applied to the 'whole ideological superstructure' of received theology; this leads, third, to a suspicion of received exegesis of the Bible; and from there, finally, to a 'new hermeneutic', whereby interpretation takes account of the new elements which previous accounts had overlooked.[48] Such a method requires 'a profound human commitment' which Segundo is not afraid to call partiality: but

[42] *Ibid.*, p. 98, note 45.   [43] *Ibid.*, p. 120 note 10; cf. p. 282 note 31.
[44] *Ibid.*, p. 137.
[45] *Ibid.*, pp. 136–7.
[46] J. A. Kirk, *Theology Encounters Revolution* (Leicester, 1980), pp. 117–19.
[47] J. L. Segundo, *The Liberation of Theology* (New York, 1976), p. 8.
[48] *Ibid.*, p. 19.

scholarly neutrality, a state of total impartiality, is 'precisely the pretence of academic theology'. In fact, there is no such thing as autonomous, impartial academic theology 'floating free above the realms of human options and biases'. Instead, such theology is 'intimately bound up with the psychological, social and political *status quo*, though it may not be aware of the fact.'[49]

Like Max Warren, Gutierrez was against any dualism into sacred and secular in examining the historical process. The Brazilian Hugo Assmann, whose radicalism led to his exclusion from Brazil, Uruguay, Bolivia and Chile, gave a further powerful critique of this tendency. His *Practical Theology of Liberation* includes a preface by Ernesto Cardinale, which referred to Che Guevara's remarks on Christians and revolution and Camilo Torres' comment that 'the revolutionary struggle is a priestly struggle'.[50] Included also is a short piece by Gutierrez that located the liberation struggle in love of the Father and solidarity with the poor.[51] For Assmann, dualism is the great enemy and one of which the Medellín documentation was in some measure guilty. To talk in ideal terms, to talk of abstract truth, very easily leads to the detachment of truth from the historical plane. Then historical reality can be 'manipulated by the powers that be'. That kind of detached thinking ends up by being a gift to the perpetrators of the so-called 'law and order' school, the guarantee of the status quo.[52] Assmann's quarrel with the Medellín meeting was that in opting for what he calls an 'analytical construct' the bishops had adopted, knowingly or unknowingly, 'an ethical and political stance'. The danger of all such detached thinking is that it evades the historical challenges: instead, 'love, a properly theological term, is indispensable in any political struggle for liberation'.[53] The post-Vatican II era had left a vacuum and it was this vacuum that went far to explain 'the almost desperate recourse to the language of liberation'.[54]

[49] *Ibid.*, p. 13.
[50] H. Assmann, *A Practical Theology of Liberation* (London, 1975), pp. 1–2.
[51] *Ibid.*, pp. 8, 11.   [52] *Ibid.*, p. 77.   [53] *Ibid.*, p. 85.   [54] *Ibid.*, p. 117.

Of other leading figures identified with the liberation movement, Dom Helder Camara became an auxiliary bishop in Rio de Janeiro in 1952. In 1955, the French Archbishop Gerlier suggested to Camara that he should address the problem of the *favelas*. Camara became a courageous and outspoken champion of the poor, making the memorable comment that when he built houses for the poor he was called a saint but when he called by name the injustices which gave rise to poverty he was called a Marxist. He himself has affirmed the use of Marxist tools of social analysis by the Christian church, while recognising the failures of Marxist rulers.[55] On the important and central issue of violence in pursuit of structural change, he has declared himself opposed, not so much on theological as on tactical grounds. Violence is seen as an ineffective method. Camara, then Archbishop of Recife, has received various threats to his life; unlike Archbishop Oscar Romero of El Salvador, gunned down, it would seem, on account of his political protests while celebrating mass in the cathedral of San Salvador, Camara continues to bear his witness, although he has been treated as *persona non grata* even by other national hierarchies, such as that in Colombia.[56] Camara has continued to combine membership of the hierarchy with social radicalism and has been a symbol of hope to many in Latin America and beyond.

Base ecclesial communities

The Brazilian brothers, Leonardo and Clodovis Boff, are two more recent contributors to the theology of liberation. They collaborated in writing *Introducing Liberation Theology* (1987), which reacted to the Medellín meeting of 1968 in terms of the theme of the Exodus, frequently employed in liberation theology. There, in the Old Testament, God took sides against Pharaoh. Medellín and the movement which has continued since has demonstrated that 'just as formerly ... Israel ... so we

---

[55] Miguez Bonino citing Camara, *Revolutionary Theology*, pp. 45–6.
[56] D. Barrett, *World Christian Encyclopaedia*, p. 241.

too cannot fail to feel his saving deliverance'.[57] The identification with the poor, so important to these writers, was expressed here by extolling their piety and sense of God, their solidarity and fortitude, their capacity for celebration and joy in the midst of conflicts, their serenity in the struggle for life.[58] Leonardo Boff has pleaded with the Roman Catholic church to drop celibacy as a requirement for priests at a time when there are less than two priests per 10,000 of the population.[59] It is the same plea made twenty years earlier, in a more muted form, by Adrian Hastings in the context of Africa, where an equivalent shortage was apparent after Vatican II.[60] Here, still more radically, authority was invited to consider ordaining women: attention was drawn to the established Lutheran practice of more than twenty-five years, and to that of the American Episcopal (Anglican) church. Even the Jewish community had overturned centuries of tradition by appointing a woman as rabbi in 1971.[61] Leonardo Boff's book placed great faith in the base ecclesial communities: they are 'helping the whole church in the process of declericalization by restoring to the People of God ... the rights of which they have been deprived ... *a new praxis must be implemented* ... They are helping the whole church to "reinvent itself"; experiment is gradually confirming theory ... in the church-as-institution ... a new way of being church in the world to-day.'[62]

The new forms of church life and ecclesiological development were compared to the gradual development of the parochial structure in the Middle Ages. As this developed in the twelfth, thirteenth and fourteenth centuries, so the development of the base communities as a churchly form will be

[57] L. and C. Boff, *Introducing Liberation Theology* (London, 1987), p. 51, quoting the Medellín documents (introduction to conclusions, no. 6).

[58] *Ibid.*, p. 56.

[59] L. Boff, *Ecclesiogenesis: the Base Communities Reinvent the Church* (New York, 1986), pp. 61–4.

[60] Hastings, *Concise Guide*, vol. 1, pp. 88–9.   [61] L. Boff, *Ecclesiogenesis*, p. 88.

[62] *Ibid.*, pp. 32–3; cf. *IBMR*, 11, no. 4 (October 1987), 'A New Ecclesiology in Latin America' (C. R. Padilla), pp. 156–64 and bibliography; G. Cook, *The Expectation of the Poor: Latin American Base Ecclesial Communities in Protestant Perspective* (New York, 1985); E. Cardenal, *The Gospel in Solentiname* (New York, 1982).

gradual.[63] In this view, the base communities have an assured future, but they would not present themselves as the only forms for the church. Nevertheless, they contribute a 'bountiful well-spring of renewal for the tissues of the body ecclesial and ... a demand for the evangelical authenticity of ecclesial institutions'.[64] Their particular strength is to 'incarnate this experience of salvation' and to make the universal church a reality 'at the grass roots'.[65] The brothers see that in these communities, 'in comradely relationships of sharing love and service', Christians experience communion. Their deep discovery of the true nature and value of the church can become a 'transparent witness to Christian commitment' in a way that would otherwise be impossible in 'our large parishes'.[66]

The Boffs list those whom they regard as leading figures as writers of liberation theology. In addition to Roman Catholics like Gutierrez and J. L. Segundo, they name leading Protestants like Emilio Castro, Julio de Santa Ana, Rubem Alves and Miguez Bonino.[67] Of these Alves, like the Boffs writing out of a Brazilian context, has taken up the Exodus theme in terms of an understanding of God as the subverter of the *status quo*, the one who breaks open the future. For Alves, theology has to stop explaining and to start transforming: to take, not orthodoxy but *orthopraxis* as the criterion of doing theology.[68] Right action must lead to a new way of doing theology.

EVANGELII NUNTIANDI

There is advantage in following through the stream of tradition which has issued from the Medellín meeting, because it serves to illustrate some of the revolutionary effects in the realm of church life, ecclesiology and theological method which continue to follow from Vatican II and, in Latin America, from the hierarchy's recognition of the need for structural change over against a social strategy of development and aid in these

---

[63] L. Boff, *Ecclesiogenesis*, p. 33.   [64] *Ibid.*, pp. 8–9.   [65] *Ibid.*, p. 22.
[66] L. and C. Boff, *Liberation Theology*, p. 59.
[67] *Ibid.*, pp. 69–71.   [68] Miguez Bonino citing Alves, *Revolutionary Theology*, p. 81.

countries. Ten years after Vatican II, Pope Paul VI issued the document *Evangelii Nuntiandi*, which embodied the reflections of the synod of bishops on where things had gone since the council closed in 1965. This synod had devoted itself to the subject of the evangelization of the modern world with 'this single objective: to ensure that the church of the twentieth century may emerge even better equipped to proclaim the gospel to the people of this century' (*EN*, 2). The gospel message was regarded as 'unique ... irreplaceable', admitting of neither indifference nor 'accommodation to the principles of other religious beliefs or of any compromise, for on it depends the whole issue of man's salvation ... it is truth itself' (*EN*, 5). Jesus' own insistence that he must preach the good news, for 'I was sent for that purpose', sums up 'in a word' his 'whole mission and mandate'. Christ's mandate to proclaim the gospel means that the church is to proclaim the kingdom by the 'assiduous preaching of the word' (*EN*, 6, 11). This kingdom and salvation is to be received by all: each individual can receive these 'fruits of grace' and this 'by a total spiritual renewal of himself which the gospel calls *metanoia*, that is by a conversion of the whole man by virtue of which there is a radical change of mind and heart' (*EN*, 10).

Evangelisation is the special vocation of the church: 'it is her essential function'. The church exists to preach the gospel. Therefore, 'evangelization is inherent in the very nature of the church' (*EN*, 14, 15). The church community can never be 'confined within itself' and cannot achieve its 'full force and value' unless it becomes a witness and 'evokes admiration and conversion of souls' (*EN*, 15). It begins, therefore, with the church herself, who needs to be continually evangelised. In relation to the world, it means 'carrying forth ... the good news to every sector of the human race' for its renewal and 'to effect this interior transformation' (*EN*, 18). This will involve the recasting of 'criteria of judgement', the values and standards of the human race, often 'inconsistent with the word of God'. This requires penetration of society and culture 'in depth', so that the gospel reaches to the 'very centre and roots of life' in a given culture (*EN*, 19, 20). Witness by groups of Christians in given communities is supremely the way that the gospel is proclaimed in a culture and by their cooperation with all others who are promoting 'the noble and good'. The rift between the gospel and culture is one of the 'unhappy circumstances' of our times (*EN*, 20, 21).

Silent witness has its place: but it is not enough (*EN*, 21, 22). Its meaning has to be 'clarified and corroborated', what St Peter called 'accounting for the hope that is in you'. Clear, unambiguous witness in word and life should proclaim 'the Lord Jesus' (*EN*, 22). The one evangelised should become the 'evangelizer': this is the test of the authenticity of his conversion, for it is 'inconceivable that a man who has received the word and surrendered himself to the kingdom should not himself become a witness and proclaimer of the truth' (*EN*, 24).

The document turned to liberation. There was recognition that evangelisation must deal also with the life of nations, delivering a message which is 'relevant ... in our age ... about liberation' (*EN*, 29). Social and economic factors have their necessary place in the eradication of injustice and the establishment of justice (*EN*, 31). The danger is, however, that preoccupation with such 'burning problems of liberation' may reduce the church's role to temporal activity only. This preoccupation can also make the church's message of liberation vulnerable to 'ideological groups and political parties' and so lose the church its authority to proclaim in the name of God (*EN*, 32). Temporal problems must be addressed, but the church 'reaffirms the primacy of her spiritual function and refuses to substitute for the preaching of the kingdom of God a proclamation of liberation of the merely human order' (*EN*, 34). Every form of temporal and political liberation 'contains within itself the seeds of its own frustration ...' (*EN*, 35).

On the highly sensitive issue of violence the document is adamant: 'the church cannot accept any form of violence and especially of armed violence ... nor the death of any man as a method of liberation'. It refers to the visit of Paul VI to Colombia in 1963, when he reminded his hearers (Camilo Torres had served as chaplain of the University of Bogota in that country) that violence is 'repugnant to the Christian spirit' and 'so far from helping may well hinder the social progress to which you rightly aspire' (*EN*, 37). Ambiguities associated with the term 'liberation' were to be removed: 'the liberation which evangelization proclaims . . . is that . . . which Christ himself announced and gave to man by his sacrifice' (*EN*, 38). Methods of evangelisation are then set out: the living of the Christian life, verbal proclamation (not least in the setting of the eucharist, by means of homilies); catechetical instruction; the use of the modern media (*EN*, 41–5) and duly directed popular religiosity or piety (*EN*, 48).

Evangelisation 'knows no frontiers' (*EN*, 49). Jesus had invested it with universality with his instruction to go out into all the world to preach the gospel to the whole creation. It is relevant therefore to the non-Christian religions. Despite their 'splendid patrimony', they have the right to know 'the riches of the mystery of Christ' (*EN*, 53). Faced even with the most admirable forms of natural religion the church has a 'special function . . . to bring men into contact . . . with [God's] living presence'. To this end the church is training 'new generations of missionaries', far from agreeing with those who say that 'the age of missionary work is past' (*EN*, 53). Contemporary atheistic humanism is assessed, associated with secularism, the 'new consumer society' with its pleasure principle and rootlessness; but with its willingness also to 'explain . . . and justify' its 'standards of authenticity' more eagerly than in previous times. Outright rejection and simple inertia are equally phenomena of unbelief (*EN*, 55, 56).

Base ecclesial communities, the group life 'flourishing more or less everywhere in the church' were given a great deal of attention by the synod of bishops (*EN*, 58). On the one hand they are commended as a 'source of hope', as long as certain ingredients are present: nourishment from the word of God; loyalty to the church of the district where they are; resistance to the temptation to challenge the established order; 'close and sincere relations' with their pastors; resistance to the illusion that they alone have a monopoly of the gospel; deepening responsibility and missionary zeal for others with an openness

to all (*EN*, 58). It would be difficult to express the danger of
any intense Christian group life more comprehensively: and
what precedes these counsels indicates that some groups, con-
sumed by 'a spirit of bitter criticism' of the church, which they
regard as 'institutional' and against which they set themselves,
had been part of the BEC's development. Such groups had 'not
infrequently ... fall[en] victim to some political group ... sect
... or faction' (*EN*, 58).

There is much else in this document, but space forbids
further comment. It cannot be left, however, without reference
to a note which will be shown to have been struck with equal
strength at the contemporary evangelical conference at Lausanne in 1974, not least by the Ugandan Anglican Bishop,
Festo Kivengere. The document lays great emphasis on the
need for united witness among Christians in a world 'in desperate need of God'. Division is one of the great obstacles to
effectiveness of evangelisation in a needy world, whether as
doctrinal dispute or in mutual recriminations among Christians. By contrast, 'the Lord's spiritual testament teaches us
that unity among Christians is not only the proof of our
enrolment in the number of his elect, but also the proof of his
mission from the Father'. Thus, the sign of unity 'is the aim and
the instrument of all evangelization'. Division among Christians is a 'very grave state of affairs which is impeding the very
work of Christ'. The Pope called for 'unceasing collaboration
with our Christian brethren with whom we are not yet united
in perfect unity', a collaboration based on common baptism
and common 'heritage of the faith'. The aim should be that 'in
the very work of evangelization' Christians 'may offer to the
world a broader common witness to Christ' (*EN*, 77).

Evangelii Nuntiandi helps to gives perspective of view on the
Roman Catholic church post-1960 and Vatican II. First, there
can be no doubting the church's deep commitment to spread-
ing the faith: 'mission,' wrote Adrian Hastings in his guide to
the documents of Vatican II 'had become a key concept in
modern theology',[69] and in documents like *Lumen Gentium, Ad*

[69] Hastings, *Concise Guide*, vol. 1, p. 215.

Gentes and *Nostra Aetate* the church had embraced it. Whether in these documents or in the later *Evangelii Nuntiandi*, the highest priority is given to proclamation, the gospel as a message to be communicated to all, committed to the church, whose prime duty is to proclaim. Although there is due emphasis on the witness of life as a part of the proclamation, a much heavier emphasis is laid on verbal preaching and witness. Dialogue, which is explored and affirmed in the Vatican II documents, is given a subordinate role.

Vatican II pre-dated the kind of developed liberation theology handled by *Evangelii Nuntiandi*. Here the key issues are present. Violence, the commitment to armed struggle, is disowned: someone like Camilo Torres, who felt that the only way to achieve change was to identify with guerrilla groups fighting the government, remained unacceptable. Some liberationists, with their strong emphasis on action, would continue to point to the kind of institutionalised violence given expression by the South African government at Sharpeville in 1960 through the police and the military, a scene all too familiar in such countries as Colombia, Chile and Paraguay: or to the less overt use of forms of assassination by death squads, devoted to the maintenance of the status quo, as seen in the assassination of Archbishop Romero in 1980. It is a classic Christian dilemma as put by Dietrich Bonhoeffer in reference to the Germany of the 1940s: is it not our duty, if we see a car in the hands of a drunken driver, not to stand on the pavement praying but to seize the wheel? The Christian conscience, however, has to struggle with the truth that 'they who take the sword will perish by the sword', that violence begets violence, that non-violent protest, as in the cases of Gandhi and Martin Luther King, in certain contexts is the better and (with Camara) the more tactically effective method of procedure.[70] It ill behoves Christians, however, outside situations of oppression and violent action by the state to judge those within them: the difference in the equation for such is the experience at first

---

[70] Cf. J. Ellul, *Violence: Reflections from a Christian Perspective* (London, 1970), pp. 135–45; *Dictionary of the Ecumenical Movement*, pp. 1055–8.

hand, in identity with the poor and dispossessed, of what oppression can do to human dignity, the sense of outrage at the denial of rights and justice to those with no voice, the weak and the vulnerable in these societies.

On the base communities, something of the strength and weakness of the new ecclesiology comes to light in *Evangelii Nuntiandi*. That they are very widespread is plain from the article on them by Clodovis Boff[71] where they are identified in Africa (Zaire, Tanzania, Cameroon, Malawi, Uganda, Kenya, Ruanda, Burundi) in Asia (India, Malaysia, China, the Philippines), as also in the west and east of Europe and North America. They bear witness to the observed phenomenon that if modern man is to be grasped by the Christian gospel, it seems that personal experience of strong community (*koinōnia*: common life) is an essential twentieth-century form to communicate it. These groups, with their depth of shared life, their openness to the Scriptures and the Spirit in a common hermeneutical endeavour, their commitment to social action and pastoral care and (at their wisest) their links in sacramental and priestly ministry to the larger whole, enable the often rootless, individualised and cosmically lonely modern to discover in relationships a Christian identity and personhood. So, in the very different tradition of the Anglican CMS, Max Warren, J. V. Taylor and Simon Barrington-Ward gave witness in this same period to the power of the small group, sometimes as 'cells of defiance' and *foci* of alternative lifestyles; sometimes as ashrams, picking up the casualties of the 'hippy' trails of the 1960s in India; sometimes in small groups in western Europe where 'one can belong without first being committed'.[72] Such groups have an essential part to play in the renewal of the church's life whether or not, as the Boffs believe, they will replace the old territorial forms expressed in parish systems, often crippled by shortage of priests, not least in Roman Catholic dioceses of Africa and Latin America, but not only there.

---

[71] C. Boff, in *Dictionary of the Ecumenical Movement*, pp. 173–7 (here the BECs are 'Church Base Communities'): cf in Nicaragua E. Cardenal, *The Gospel of Solentiname*.

[72] *IBMR*, 12, no. 1 (January 1988), pp. 12–13, 14–15.

What, finally, of the challenge to theological and missiological method put by the liberation theologians? Surely, the emphasis on context and action (*praxis*) leading to reflection is a profoundly Christian one, especially in its integral form, so that faith and works become indivisible and radical Christian energy of mind and spirit is expressed in deeds, 'faith working through love' (Gal. 5:6). Such a programme, however, does not involve jettisoning those hard-won skills which Gutierrez, Assman and the Boffs have acquired from the theological tradition bred in the western European universities and used to effect in criticism of that tradition; nor the end of a properly objective approach to reality. But observation and analysis are not enough: much of the European tradition has sickened through over-emphasis upon them. Whether the Johannine Jesus' or Marx's insistence or that of the Jocist cells and the Medellín bishops that action must be associated with understanding is surely theologically and missiologically healthy. In so far as the stress on the 'hermeneutical circle' and identification with the poor as a point of departure makes any critics examine their own context and its hidden effect upon the theological agenda this, too, is to the good, so long as certain contexts are not held to debar their occupants from any voice at all. As with R. H. Tawney at the Jerusalem Conference of 1928, the values of the kingdom and their structural application are also a part of the Christian missionary enterprise, so that the Christianisation of societies should be as much an aim as it was for those who embraced the *Volkskirche* approach to tribal life. At these points, and others, the church at large has much to learn from the liberation theologians and much to lose if there is a retreat into a 'sanctuary Catholicism' or a 'privatised Protestantism', interested only in a vertical religion and an individualised charity. To achieve a creative interaction, there is great need for that universal hermeneutical community which, by mutual attention, enables the proportion of truth, an arena where local theologies interact creatively for the good of the whole body.

CHAPTER 7

Mission as proclamation and church growth
1970–1980

At the time of the integration debate, as early as 1947, faced with the possibility of the demise of the IMC, Max Warren had prophesied that it was not 'right beyond the region of possibility that the fundamentalist churches and mission bodies may some time in the next few years try and [sic] constitute an international organisation of their own'.[1] Norman Goodall, recipient of the memorandum in which this appeared, wrote later that Warren had written 'with some prescience'.[2] Warren continued that he had noted what he called 'a mounting tide of fundamentalism and not only in North America'.[3] At least one informed observer, Ralph Winter, saw the emergence of world evangelicalism and its congresses of the 1960s and 1970s as a direct product of the Ghana Assembly of 1958. The development was the 'child of Ghana' and the subsequent absorption of missionary concerns into the WCC. World gatherings like the Berlin Congress on Evangelism of 1966, the Wheaton Congress on the Christian World Mission also of 1966 and the Lausanne International Congress on World Evangelization of 1974 were seen by Winter and others as a response to this.[4] The evangelical leaders disavowed any attempt to replace the IMC. Nevertheless, in the decade from 1970 to 1980 the Lausanne Congress issued in a continuation committee which mounted further consultations, ending the decade with a

---

[1] M. A. C. Warren in N. G. Goodall, Memorandum, March 1947, p. 3: YDS Archive.
[2] N. G. Goodall, *Second Fiddle* (London, 1979), p. 103.
[3] Warren, Memorandum, p. 8; cf. Goodall, *ibid.*, p. 103.
[4] Wheaton Declaration in *IRM*, 55, no. 215 (October 1966), pp. 458–76; R D. Winter 'Ghana: Preparation for Marriage', *IRM*, 67, no. 267 (July 1978), p. 352.

meeting held in the same year as the WCC's Melbourne meeting of the CWME in 1980. The parallel meeting for evangelicals was held at Pattaya in Thailand and produced pamplets on the Christian witness to Jewish people, Muslims, Hindus and Buddhists.[5]

CONSERVATIVE EVANGELICALS AND THE WCC

In 1966 J. A. Mackay had written an article for *Christianity Today*, the evangelical journal, entitled 'What the Ecumenical Movement Can Learn from the Conservative Evangelicals'.[6] As a WCC leader who had sympathy with the evangelicals, he wanted to emphasise the contribution to the ecumenical movement which the evangelicals could make in the sphere of mission, in their welcome emphasis on conversion and in their stress on the Bible: on the last, had he not been present when the Norwegian evangelicals had argued successfully for the inclusion of 'according to the Scriptures' to the WCC theological basis ('a fellowship of churches which accept our Lord Jesus Christ as God and Saviour')?[7] Certainly, between 1960 and 1980 the WCC was made increasingly aware of a third force with which it had to engage in debate, over and above post-Vatican II Roman Catholicism and the friendly, but often theologically critical, stance of its Orthodox membership.

Two things at least stood out for any body addressing world evangelicalism in this period: first, it stood at a disadvantage over against the Orthodox or Roman Catholics, though in similarity with the WCC, in that it had no single ecclesiology (some would say little ecclesiology at all) from which to engage in debate. Its wiser leaders, such as John Stott, Andrew Kirk and Christopher Sugden, tried to lay emphasis on the doctrine of the church and its importance;[8] but the membership was

---

[5] Lausanne Occasional Papers in *How Shall They Hear? Consultation on World Evangelization. Thailand Reports* (Wheaton, Ill., 1980), nos. 7, 13, 14, 15.

[6] *Christianity Today* (27 May 1966), p. 17.   [7] *Ibid.*, pp. 22–3.

[8] See *Lausanne Covenant* para. 6 in J. D. Douglas (ed.), *Let the Earth Hear His Voice. International Congress on World Evangelization in Lausanne* (Minneapolis, 1975), pp. 1–9 (hereafter *COWE/I*). For Sugden see Bassham, *Mission Theology* (Pasadena, 1979), pp. 233–4.

inevitably as widely disparate as the membership of the WCC, and unlike members of that body was not representing its churches in their capacity as members of world conferences. Secondly, there was no doubting the growing distrust, even hostility, to the WCC in the evangelical world. At the Berlin Congress on Evangelism in 1966 this was so marked that W.J. Hollenweger, then study secretary of the WCC, sought out Billy Graham, whose evangelistic organisation had mounted the meeting, to remonstrate. He was assured that confrontation and polarisation was not the intention of the evangelical leaders.[9] Despite this, an observer like Eugene Smith, executive secretary of the WCC in New York and, like Mackay, basically sympathetic to the evangelicals and their theological and evangelistic concerns, after a visit to the Wheaton Congress of 1966 wrote of an experience of 'distrust of the ecumenical movement within this group [which] has to be experienced to be believed'.[10] Smith himself knew that there were gradations within evangelicalism, from the virulent opposition to all things ecumenical of a Carl McIntire, a leading fundamentalist voice in North America with his International Council of Christian Churches (founded 1948), an alternative structure to the more ecumenical National Council of the Churches of Christ in the USA, to the more sympathetic evangelicals. Smith was also aware of the growing strength of the movement and wrote of it in the *Ecumenical Review*: where the more 'ecumenical' mission bodies had increased their missionary force by some 4.5 per cent from 1952 to 1960, the conservative evangelicals had expanded by 149 per cent. Total numbers of missionaries of the 'mainline' churches in the Division of Foreign Missions of the National Council was 10,324 in 1960, of the conservative evangelical bodies 16,066. He noticed also that the long-established journal *The Christian Century*, ecumenically sympathetic, had been overtaken in circulation by the much more recent evangelical journal *Christianity Today*

---

[9] *Ecumenical Review* (hereafter *ER*), 19, no. 1 (January 1967), pp. 88–9.
[10] E. Smith, 'The Wheaton Congress in the Eyes of an Ecumenical Observer', *IRM*, 55, no. 215 (October 1966), p. 480.

(founded 1955), which now had 38,200 subscribers against 37,500 of *The Christian Century*. One attempt to meet the divergence was joint authorship of certain pamphlets by WCC and evangelical writers, for example a production between Lesslie Newbigin of the WCC and Leslie Lyall of the CIM, which had become the Overseas Missionary Fellowship after China became closed, following the expulsion of missionaries by the Communists after 1948.[11]

Whether or not the Ghana Assembly of 1958 was the turning-point, evangelical distrust of the WCC came to be focussed on the Uppsala meeting of the WCC of 1968. The radicalism of the period, already noted, had caused the WCC leadership also to move in increasingly radical directions. The WSCF meeting at Strasbourg in 1960, was a sign of this, again noted earlier here. Hans (J. C.) Hoekendijk laid strong emphasis on God's work in the world and gave what some have viewed as quite different and new content to the term *Missio Dei* (mission of God) as used by Karl Hartenstein at Willingen in 1952.[12] Hoekendijk used the term to denote the totality of God's activity, thereby by-passing the church and stressing the God-World movement (as distinct from the God-Church-World movement) towards the establishing of the kingdom. Hoekendijk wrote:

the Church-centric conception, which since Jerusalem 1928 appears to have been the single, almost uncontested, dogma in the theory of missions, has clasped us so tight ... that we ourselves hardly realize how far the churchification of our thought has gone. From this crushing embrace we shall never escape, until we learn to ask again ... what it means when we repeat again and again our beloved missionary text. "This gospel of the kingdom must be preached in all the world" and to attempt to find our solution of the problem of the Church in this framework of Kingdom-Gospel-Witness (apostolate)-World.[13]

Hoekendijk's favourite phrases that 'kingdom and world

[11] *ER*, 15, no. 2 (January 1963), pp. 182–91.
[12] Bosch, *Witness to the World* (London, 1980), pp. 179–80.
[13] *EMZ* (January 1952), p. 9; trans. in W. Andersen, *Towards a Theology of Mission* (London, 1955), p. 39.

belong together', that 'church-centric missionary thinking is bound to go astray' because based on an 'illegitimate centre',[14] the search for *shalom* (Hebrew: peace, used in the Old Testament of God-given communal well-being) became part of the ecumenical currency. Hoekendijk's writing and speaking were invigorating and biblically arresting: nevertheless they provided for a de-sacralising of mission and a depreciation of the church as the agent of God's mission, at best regarding it as a 'function of the apostolate'.[15] In the climate of the 1960s this emphasis resulted in such catch-phrases as 'the world sets the agenda', much in use at the Uppsala meeting of 1968,[16] and a predominantly horizontal view of Christian mission which adopted the revolutionary movements of society as the activity of God's spirit and allied itself with social betterment in the name of 'humanisation'.[17] In WCC circles it also led to the depreciation of the local church and local ministers. J. V. Taylor, who played a leading role in the important Section II at Uppsala on 'Renewal and Mission', noticed as regrettably typical of WCC gatherings 'too few women ... too many clergy ... what was more serious, hardly any of them parish priests. This fact, I fear, reflects the disdain ... of the WCC towards the life of the ordinary local congregation and its ministry.'[18]

Donald McGavran had crystallised some of the evangelical concerns in his question to the Uppsala meeting: 'Will Uppsala betray the two billion?', those whom the Vatican II document *Ad Gentes* had also specified as people in the world who had never, or hardly ever, had the gospel preached to them.[19] The question was a sign that the specifically missionary and evangelistic dimension, for which the IMC had stood, was perceived as under threat by evangelical leaders. To read the Uppsala 1968 Section II report 'Renewal and Mission'

[14] J. C. Hoekendijk, *The Church Inside Out* (London, 1967), pp. 38–9; cf. J. Aagaard, *Studia Theologica*, 19 (1965), pp. 248–50.
[15] Hoekendijk, *Church Inside Out*, p. 41; cf. *IRM*, 41, no. 143 (July 1952), pp. 324–36; Andersen, *Towards a Theology of Mission*, pp. 37–8.
[16] N. Goodall (ed.), *The Uppsala Report 1968*, (Geneva, 1968), p. xvii.
[17] Bosch, *Witness to the World*, pp. 35–6.
[18] J. V. Taylor, CMS *Newsletter*, no. 370 (April 1973).
[19] *Church Growth Bulletin*, 4, no. 5 (May 1968), p. 1; *Ad Gentes* ch. 2, para. 10.

alongside the documents issuing from Vatican II, as explored in the last chapter, is to understand why the evangelicals could have come to the view that their own emphases were more likely to be conserved and stated with a positively biblical note on such matters as proclamation and witness by the Roman Catholic church than by the WCC. There appears to have been general unease over the section,[20] despite advocacy by J. V. Taylor and D. T. Niles, the first of whom was particularly anxious to hold together the 'gospel of personal conversion and the gospel of social responsibility':[21] for the evangelicals this unease was voiced by John Stott, the English evangelical leader, and echoed by the African minister Buana Kibongi of the Evangelical Church of the Congo. Stott said that he failed to find in the report any concern for spiritual hunger comparable to that which had been pressed in regard to physical hunger and poverty. The prior concern of the church should be in relation to the millions of people who, being without Christ, were perishing. The World Council, in its basis, confessed Jesus is Lord: 'the Lord sends his Church to preach the Good News and make disciples. I do not see this assembly very eager to obey its Lord's command. The Lord Jesus Christ wept over the city which rejected him. I do not see this Assembly weeping similar tears.' Kibangi said that Stott had 'voiced what he would have said' and criticised the lack of overt biblical testimony in the text of the document (a particularly striking contrast to the Vatican II documents in this respect, certainly): 'we should wear the Scriptures as spectacles and then we should see the Scriptures' Lord'.[22] Reflecting later on the Uppsala assembly, the North American evangelical leader A. F. Glasser wrote that, despite what he saw as Stott's courage in standing out against the WCC consensus, the evangelical voice had not been heard at Uppsala and that the Section II document remained manifestly unsatisfactory despite the efforts of Stott and McGavran.[23]

[20] Goodall, *The Uppsala Report*, pp. xix, 21–38.   [21] *Ibid.*, p. 24.
[22] *Ibid.*, p. 26.
[23] *EMQ*, 5, no. 3 (Spring 1969), pp. 129–50.

3

The decade of 1970 to 1980 continued to demonstrate this evangelical–ecumenical tension. It was a decade in which the WCC adopted the Programme to Combat Racism in 1970, when there was a call for a moratorium on missionaries sounded by the African leader, John Gatu, in 1971 and taken up by the All-African Council of Churches at its Lusaka meeting of 1974; and of the WCC–CWME meeting at Bangkok of 1973. The last, with its heavy emphasis on experiential learning and apparent lack of theological content, roused even an experienced and committed ecumenist like Bishop Stephen Neill to ask whether the WCC had lost its sense of Christian direction.[24] From other theologically minded evangelicals there came weighty theological critique of such tendencies. The German missiologist, Peter Beyerhaus, author of a fine study on nineteenth-century missionary developments[25] produced with others the Frankfurt Declaration of 1970. Beyerhaus saw this statement as standing in historical relationship to the Barmen Declaration of 1934, composed by Karl Barth and others, because it stood against 'the distortions of missiological thinking ... since the integration of the International Missionary Council with the World Council of Churches', especially as represented in Section II of the Uppsala report. Like the Barmen Declaration, it was cast in the form of seven affirmations, the seventh of which affirmed 'the reality of Christ's second coming for an eschatological approach to mission over against an ideology of progress or revolution'. It was not, he wrote, a call to separate from the CWME, but that there should be a return to former biblical tradition as expressed at the Whitby, Ontario, meeting of 1947 and the Willingen meeting of 1952.[26] The split in Germany between conciliar and evangelical missionary agencies had become final after the Bangkok meeting of 1973.

[24] S. C. Neill, *Salvation Tomorrow* (London, 1976), pp. viii–x; *The Churchman*, 89, no. 3 (July–Sept., 1975) p. 234.
[25] P. Beyerhaus, *Die Selbstständigkeit der jungen Kirchen als missionarisches Problem* (Uppsala, 1956).
[26] *New Dictionary of Theology*, P. Beyerhaus, 'Frankfurt Declaration', p. 263; Beyerhaus, *Missions – Which Way?* (Grand Rapids, Mich., 1971); Beyerhaus, 'Mission and Humanization' *IRM* 60, no. 237, pp. 11–24.

Beyerhaus and others followed up with the Berlin Declaration on ecumenism of 1974, in which they essayed 'a radical critique of the recent theological direction of the WCC'.[27] It was no less than the truth when John Stott, in his introductory address to the Lausanne Conference of 1974 on 'The Biblical Basis of Evangelism', said to his fellow evangelicals: 'we all know that during the last few years, especially between Uppsala and Bangkok, ecumenical–evangelical relations hardened into something like a confrontation'.[28]

LAUSANNE 1974

To read the 1,500-page account of the Lausanne Congress of 1974 is to be transferred from a world of polemics into an international gathering of Christian leaders which can stand comparison with any of the great missionary conferences of the century, whether the Edinburgh Conference of 1910, the Jerusalem Conference of 1928 or the Tambaram Conference of 1938. The conference was notable for the maturity of judgement of its participants, not least those from Latin America like René Padilla, Samuel Escobar and Orlando Costas and from Africa (Bishop Festo Kivengere, the Ugandan Anglican) and Asia (B. V. Subamma, leader of a Christian ashram approach from India and Jonathan Chao, dean of the school of theology at Hong Kong), the breadth of its engagement internationally and missiologically and its success in holding together the evangelistic note, mission as proclamation, with the stress on social justice, concern for the poor and socio-political involvement. The conference, entitled 'Let the Earth Hear His Voice', was comparable in size to the assembly for Vatican II, and had 2,473 participants who broke down into 660 from Asia and Australasia; 370 from forty-seven countries in Africa; 219 from twenty-one countries in Latin America and some 1,100 from Europe and North America.[29] Like the Berlin Congress of

---

[27] *New Dictionary of Theology* (Leicester, 1988), p. 90; W. Künneth and P. Beyerhaus, *Reich Gottes oder Weltgemeinschaft?* (Bad Liebenzell, 1975); H. Berkhof, 'Berlin versus Geneva', *ER*, 28, no. 1 (January 1976), pp. 80–6.
[28] *COWE/I*, p. 65.   [29] *COWE/I*, p. 18.

1966, the conference was sponsored by the Billy Graham Evangelistic Association. It was chaired by A. J. Dain, who had served for some years as a lay member of a missionary society before ordination and was then a suffragan bishop in the Anglican diocese of Sydney, Australia.

Recognised interpreters have noticed the steady movement in post-second world war evangelicalism in the direction of affirming the social dimension in the Christian calling. The baleful effect of an extreme reaction against the social gospel of the pre-war period and earlier, especially in North America, which had led to a swing against its own history, as exemplified in figures like William Wilberforce and Lord Shaftesbury in England, had been critically observed. In an important book of 1947 called the *Uneasy Conscience of Modern Fundamentalism*, Carl Henry, a well-known North American evangelical, had written: 'fundamentalism, in reacting against the Social Gospel, seemed also to react against the Christian social imperative ... it does not challenge the injustice of totalitarianism, the soullessness of modern education, the evils of racial hatred ... the inadequate bases of international dealings ... There is no room ... for a gospel that is indifferent to the needs of the total man nor of the global man.'[30] At the Berlin Congress of 1966, two black evangelicals had protested at the lack of a social dimension to the message: the evangelist, W. E. Pannell, had pointed out that to lack this element resulted in a tacit support for the status quo. To declare, as one member of the conference had done, that morality cannot be legislated for is 'worse than spitting in the wind'. He for one, speaking as a Negro, was 'frankly a bit weary of hearing that Lord Shaftesbury and William Wilberforce effected social change in England'. To this the black American Baptist, Louis Johnson, added that 'law did for me and my people in America ... what ... evangelical preaching never did in 100 years'. Carl Henry, who co-edited the report of the Berlin Congress, *One Race, One Gospel, One Task*, renewed his criticism of twenty years earlier:

---

[30] C. Henry, *The Uneasy Conscience of Modern Evangelicalism* (New York, 1947), pp. 30, 33, 42, 45; Bassham, *Mission Theology*, p. 176; Bosch, *Transforming Mission*, p. 404.

'Christian denial of neighbourly love may in fact become an offense to the world that prevents effective hearing of the gospel.'[31]

There had been preparation, therefore, in the 1945–70 period for a recovery of a social emphasis in the evangelicals' message. Stott himself had used the equation after the Uppsala meeting of 'mission = witness plus service'.[32] The tendency towards Gnostic and dualist separation of the spiritual from the bodily, message from deed, conversion as purely vertical experience related to God rather than one which also related the Christian to the neighbour was clear enough to the philosophically minded Francis Shaeffer, leader of the evangelical community, L'Abri, in Switzerland: as a participant at Lausanne, he drew attention to what he called the Platonic element in evangelicalism, so damaging and so deadly: it is 'equally spiritual to give when my brother needs a pair of shoes'.[33] As well as doctrinal orthodoxy, there was need for 'orthodoxy of community', a different way of expressing the *orthopraxis* of the Latin Americans. It was the representatives from this subcontinent that drove home the message of social involvement. René Padilla, then secretary of the International Fellowship of Evangelical Students based in Argentina, while eschewing the emphases in the theology of liberation, which resulted in 'eschatology [being] absorbed by the Utopia and the Christian hope ... confused with the worldly hope proclaimed by Marxism', nevertheless, believed that 'Jesus' work had a social and political dimension ... the kingdom of God'. There was 'no place for an "otherworldliness" ... for statistics on "how many souls die without Christ every minute" if they do not take into account how many of those who die, die victims of hunger'. The church was not an 'otherworldly religious club' but 'a sign of the kingdom of God ... given a mission

[31] C. F. H. Henry and W. S. Mooneyham, *One Race, One Gospel, One Task: World Congress on Evangelism Berlin 1966*, 2 vols. (Minneapolis, 1967), II, pp. 378, 205; Bassham, *Mission Theology*, pp. 225–7.

[32] *Church Growth Bulletin*, 5, no. 2 (November 1968), p. 39; cf. *IRM*, 60, no. 237 (January 1971), p. 14.

[33] *COWE/I*, pp. 378, 371–2, 377.

oriented toward the building of a new humanity ... performed only through sacrifice'. There was need for a cosmic, rather than simply an individual, view of sin and for a comprehensive salvation to wholeness, total humanization and eternal life.[34] Samuel Escobar, another Latin American, compared an evangelicalism which concentrated only on 'souls' to the *conquistadores*' execution of those they conquered, towards their 'spiritual' salvation: evangelicals should cease to be exercised by guilt over their care for the body in hospitals, health centres and student centres. In a response later, he stated that he did not believe that to work out the social implications of the gospel led to neglect of evangelism. The problem with the old style of social gospel had been practice based on poor theology.[35] Among the Europeans, George Hoffmann asked for 'love without strings' and Michael Green emphasised that God had joined evangelism, worship, service and fellowship and they cannot be divided. Evangelicals ran the risk of separating the gospel from the kingdom of God.[36]

Before turning to the Lausanne Covenant, the document which drew together the theological and missiological consensus of the congress, some of the other contributors should be mentioned. Billy Graham, who had assumed a similar role to the other great American evangelist noted in this book, D. L. Moody, as an inspirer and enabler of world mission, in an introductory address, 'Why Lausanne?', struck a firm note against modern relativism: modern permissiveness in the realm of belief had moved the church's stance: 'not Christ "the one way" according to God's revelation but "many ways" according to one's culture and inclination. To this evangelicals must return a resounding "No".' But he showed himself aware, too, of the contextual issue when it came to the missionary or evangelist: 'when I go to preach the gospel I go as an ambassador for the kingdom of God – not America'. He made the point that whereas conferences like that at Edinburgh in 1910 had been comprised of those with specifically missionary interests,

[34] *Ibid.*, pp. 129–33, 116–20.   [35] *Ibid.*, pp. 303–18, 324.
[36] *Ibid.*, pp. 175–6, 708.

WCC conferences were made up of what he called 'church-men', by which was meant ecclesiastical leaders, inevitably drawn to an overview of the church's entire task and therefore not having that same concentration on evangelism and missionary proclamation that Edinburgh (or, by implication, Lausanne) could give. Finally, he challenged the WCC meeting of 1975 (then intended for Jakarta but finally held at Nairobi) to study any biblical declaration on mission or evangelism which might come from Lausanne 'carefully and prayerfully', with a view to 'adopting more evangelical concepts of evangelism and missions'.[37] Whether or not for this reason, the Nairobi meeting of 1975 is likely to have encouraged Graham in this respect.

Peter Beyerhaus warned the conference against what he saw as theological distortions of the modern, especially liberation, theology of mission. Such theologies easily reversed God's order and moved from New Testament to Old Testament: so *shalom*, the gifts of God's kingdom and his liberation, was rediscovered but in isolation from Christ himself, the Lord and bringer of the kingdom: 'it is shocking to discover how to-day some theologians and church leaders even draw parallels between the New Testament salvation and that salvation which is brought ... by present-day ideologies and religions. Jesus, as far as he is still referred to by them, is reduced to the type of liberator ... from Cyrus to Mao Tse-tung ... this is a terrible distortion of the biblical Gospel of the kingdom.' To embrace such views was to exchange one's theological birthright for 'an ideological pottage of lentils'. He had some wise words on the relationship of the individual Christian to the church, which in turn was representative of the kingdom; this gave perspective to the issue of church growth (to be examined later as an understanding of mission which was close to the heart of Donald McGavran and his school). For Beyerhaus, McGavran was in danger of turning the kingdom of God in a triumphalist direction, a kingdom of glory, post-millennial and mistaken. Whether on this front or in forms which he associ-

[37] *Ibid.*, pp. 26–7, 29–30, 34.

ated with the WCC, Beyerhaus rejected earthly utopias as
having any equivalence with the biblical kingdom of God. He
referred the conference to the Berlin Declaration on ecumenism
noticed earlier.[38] Beyerhaus had reasserted a German theological and eschatological critique of American views which went
back to Warneck.

There was an eloquent appeal to the conference in terms of
missionary methods to affirm the role of Christian ashrams in
evangelism, not least among women, by an Indian doctor,
B. V. Subamma. These communities of study, service and
meditation, where they were adopted, showed the church to be
adaptable to sub-cultures. There was a need, she said, for a
freedom of response so that 'each ethnic unit in each land'
could 'follow its own culture'. In India, she believed also that
as with women doctors, there was a need for women to be
ordained as ministers, and she showed herself aware of developments in, for example, the Lutheran churches in Japan,
Germany, the US and Scandinavia in this respect.[39] With this
appeal for cultural awareness in India went a similar appeal
from an elder of a Messianic Assembly in Jerusalem to restore
the Jewishness of Jesus to Jews; an appeal for generous and
honest study of Islam towards informed dialogue by F. S.
Khair-Ullah; a highly polemical piece on evangelism among
Buddhists and Confucianists by a Buddhist convert to Christianity, something of a modern Tertullian, Lit-sen Chang, who
saw these alternatives as 'strongholds of Satan'; and a recognition of the truth in Marxist critiques of religion and the
genuine altruism of its expressions on issues of social justice by
the Japanese pastor, Junji Hatori.[40]

Questions of great importance to evangelicals were
addressed by a section of the conference concerned with the
visible church and its relationship to the kingdom of God. How
were the ubiquitous and multiple evangelical para-church
agencies to be viewed in the understanding of the church? In so
far as the church is the place where the rule of Christ is seen

and to which the converted come, para-church structures have
to see themselves as part of the church. They can never replace
the church or present a full gospel, because the church is part of
the gospel message. On the broader front of the kingdom,
Andrew Kirk quoted John Bright to excellent effect: the early
church never imagined that it could bring in the kingdom. It
was sent rather into the world as a missionary witness to a
kingdom already set up.[41] To Jonathan Chao, neither para-
church structures nor denominations could be justified and
were equally barriers to the real need, visible unity. It was
quite mistaken for a church growth advocate like C. P.
Wagner, associate of Donald McGavran, to hold it permissible
for para-church agencies to by-pass the indigenous church 'if
the latter is not doing a good job'. The church was not
'disposable' in this way. Such agencies and denominations, too,
were assertions of autonomy which were basically schismatic
and so a barrier to the proper function of bodily life for
evangelism and church growth. Bishop Festo Kivengere of
Uganda held equally that 'denominational ghettoes' were a
tragic hindrance to the mission of the church.[42]

The conference addressed violence, which few felt to be
justifiable,[43] the ethics of war in a nuclear age, for which Carl
Henry drew on Reinhold Niebuhr to judge that 'the effort of
pacifism to make the peace of the kingdom of God a present
historical possibility' places a premium on surrender to evil.[44]
It considered questions of clan and group conversion over
against the individual, with informed comment from the
anthropologist A. R. Tippett, and Bishop David Gitari from
Kenya,[45] and the difficult question of syncretism in relation to
cultural context, especially in Africa (Byang Kato, General
Secretary of evangelicals of Africa and Madagascar). It was
held that, unless certain basic elements of the gospel remained,
'syncretism reaches such proportions that a totally new
"gospel" appears'.[46]

[41] *Ibid.*, pp. 1081, 1073.   [42] *Ibid.*, pp. 1103–13, 403.   [43] *Ibid.*, pp. 1091–2.
[44] *Ibid.*, p. 1179.   [45] *Ibid.*, pp. 849–52, 972, 116–26.
[46] *Ibid.*, pp. 1216–23, 1227.

John Stott was mainly responsible for the drafting of the
Lausanne Covenant, to which the large proportion of those
present subscribed and which remained influential in the
stream of tradition to which Lausanne gave rise. The salient
points related; first, to the uniqueness and universality of
Christ: 'we ... reject ... every kind of syncretism and dialogue
which implies that Christ speaks equally through all religions
and ideologies', though general revelation of God in nature
was recognised, a revelation which, however, was not salvific:
to perceive God in nature is not to experience salvation.
Christian presence was recognised as 'indispensable to evangelism' and the kind of dialogue 'whose purpose is to listen
sensitively in order to understand'. But proclamation, as for the
Roman Catholic documents examined in the last chapter, was
still regarded as basic to the task of evangelism: 'evangelism
itself is the proclamation of the historical, biblical Christ as
Saviour and Lord, with a view to persuading people to come to
him personally and so be reconciled to God'.[47] Secondly,
however, the emphasis on social justice was strong. Here, Stott
himself changed his mind from earlier positions.[48] Whether or
not through his drafting, paragraph 5 of the covenant stressed
God's concern for justice, for liberation from every kind of
oppression, for freedom from exploitation for those created in
His image and so having an intrinsic dignity; and a note of
penitence is struck, because evangelicals have 'sometimes
regarded evangelism and social concern as mutually exclusive'.
Social action is not evangelism nor is political liberation salvation, but 'we affirm that evangelism and socio-political
involvement are both part of our Christian duty'.[49] Visible
unity was strongly affirmed as a goal (though the qualifier 'in
truth' was added) and was seen as God's purpose for the
church. Simplicity of lifestyle was embraced. On cultural

---

[47] Lausanne Covenant para. 4; *COWE/I*, p. 4 G H. Anderson and T F. Stransky
(eds.), *Mission Trends*, 5 vols. (New York, 1974–81), vol. II, p. 243; *New Dictionary of
Theology*, pp. 240–1.

[48] Bassham, *Mission Theology*, p. 232; Stott, *Christian Mission in the Modern World*
(London, 1975), p. 23.

[49] *COWE/I*, pp. 4–5.

questions, 'the gospel ... evaluates all cultures according to its own criteria of truth and righteousness and insists on moral absolutes in every culture'.[50]

All in all this was a notable international Christian gathering. Stott and others in the evangelical world had moved in their understanding of the Great Commission, which, on Stott's own account, at Berlin in 1966 had been strictly in terms of evangelism. He wrote in a book of 1975 following Lausanne: 'I now see more clearly that not only the consequence of the commission but the actual commission itself must be understood to include social as well as evangelistic responsibility unless we are to be guilty of distorting the words of Jesus.'[51] How far Stott and the Lausanne Covenant had really carried the evangelical constituency has been doubted: 'to the right of Stott there were two for every one who joined him'.[52] Mar Osthathios, a Syrian Orthodox critic, regarded Stott also as a 'liberal spokesman for the evangelicals' and discerned in his book *Christian Mission in the Modern World* something of the same underlying dichotomy that David Bosch, the Dutch Reformed missiologist, also identified. Salvation as 'interior freedom' was only half the truth for Mar Osthathios, which love of neighbour fills out. Both Bosch and Osthathios discerned a basic division between evangelism and social action, what Bosch calls a 'two mandate approach'. This he held to be inadequate and theologically insupportable, because it lacks the 'holism' of the New Testament, which binds the two together into a single obedience in discipleship. This caused Bosch to favour the response of a so-called radical discipleship group to Lausanne, made by participants: they had written 'there is no biblical dichotomy between the word spoken and the word made visible in the lives of God's people ... we must repudiate as demonic the attempt to drive a wedge between evangelism and social concern'. As Bosch saw it, this fatal dichotomy emerged again at Pattaya in 1980 and beyond in

[50] *Ibid.*, pp. 6–7.   [51] Stott, *Christian Mission*, p. 23.
[52] Hutchinson, *Errand to the World* (Chicago, 1987), p. 196.

the Lausanne tradition, though it had been heavily criticised by the membership at Pattaya.[53]

Regardless of the validity of such criticism, however, Lausanne had shown that progressive evangelicalism recognised the need for 'holism' in the proclamation of the gospel. It had also shown that the evangelicals were aware of the cultural relativities involved in any proclamation. This theme was pursued by the Lausanne committee in a consultation at Willowbank, Bermuda. This produced the Willowbank Report of 1978, the main thrust of which was the recognition that 'no theological statement is culture free' (para. 5 (b)).[54] Stott collaborated with Robert Coote to edit a collection on cultural themes entitled *Down to Earth*. In a series of pamphlets, of which the Willowbank report was one, the Lausanne committee published on such themes as the so-called 'homogeneous unit principle' (which will be examined here when Donald McGavran is treated), and, in a series of booklets from Pattaya representing consultations at that conference, on Christian witness to Jewish people, Muslims, Hindus and Buddhists. One striking comment from the pamphlet on Jewish people must suffice: 'Christian life-style conditioned by western culture seems rather devoid of the intensity which the Jew recognises as the way life should be lived. The Christian life seems too austere with a multiplicity of taboos'.[55] Such comments gave evidence of a willingness for self-criticism in response to genuine dialogue which was a welcome mark of the Lausanne tradition.

'FAITH MISSIONS'

At an earlier stage of this history, the importance in the evangelical missionary world of the so-called 'faith missions'

[53] *IRM*, 66, no. 261 (January 1977), pp. 81–2 (Mar Osthathios); Bosch, *Transforming Mission*, pp. 405–8; Anderson and Stransky (eds.), *Mission Trends*, 5 vols. (New York, 1974–81), vol. II, 'A Response to Lausanne: Theological Implications of Radical Discipleship', pp. 249–52; *IRM*, 63, no. 252 (October 1974), pp. 570–4, 574–6.
[54] *New Dictionary of Theology*, pp. 164–7, 183–4.
[55] Lausanne Occasional Papers no. 7, 'Christian Witness to the Jewish People', in *How Shall They Hear?*, p. 10.

was mentioned. The China Inland Mission of Hudson Taylor remained the example to which many looked. In the post-1945 period evangelical missions of this kind, mainly American based and staffed, grew remarkably. If they were affiliated to a wider body, it was likely to be the IFMA (Interdenominational Foreign Mission Association, founded 1917) or the EFMA (Evangelical Foreign Missions Association, founded 1945) in the US. The main distinguishing marks of these missions were a strongly conservative theology, an interdenominational membership, suspicion of, or opposition to, ecumenism as expressed by the WCC and principles of Christian giving which looked to, if they did not imitate, Hudson Taylor's refusal to appeal publicly for money. In a study which compared the life of these missions between 1938 and 1960 they were shown to have grown remarkably: so the African Inland Mission grew from 148 to 486 missionaries, of whom it was noteworthy that 422 were North American: the Sudan Interior Mission from 211 to 1,285, of whom 1,023 were North Americans: the Evangelical Alliance Mission from 95 to 744 and the Wycliffe Bible Translators (WBT), about whom more will be written shortly, from 25 to 832, of whom 762 were North Americans. Other such missions were the New Tribes Mission (NTM), the Regions Beyond Missionary Union and the Sudan United Mission. By 1960, NTM had one-third of the missionaries and one-quarter of the cash resources of all the unaffiliated mission groups.[56] Since 1945, North America has produced 279 fresh missionary societies which compares with a total number up to then of 228, and in 1976 the total North American missionary force was calculated as 35,458 missionaries. Of this upsurge, W. R. Hogg, historian of the IMC and a sympathetic interpreter of mission history, wrote: 'one reports frankly and with sadness that some among these are parasitic. Some are contentiously divisive ... their approach [being] an "anti-this" "anti-that" spirit ... they pose a problem'; or create what the Danish missiologist, Johannes Aagaard, called

---

56 H. Lindsell in W. Harr (ed.), *Factors of the Christian World Mission* (New York, 1962), pp. 189–230.

'great confusion'.[57] Conservative evangelical bodies now account for 66 per cent of the funds and 88 per cent of the personnel of North American missionary agencies. Unaffiliated missionary societies increased from 7,000 to 17,000 between 1960 and 1980.[58]

Two bodies which have caused much debate, because their work has been concerned with the survival of primitive tribes in Mexico or Latin America or elsewhere, have been the WBT and the NTM. WBT was founded in 1934 by W. Cameron Townsend and L. L. Legters. Townsend had himself been a Bible translator in Guatemala. His vision of reducing the languages of the unreached tribes by the use of the science of phonetics and modern linguistic skills led to the formation of the Summer Institute of Linguistics (SIL) in 1934. Men like Eugene Nida and Kenneth Pike, who gained considerable reputations in this specialist field of study, attended these schools in the 1930s. By 1942 there were 130 students enrolled with a view to missionary translation work. By 1970, 12,000 missionaries had been given linguistic training. Townsend collaborated with the Missionary Aviation Fellowship before forming Wycliffe's own Jungle Aviation and Radio Service (founded 1948) to assist their workers in jungle settings in Peru and Amazonia, which WBT entered in 1946. In the 1950s, WBT became involved in the aftermath of an incident which caught the imagination of the Christian world, when five missionaries of the Missionary Aviation Fellowship, including a pilot called Nate Saint, were martyred by Huaorani (Auca) Indians in Ecuador in 1956. This was a tribe which had suffered at the hands of white people previously[59] and retaliated on the missionaries in the manner of J. C. Patteson's martyrdom in the Pacific in the 1870s. What claimed wide attention was that the widow of one of the martyred men,

---

[57] W. R. Hogg in R. P. Beaver (ed.), *American Missions in Bicentennial Perspective* (Pasadena, 1977), pp. 388–9; J. Aagaard, 'Some Main Trends in Modern Protestant Missiology' *Studia Theologica*, 19 (1965)), p. 250.

[58] W. R. Hutchison, *Errand to the World*, p. 193; R Coote, *IBMR*, 6, no. 3 (1982), pp. 118–23.

[59] D. Stoll, *Fishers of Men or Founders of Empire?* (London, 1982), p. 281.

Elisabeth Elliot, and the sister of the pilot, Rachel Saint, returned to the tribe in 1958 under WBT's auspices. Although frequently referred to as 'Aucas', this was the name (savages) given them by their neighbours, the Quichua, their true title being Huaorani. Under the tuition of Rachel Saint one Huaorani Indian woman, Dayuma, became a key figure in the penetration of the tribe by the missionaries, and in due course a version of the New Testament in their language resulted. Some of the missionaries' killers became elders of the new church. The usual complexity of motive has been discerned by modern commentators, but it remains an outstanding story of missionary heroism.[60]

The picture given us of Cameron Townsend (1896–1982) is of a remarkable Christian leader who harnessed the technological aids of the twentieth century to the needs of Stone Age societies in the form of radio, scientific phonetics, translation by 'dynamic equivalence' and air travel. While he was fundamentalist in his theology, perhaps naive in political relationships and open at times to the charge of disingenuousness in the presentation of WBT as a strictly linguistic and so 'scientific' organisation, he still displayed an authentically Christian character and devotion. An example of this was his letter to his fellow missionaries at the time of the assassination of Martin Luther King, urging integration and shared social life with black Christians, a profoundly Christian exhortation.[61] By underlining the 'non-sectarian' nature of their work, he was able to convince Roman Catholic authorities in state and church that Bible translation, which reduced the tribal languages to written form, could only asssist the aims of bringing civilisation and Christianity to the tribal people, which the authorities sought. In his division of the SIL from the WBT he has been fairly criticised by both friend and foe: the same organisation was made to wear a different face for supporters in North America (WBT), with their missionary interest, from

[60] E. E. Wallis and M. A. Bennett, *Two Thousand Tongues To Go* (New York, 1959), pp. 47–8, 64–5, 94, 108, 127, 181, 183, 216–27; *CDCWM*, pp. 667–8; E Elliott, *Through Gates of Splendour* (London, 1957); D Stoll, *Fishers*, pp. 278–94.
[61] M. and J. Hefley, *Uncle Cam* (London, 1975), pp. 228–9.

governments and church authorities prepared to back the tribal work (SIL). In Townsend's defence, however, it must be added that he was open to all about the intention of translating the Bible, a basically religious purpose, but was anxious to define his workers as translators rather than traditional missionaries.

It was in keeping with the portrait that Wycliffe's planes gave lifts to Roman Catholic monks and nuns in jungle settings, treating them as 'brothers and sisters in the Lord'. This, however, aroused criticism and suspicion in the umbrella organisation, the IFMA. In correspondence with them Townsend wrote, 'we feel very strongly that the way our critics want us to treat the monks and nuns is unscriptural ... we simply can't do it'. WBT subsequently withdrew from IFMA.[62] In 1970, despite the loss of support that this caused, Wycliffe had 2,150 translators in the field and by the 1980s this became 4,300, with an income in 1980 of 26.5 million dollars.[63]

The NTM (founded 1942) has proved possibly more controversial than the WBT. This is not the place to give a thorough examination into the rights and wrongs of the debate which has included accusations of tribal genocide, improper inducements and cultural assault on tribal peoples. One tribe, the Yuqu people, was said to have been reduced, during the New Tribes Mission's presence, from some thousands to 124 persons,[64] but in other areas, as in the case of the WBT with the Huaorani, the population is either stable or increasing.[65] In 1971 a group of anthropologists produced the 'Declaration of Barbados' (printed in the *IRM* of July 1973) which sought for an end to cultural dominance by the state authorities of the Indians of Latin America, granting of rights and land and the same access to social, educational and health facilities as the rest of the population. It contained an extensive indictment of the missions, who were accused of being a part of the colonial process, lacking respect for the Indian culture, acquiring

---

[62] *Ibid.*, pp. 186–92.   [63] Stoll, *Fishers*, p. 5.
[64] J. Pettifer and R. Bradley, *Missionaries* (London, 1990), p. 145.
[65] Stoll, *Fishers*, p. 279; personal interview with B. Challoner, NTM missionary in New Guinea.

Indian land and property and living in a sumptuous and lavish manner 'often [by] exploitation of Indian labour', improper inducements amounting to blackmail and the removal of Indian children to residential schools, so turning them into 'marginal individuals' in their own societies while imposed upon by the missions' 'puritanical' ethics. Some of these charges were repeated at a more popular level by Norman Lewis, who found that the NTM had 2,500 missionaries working in 159 different tribal settings.[66]

In response to this indictment, the WCC convened a meeting in 1973 between anthropologists and missionaries, including some of those who had made the accusations, together with three indigenous Indians from Paraguay and Panama. This group produced an answering statement, 'The Asuncíon Declaration'. It described the church's task in terms of renunciation of all ideologies and exploitation and undertook to work for the liberation of the Indian.[67] Two anthropologists who had been involved in the Barbados declaration softened their attitudes at Asuncíon: they did not wish to 'do away with the missions' of the churches, but only with a certain type of 'missionary activity' 'considered to be colonialist and oppressive'.[68]

DONALD McGAVRAN (1897–1990)

No consideration of the conservative evangelical contribution to world mission could omit Donald McGavran. The son of a missionary who was also a professor of missions, McGavran was an example of the many who, as young men, were drawn into committed discipleship and missionary service in the early years of the century through the YMCA and the Student Volunteer Movement. His commitment to missionary service dated from a SVM meeting at Des Moines in Iowa in December 1919. This resulted in service in India in the 1920s

---

[66] *IRM*, 62, no. 247 (July 1973), pp. 268–74; N Lewis, *The Missionaries* (London, 1988), p. 129.
[67] *IRM*, 62, no. 247 (July 1973), pp. 275–7.   [68] *Ibid*., p. 278.

as a member of the Disciples of Christ mission.[69] Earlier in this record McGavran appeared as an associate with J. W. Pickett in an investigation which resulted in Pickett's *Mass Movements in India*. During the 1930s McGavran's mission, noting his enthusiasm for 'people movements' engendered by Pickett's study, set him in a field where such theories of group conversion could be tested; on his own account,

for the next eighteen years I devoted myself to the evangelization of one caste, the Satnamis. I wish that I could record that I was hugely successful but this is not the case. Perhaps 1000 individuals were won to Christian faith but no castewide movement to Christ resulted. By 1950 conversions from that caste had almost ceased. True, there were fifteen small village churches but the movement had stopped.[70]

One may ask of how many missionaries it could be said that they were responsible for 1,000 people becoming Christians: McGavran's refreshing honesty and apparent disappointment with his work should not disguise that this theorist of church growth, as he was to become, had been a practitioner of considerable experience and achievement.

In 1955 McGavran published his first and very widely studied book *The Bridges of God*. His mission, showing some imagination, had deployed him in research into the growth of churches in various parts of the world, an experience which was to lead to his second book *How Churches Grow*. At the age of sixty-one, McGavran made the brave decision to resign from his missionary society in order to set up an institute of church growth. After various unsuccessful approaches to seminaries in the US, the North-West Christian College, Eugene, Oregon, showed itself ready to back this venture. McGavran opened the institute with one student in January 1961.[71] From this humble beginning and after a move to Fuller Theological Seminary in Pasadena, California, in 1965, McGavran developed the School of World Mission, which by 1983–4 had 400 students and a large faculty of teachers.

[69] *IBMR*, 10, no. 2 (April 1986), pp. 53–8.   [70] *Ibid.*, p. 56.   [71] *Ibid.*

Church growth

Whatever his considerable qualities as Christian missionary
and inspirer of studies in church growth, McGavran had
defects as a writer and thinker. His arguments are frequently
buttressed by statistics of doubtful validity, questionable exegesis of the New Testament evidence and, especially in his later
writings, impatience with alternative views to his own. This
said, he presented missionary thinkers with certain leading
insights which continue to stimulate debate and with a missionary vision which has confronted the Christian church often
uncomfortably with the needs of the unevangelised millions. In
the *Bridges of God*, he built on his experience with J. W. Pickett
in the 1930s and on Pickett's conclusions on mass movements to
draw a sharp contrast between the so-called 'mission station'
approach, as he had known it in India, and 'people movements'. He recognised, as Gutmann and Keysser had done,
that 'a people is not an aggregate of individuals ... a true
people is a social organism'.[72] Without denying the importance
of individual conversion, McGavran had discerned that Westerners who concentrated on outstanding individual conversions like those of 'Paul, Sadhu Sundar Singh, Kagawa and
Sun Yat Sen'[73] were reflecting what in the West is 'an
extremely individualistic process'.[74] Certainly, nothing was
gained in belittling conversion, for 'any people movement to
Christ depends in great measure on the number of truly converted persons in it': but peoples become Christian 'as a wave
of decision for Christ sweeps through the group mind', a
movement which transcends by far the individual decisions
which also comprise it.[75] The danger of the mission station
approach was that it extracted individuals from their social
setting, thereby hindering rather than advancing the spread of
the gospel. It was, as Kenneth Grubb described it in his
foreword, 'a static conception'.[76]

[72] D. A. McGavran, *The Bridges of God* (London, 1955), p. 9.
[73] *Ibid.*, pp. 107–8.
[74] *Ibid.*, p. 8.   [75] *Ibid.*, pp. 11–12.   [76] *Ibid.*, p. v.

The second leading insight associated with McGavran is the so-called 'homogenous unit principle'. One of his research students claimed to discern it in McGavran's earliest work, and in citing this McGavran did not disagree.[77] In the *Bridges of God* McGavran had drawn a distinction between discipling and perfecting of peoples. The first stage, especially in people movements, pre-dated the ethical revolution which would follow once the life of a social organism became reorganised around Christ as its governing authority.[78] It was at the discipling stage that McGavran held, in face of some controversy, that most people became Christians when evangelised by those who shared their cultural, linguistic and social background: 'people like to become Christians without crossing racial, linguistic or class barriers. This principle states an undeniable fact.'[79] It was a view which his colleague C. P. Wagner was to express in his title *Our Kind of People*. Wagner himself pointed out that it was radically to misunderstand McGavran to suppose that he was proposing racist or class-based churches. The analysis was of the initial stage, when the gospel is shared among the like-minded. In the later 'perfecting' stage, McGavran put his faith in the Spirit of Christ, who would cause such culturally similar Christians to move out from association with their own kind towards a universalism where there is 'neither Jew nor Greek ... barbarian, Scythian'.[80] He wrote: 'if class distinctions continue they do so in spite of the Christian faith ... brotherhood is part of the basic theology of the Christian church'.[81] On church growth in general, McGavran laid great emphasis on numerical increase, pointing to the occurrence of numbers in Luke's account of the early church and its development in Acts. This caused him to question any mission strategy which did not show numerical results, not least the 'mission station' approach; and what he viewed as the massive over-funding by mission boards of areas of low response, often to the

---

[77] D. A. McGavran, *Understanding Church Growth* (New York, 1984), p. 163. The third edition of 1990 is used here. McGavran accepted the work of James C. Smith.

[78] McGavran, *The Bridges of God*, pp. 14–15.

[79] McGavran, *Understanding Church Growth*, p. 163.

[80] *Ibid.*, p. 169.   [81] *Ibid.*, pp. 174–5.

detriment of more responsive, but under-resourced, alternatives. For him, the 'numerical approach is essential to understanding church growth'[82] and he poured scorn on the idea of
shepherds who searched for lost sheep but paid no attention to
the numbers recovered. He failed, however, to convince critics
like Lesslie Newbigin that the New Testament put such an
overwhelming stress on numerical increase, and others were
uneasy with his theological basis and his wish for demonstrable
'success'.[83]

On issues of social justice, McGavran appeared ambivalent.
He could affirm Christian involvement in the Civil Rights
campaign associated with Martin Luther King, but only as a
kind of parenthesis, a temporary diversion from evangelism
and church growth:[84] and yet a just society, created by the
multiplication of Christians and church communities,
remained his aim. He was able to acknowledge that in one
specific instance, that of the fishermen of Kerala in India, the
espousal of their case and the redressing of injustice as the
result of Christian initiative had led to church growth. He was
clear that the 'Bible shows a steady preference for the poor',[85]
but he is at his most polemical over mission strategies which
allowed social justice and conditions of poverty to dictate:

the sentimental supposition of some that 'Christian presence',
'working for secularization', 'witnessing to Christ by kind deeds',
'industrial evangelism that seeks to improve labouring conditions',
'discerning God in the revolution and lining up with him' will
through some mysterious process result in as much communication of
the gospel as they should hangs in mid-air without a shred of biblical
or rational evidence to support it ... Churching these billions will
never happen ... as an unplanned by-product of kind Christian
activity.[86]

Despite his own work as director of a leprosarium, he repudiated the growing emphasis on 'holism', an understanding of the

[82] *Ibid.*, p. 67, cf. p. 68.
[83] L. Newbigin, *The Open Secret* (Grand Rapids, Mich., 1978), p. 140; R Gill, *Beyond Decline* (London, 1988), pp. 72–7; D. Bosch, *Witness to the World*, p. 208.
[84] McGavran, *Understanding Church Growth*, pp. 22–3.   [85] *Ibid.*, p. 199.
[86] *Ibid.*, p. 285.

gospel as expressed in both word and deed: 'world evangelization is a chief and irreplaceable work of the church': such
'holistic' emphasis was an attractive but mistaken alternative
to the basic task of proclamation and church growth.[87]

NAIROBI WCC 1975

While McGavran's anxieties at and after the WCC meeting at
Uppsala of 1968 spoke for many conservative evangelicals,
there were solid grounds during the decade 1970–80 for
discerning the kind of convergence that was claimed by
others.[88] Figures like Emilio Castro from the Evangelical
Methodist Church of Uruguay, editor of the *IRM*, director of
CWME from 1973–83 (and general secretary of the WCC from
1985), represented in his stance some of the evangelicals' insistence on mission as proclamation, along with the Latin
American emphasis on social justice, which had also been
present at Lausanne. At the WCC meeting at Nairobi of 1975,
next in line to Uppsala, Bishop Mortimer Arias of the
Evangelical Methodist Church in Bolivia was another important bridge figure. His address to the assembly, 'That the
World May Believe', which saw world evangelisation as the
primary calling and responsibility of the churches, drew
equally on the Lausanne Congress and the Roman Catholic
Synod of Bishops as evidence of the recognition of this calling
by the world Christian community. He reassured many
evangelicals and set a new and different tone from what David
Edwards had called the 'secularising radicals' of Uppsala.[89]
His stress on an integrated presentation of the gospel, truly
incarnated, an approach to the whole person 'individual and
social, physical and spiritual, horizontal and vertical', which
was described as 'holistic and integral', gained wide acceptance. Arias drew equally on Donald McGavran, addressing

---

[87] *Ibid.*, pp. 64–5.
[88] R. Bassham, *Mission Theology*, p. 358; D. Bosch, *Transforming Mission*, p. 408.
[89] *IRM*, 65, no. 257 (January 1976), p. 14, pp. 13–26 (Arias' address): K. Slack, *Uppsala 68 Report* (London, 1968), p. 84; cf. Bassham, *Mission Theology*, p. 99; Bosch, *Witness to the World*, pp. 192–5.

issues of church growth, and on Philip Potter, representing the
mainstream of the WCC, in this address.

In response to it, John Stott welcomed the notes struck, the
reference to Lausanne and its preoccupation with the 2,700
millions still unevangelised in the world. He added, however,
'would it be unfair to say that the bishop's address is not typical
of recent ecumenical utterances? ... Evangelism has become
largely eclipsed by the quest for social and political liberation',
as against the ecumenical movement's earlier missionary
passion. He recalled the assurance at the New Delhi meeting of
the WCC in 1961 that the IMC's work would become central
to the concerns of the WCC as the IMC was wound up. Stott
disagreed with M. M. Thomas, who had claimed a consensus
between Bangkok, Lausanne and Rome on 'comprehensive
salvation', however. Lausanne, Stott said, had drawn a sharp
distinction between salvation and political liberation.[90] He
himself was far from wanting to ask the WCC to drop its social
and political concerns, but he remained conscious of a wide
divergence between 'Geneva and Lausanne', by which 'ecumenical leaders generally questioned whether evangelicals had
a heartfelt commitment [to] social action ... [and] evangelicals questioned whether the WCC had a heartfelt commitment
to worldwide evangelism. They say they have but I beg this
Assembly to supply more evidence that it is so.'[91] By the end of
the assembly, however, Kenneth Slack reported that most
members felt that 'there was more danger from undue stress on
an evangelism of individuals than the other way', despite the
widely expressed anxiety, given expression by Stott, that liberation in the political, social and economic sense was in danger
of replacing 'salvation from sin at the heart of the redeeming
gospel'.[92]

After Nairobi 1975, the evangelicals gave further evidence of
engaged dialogue with those of other views by mounting a
series of consultations with representative Roman Catholic
figures. These meetings took place between 1977 and 1984 and

[90] *IRM*, 65, no. 257 (January 1976), pp. 30–3.   [91] *Ibid.*, p. 33.
[92] K. Slack, *Nairobi Narrative* (London, 1976), p. 86.

were given permanent record in a book jointly written by the
Roman Catholic Basil Meeking and John Stott, *The
Evangelical–Roman Catholic Dialogue on Mission*. Evangelicals like
Peter Beyerhaus, Bishop Donald Cameron of the Anglican
diocese of Sydney, the Africans Kwame Bediako and Gottfried
Osei-Mensah and the Latin American Orlando Costas met
with Monsignor Pietro Rossano, Father Thomas Stransky,
Sister Joan Chatfield and others in Venice (1977), Cambridge
(1982) and France (1984). Stott, Meeking and Joan Chatfield
were present at all the meetings, which faced squarely the
continuing divide on the place of the church, the contrast
between Roman Catholic 'optimism' and evangelical 'pessimism' on the redemption of the human race without explicit
repentance and faith, leading to a different approach to
culture: where Roman Catholics stressed continuity with cultures formed prior to the entry of the gospel, evangelicals
stressed discontinuity. Equally, where Roman Catholics
emphasised that the gospel and the church were inseparably
related, so that the gospel was found within the church, for
evangelicals the reconciliation afforded by the gospel to individuals then resulted in their relationship to the church. Whatever differences were acknowledged, joint undertakings
towards common witness, the relief of need, common social
thought and action and evangelism were strongly affirmed; and
common worship was to follow so long as there were no 'indis-
criminate approaches to sacramental worship', which might
override conviction held on either side.[93] The evangelical representatives acknowledged openly that because of their
emphasis on the value of the individual they had 'traditionally
neglected the doctrine of the church'.[94]

To sum up: in the period after 1970 there was a notable
advance in evangelical thinking over issues such as social
justice, the poor, dialogue as a valid approach to other faiths
and, despite McGavran's hesitations, an affirmation of 'holistic' mission, without loss of stress on proclamation as central to

[93] B. Meeking and J. Stott, *The Evangelical–Roman Catholic Dialogue on Mission* (Exeter, 1986), pp. 31, 35, 44, 45, 73, 83–9.
[94] *Ibid.*, p. 65.

the evangelical understanding of mission. The title of the Manila Conference, following Lausanne, in 1989, 'Proclaim Christ until He Comes', with its sub-title 'Calling the Whole Church to Take the Whole Gospel to the Whole World', expressed both the continuing emphasis on proclamation and this newly comprehensive outlook. This conference, Lausanne II, on its own admission was inspirational in intention.[95] Nevertheless, it contained strong sections on the poor,[96] on dialogue as a valid procedure[97] (E. Stanley Jones was upheld as a model to good effect) and the holistic approach to mission was given firm expression by many contributors, among them Bishop David Gitari of Kenya, Bishop Michael Lazario, Tom Houston, Caesar Molebatsi and others. The basic dichotomy, which David Bosch discerned among evangelicals, between evangelism understood as proclamation and the acts of neighbourly love which gave the gospel embodiment, was still present: but the first was put firmly in the context of the second: 'evangelism is primary because our chief concern is with the gospel ... yet Jesus not only proclaimed the kingdom of God, he also demonstrated its arrival by works of mercy and power. We are called to-day to a similar integration of words and deeds ... we also affirm that Good News and good works are inseparable'.[98] Here there was substantial agreement between strands of the WCC, Roman Catholic thinking, the Orthodox and the evangelicals: where there were differences they were of emphasis, with the evangelicals stressing supremely the gospel message and its centrality: its proclamation in the context of the needy and unevangelised billions, but making increasingly common cause on issues of social justice and the poor, with a willingness to struggle with their understanding of the importance of the church. In terms of wholeness of Christian mission, the decade of 1970–80 had given some notable examples of the Christian community's need of its separate constituents: the Latin Americans had injected an

[95] J. D. Douglas (ed.), *Proclaim Christ until He Comes: International Congress on World Evangelization in Manila* (Minneapolis, 1990), pp. 13–14.
[96] *Ibid.*, pp. 150–61, 295–300.   [97] *Ibid.*, pp. 179–89.   [98] *Ibid.*, p. 30.

essential element into Lausanne in 1974, a refusal to allow suspicion of the old-style social gospel to permit escape from issues of social justice: the influence of Stott and others after Uppsala, which brought a greater acknowledgement of the missionary and evangelistic dimensions to Nairobi in 1975: and the Roman Catholic and Orthodox insistence on the importance of the visible church and the rooting of theology and mission in worship and prayer. Lausanne II gave explicit intent to seek 'to bear witness to the gospel of reconciliation by seeking areas of agreement with the historic Orthodox, Latin and Coptic traditions',[99] one sign of many that the opportunities for wholeness of Christian understanding in the twentieth century had been grasped by this evangelical strand of missionary tradition.

[99] *Ibid.*, p. 374.

CHAPTER 8

Pluralism and enlightenment 1980–1990

The decade of the 1980s proved to be a momentous one in the history of the world. Historians may well judge the year 1989 to be of similar significance to 1789 as one of the great climacterics of the modern period. Earlier in this history Marxist communism was described as a formidable contender to Christianity, sharing similar beliefs that it was universal in scope and had history on its side. After 1917 it had dominated Russia and, through Russian influence after 1945, Eastern Europe. After 1948 it had become the prevailing philosophy in China, leading to the expulsion of expatriate missionaries in 1949. Areas of the East like Korea and Vietnam had Communist governments over part of their territory. Cuba, under an ideologically motivated leader in Fidel Castro, constituted a permanent thorn in the side of the government of the US. In 1989, however, the world looked on in growing astonishment as one after another of the Communist régimes of Eastern Europe were overthrown: Hungary, Poland, Czechoslovakia and the German Democratic Republic, with its symbol of ideological division in the capital, the Berlin Wall, dismantled: followed by Romania and its tyrannical dictator, Ceauşescu, all passed one after another into some form of democratic government. Above all, the USSR, whose president Mikhail Gorbachev had initiated much of the new order, rejected Leninism with its means of enforcement by secret police in the KGB and replaced its Communist rulers.

While the decade saw the phenomenon of world communism fundamentally reshaped, Islam became an increasingly significant force in world developments. In the 1970s Islamic countries had become aware of the economic dependence of the industrial nations on their control of oil. In 1971 the price of oil produced in the Middle East began to rise. In 1973 it rose by nearly 200 per cent in one year. Apart from the economic consequences on the industrial economies of the West, and its effect on the poorer nations of the so-called Third World, Islamic nations had given notice of their political strength. In relation to Israel, they would wish to exert this influence on behalf of Palestinian Arabs. In Iran, the government of the Shah, pro-Western in its approach to industrial technology and social mores, was replaced by religious leadership which, in the person of Ayatollah Khomeini and his form of religious theocracy, was to be described in the West as 'Islamic fundamentalism'.

As far as world-wide Christianity was concerned, the decade opened with the signs of both convergence and divergence. Both the CWME meeting at Melbourne and the evangelical equivalent at Pattaya in Thailand in 1980 claimed to look back to the Edinburgh Conference of 1910. They provoked one attender (Simon Barrington-Ward, the general secretary of CMS) to call them 'mirror images of each other'. Another, the Roman Catholic Paulist, Thomas Stransky, expressed regret that there should be such a manifestation of disunity: Stransky looked instead for 'mission-in-unity' and 'unity in mission'.[1] The presence of Emilio Castro, future general secretary of the WCC, at both meetings was an example of a Christian figure capable of bridging the ecumenical–evangelical divide. A similar uniting signal in print was the joint production by the Roman Catholic Church and the WCC of the document *Common Witness*. This quoted Pope John Paul II and *Redemptor Hominis:* 'in this unity in mission, which is demanded principally by Christ Himself, all Christians must find what already unites them, even before their full communion is achieved':[2] and again, 'the credibility of the gospel message and of Christ

---

[1] *IRM*, 69, no. 273 (January 1980), p. 48 (Stransky); *IRM*, 73, no. 289 (January 1984), p. 51 (Barrington-Ward).
[2] *Common Witness* (Geneva, 1982), p. 10, quoting *Redemptor Hominis*, paras. 11, 12.

Himself is linked to Christian unity ... it is possible for us to collaborate frequently in the cause of the Gospel'.[3] Attempts at bridge-building between Roman Catholics and evangelicals have already been noted in the conversations which took place between 1977 and 1984 under the leadership of Basil Meeking and John Stott. Two further very significant documents, which carried the same possibilities of convergence, were the WCC production *Mission and Evangelism – an Ecumenical Affirmation* (1981), which reassured evangelicals that these realities were as important as Mortimer Arias had indicated at Nairobi in 1975, and in which the hand of the reconciling figure of Emilio Castro had an important influence:[4] and, most significant of all for the future because of its ecclesiological importance, the Lima document *Baptism, Eucharist and Ministry*.[5] At the Vancouver meeting of the WCC in 1983 and at the San Antonio meeting of the CWME in 1989, held at the same time as the Lausanne movement's 'Lausanne II' at Manila, evangelicals expressed regret for stereotypes of the WCC which had been challenged at Vancouver;[6] and, at San Antonio, urged that in future parallel conferences on the same site be arranged.[7]

In a world of pluralist belief, the WCC continued to explore dialogue with other faiths, now an accepted procedure, whatever differences of emphasis might exist, in the Vatican II documents and those of the Lausanne tradition also, however much priority these might give to proclamation as a form of mission. Stanley Samartha (*b.* 1920), first director of the WCC sub-unit on Dialogue with People of Living Faiths and Ideologies, was a guiding influence and enabler of such dialogue: this programme developed from a meeting at Kandy in 1967 and another at Ajaltoun in 1970 but was seen to have received a set-back at the Nairobi meeting of the WCC of 1975, difficul-

[3] *Common Witness*, pp. 51–2.
[4] *IRM*, 73, no. 289 (January 1984), p. 119; full text at pp. 427–47.
[5] *Ibid.*, 72, no. 286 (April 1983), pp. 157–98; WCC, *Faith and Order*, paper no. 111 (Geneva, 1982).
[6] *IRM*, 72, no. 288 (October 1983), p. 599.
[7] *Ibid.*, 78, no. 311/12 (July–October 1989), pp. 404, 431–5; *The San Antonio Report* (Geneva, 1990), appx. 8, pp. 190–4.

ties that Samartha was held to have overcome at the later meeting at Chiang-Mai in 1977. The WCC formally accepted the *Guidelines on Dialogue*, formulated at Chiang-Mai, in 1979.[8] Samartha himself produced *Courage for Dialogue*, a thoughtful and stimulating examination of some of the issues: then, and since, he has wanted to reopen the use of the term 'syncretism', feared by evangelicals as leading to a betrayal of the gospel, but with a creative Christian past (for example, in the relationship of the gospel to Hellenistic culture) which Samartha believed offered possibilities for the future.[9] Other religions could act as catalysts. For example, Asian Muslims might help English Christians to rediscover the gospel;[10] and, however much they are divided on their 'ultimate hope for humanity' they can cooperate on 'provisional goals' in terms of compassion and service. 'Pluralism,' wrote Samartha, 'does not relativise Truth. It relativises different responses to Truth.'[11] He made the proposal that to overcome the personal–impersonal divide between Christianity and Eastern religions, Hindu and Buddhist, the Eastern approach to truth as 'impersonal' be viewed instead as 'trans-personal' or 'supra-personal'.[12] Samartha was no doubt aware that there has been a strand of Orthodox theological tradition which has used the impersonal in relation to God in the interests of stressing the mystery of the Godhead.

HOCKING AND HOGG

In the period covered by the second part of this book, significant contributions were made on issues of the Christian's relation to other religions by such figures of the earlier period as W. E. Hocking and A. G. Hogg; and, after 1950, by theologians like John Hick, Wilfred Cantwell Smith and, more

---

[8] *ER*, 34, no. 2 (1982), p. 192; *IRM*, 72, no. 285 (January 1983), pp. 83, 122; WCC, *Guidelines on Dialogue with Peoples of Living Faiths and Ideologies* (Geneva, 1979).

[9] S. J. Samartha, *Courage for Dialogue* (Geneva, 1981), pp. 58–9; see *IBMR*, 16, no. 2 (April 1992), pp. 49–53.

[10] *Ibid.*, pp. 76, 155.   [11] *ER*, 42, nos. 3 and 4 (1990), p. 253.

[12] Samartha, *Courage*, pp. 145–6.

recently still, by Paul Knitter, Gavin D'Costa and Alan Race. Up to 1970 the position has been excellently set out by the Swedish scholar and staff member of the WCC at the time, C. F. Hallencreutz, in *New Approaches to Men of Other Faiths*. In 1988, the fiftieth anniversary of the Tambaram Conference, with its powerful reminiscences of Hendrik Kraemer and other participants at the IMC meeting of 1938, demonstrated the continuing debate in the area. Hocking's *Living Religions and a World Faith* continues still to echo with modern resonances. Hocking tried to characterise the world-view as he saw it developing in a world culture of growing unity: 'localness ... seen with the staleness of ancient subjectivities, like a stuffy air ... God is in the world but Buddha, Jesus, Mohammad are in their little private closets and we shall thank them but never return to them.' 'Such,' he wrote 'is the spirit of world citizenship at the moment.'[13] The question posed was whether a world culture also needed a world religion[14] to meet the 'universal craving' for an 'absolute' which 'holds good for all ... in all places at all times'.[15] Other religions were emphatically not on the way to death. Duncan Black Macdonald's forecast in the *Moslem World* of 1932 could be shown to be manifestly mistaken: had there not been an increase of Muslim printing presses from 200 in 1900 to 880 in 1935, a fact which might have convinced him that Islam was not on the way to death?[16] In its early years Christianity was 'vigorously syncretistic',[17] though Hocking admits that it was as much resistant to, as absorptive of, other ancient religions and philosophies.[18] He believed that the way forward was by what he called 'reconception' but not by the kind of accommodation which compromised religious truth: he hoped for a 'new perspective' which, in time, would be seen to 'belong quite naturally to what had always been present ... unnoticed ... by us'.[19]

Hocking held that 'our present Christianity does not include

[13] Hocking, *Living Religions and a World Faith* (London, 1940), p. 231.
[14] *Ibid.*, p. 14.
[15] *Ibid.*, p. 32.   [16] *Ibid.*, pp. 119, 129.   [17] *Ibid.*, p. 184.
[18] *Ibid.*, pp. 184–5, 155.
[19] *Ibid.*, p. 191.

all that other religions have';[20] for instance, in Islam 'one is aware of a dignity, a sweep, a sense of the instant majesty of God which we lack ... the Muslim never forgets that it is God with whom he has to do'.[21] With Hinduism and Buddhism, the emphasis on the 'impersonal element of ultimate truth' is of value, because 'impersonality belongs to the vast inner spaces of God's being'.[22] Despite the West's declared belief in 'a radically impersonal world process', Hocking discerned, by contrast, among Western thinkers, 'faith in the significance of the particular event and of the individual person' as a 'sub-conscious factor in the western intuition of the world'; and this related to the Christian view of history as 'personalised in its invisible structure'.[23] For the Christian believer to say, at the outset, that all is included in Jesus Christ, as an a priori basis for approaching other faiths, was simply 'unacceptable': and, in the face of such an attitude, the 'non-Christian religions' should 'hold their own', at least until they 'find themselves in fact understood, translated and included in the growing power of a religion which, in achieving its own potentiality, achieves theirs also'.[24]

Hocking had been one of Kraemer's critics. So had A. G. Hogg, who reiterated his belief that God was to be found in the experience of Hindu believers, stated at Tambaram in 1938, in his *The Christian Message to the Hindu*. Hogg, who had been so severe on the fulfilment school of J. N. Farquhar and others in their claim of a form of continuity between Hinduism and Christianity, and who had rethought his own path from a liberal Christianity to a biblical and historical form in the face of Hindu views of karma, nevertheless could speak of offering the gospel 'to saintly souls who, although without Christ, are manifestly leading a life that is hid in God – possibly more deeply hid in God than our own'.[25] There was an ever-present danger of presumption. He went on:

[20] *Ibid.*, p. 254.   [21] *Ibid.*, p. 255.   [22] *Ibid.*, p. 258.
[23] *Ibid.*, pp. 268–9.
[24] *Ibid.*, p. 262.
[25] Hogg, *The Christian Message to the Hindu* (London, 1947), p. 29.

I do not see eye to eye with those who have looked for a sympathetic line of missionary approach in the conception that Christianity is the *finding* of that for which Hinduism has been only the *seeking*. Hindu faith has known a finding as well as a seeking ... Hindu saints who have testified that their seeking has become a finding [which] ... has come to them ... as self-authenticating. They *know* that they have met God ... it is no part of our Christian duty to deny the actuality of that meeting.[26]

For Hogg, the text repeated by Kraemer, where the Johannine Jesus declares that 'I am the Way, the Truth and the Life: no one comes to the Father but by me' (John 14:6) did not require Christians to believe that, except through Christ, no one could come to *God*: but, rather, that 'the wonderful simplicity of fellowship, with all barriers down, which was our Lord's own new way of knowing the Father' was what he intended to stress 'when he said that no one but himself could reach the Father'.[27]

Hogg is an interesting bridge figure. He looked back to D. S. Cairns, so influential at the Edinburgh Conference of 1910 and on its views of other religions. He befriended and corresponded with Lesslie Newbigin in the 1930s and it would seem that the two men had much in common in their biblical and philosophical outlook and their Indian experience as fellow missionaries. It is all the more interesting to discover that, at the Tambaram celebrations of 1988, Bishop Newbigin stated that, in the debate between Hogg and Kraemer (essentially about the possibility of the revelation of God and the experience of God among people like the Hindus whom he and Hogg knew so well) the bishop found himself increasingly on Kraemer's side of the debate; though we may note that on individuals, as distinct from the systems which they inhabit, he has written something very like Hogg in a book of 1989: 'anyone who has had intimate friendship with devout Hindus and Muslims would find it impossible to believe that the experience of God of which his friend speaks is simply an illusion or fraud'.

---

[26] *Ibid.*, p. 32; cf. E. J. Sharpe, *The Theology of A. G. Hogg* (Bangalore, 1971), pp. 206-13.
[27] Sharpe, *Hogg*, p. 214.

Nevertheless, Kraemer's supreme emphasis on the uniqueness of God's redemptive action in history in Jesus Christ was pivotal: if this is the fact, as the New Testament claims, such an 'act of matchless grace', Newbigin wrote, cannot become part of a 'syllabus for "comparative study of religions"'.[28]

CANTWELL SMITH AND HICK

In the 1960s and 1970s two theologians of religion, Wilfred Cantwell Smith and John Hick, made important contributions to thinking about the relationship of Christianity to other faiths. Hick admired Cantwell Smith's *The Meaning and End of Religion*, first published in New York in 1963 and to which he contributed a foreword in the second edition. Cantwell Smith, like Hocking, was confronting the questions of 'how to turn a nascent world society into a world community', and how to find meaning in modern life at the individual level.[29] He showed great erudition in this book. Over against the Indian philosopher Radhakrishnan's charge that it was the Jews who had 'invented the myth that only one religion can be true', Cantwell Smith demurred: it was truer to say, 'what the Jews asserted was that only one God is real'.[30] What had specially emerged in the Christianity of the ancient world was the element of choice, a right and a wrong way to worship God. The previous 'unselfconscious co-existence' with numerous patterns of worship had given way to Christian refusal 'to participate in ceremonies of the traditional ritual' to the point of execution and loss of life for the Christians' choice. What Cantwell Smith wanted to stress was that once more, like the Jews, Christians were standing for the true worship of the true God; and that, for example, the New Testament showed no sign of a new 'religion', a Western term of much later coinage. As a profound and sympathetic student of Islam, Cantwell Smith held Muslims responsible, by way of their strong identi-

---

[28] *IRM*, 77, no. 307 (July 1988), p. 328; L. Newbigin, *The Gospel in a Pluralist Society* (Grand Rapids, 1989), p. 174.
[29] W. Cantwell Smith, *The Meaning and End of Religion*, 2nd edn (London, 1978), p. 8.
[30] *Ibid.*, p. 30.

fication of themselves over against other 'religions', for what he
calls 'reification', for a development of the use of the term
which, he believed, would be best dropped altogether.
Buddhism as taught in India was to be thought of as a community or a tradition but not as a Buddhist 'religion';[31] Muslim
students were baffled by the Chinese who, at one and the same
time, claimed to be Buddhist, Taoist and Confucianist. In his
later *Faith as Belief*, Cantwell Smith showed his preference for
the term 'faith', with its aspects of serenity, courage, loyalty
and quiet confidence and joy; the Hindu wished, in his faith, to
be human 'in a cosmic sense'; the Buddhist looked to cosmic
goals and values, the Jew wanted supremely to be human and
Jesus himself was presented by Christians as 'true humanity',
not just for Christians but for all. The need was for the stress to
lie not on 'religions', but on the faith which makes for humanity in whatever tradition it might be found.

John Hick took this a stage further. In a famous contrast
between the universe as viewed by Ptolemy and Copernicus,
where for the second the earth ceased to be the centre of the
universe but moved round the sun, he called on Christians to
see Christian revelation no longer as central in the religious
firmament but to see God as central. God was found in every
religious tradition and one of these was the Christian tradition,
with its salvation in Christ:

in its essence Christianity is the way of life and salvation which has its
origin in the Christ-event. It will continue as a way of salvation ...
the needed Copernican revolution [is when there is] a shift from the
dogma that Christianity is at the centre to the realization that it is
God who is at the centre and that all the religions of mankind,
including our own, revolve around him.[32]

In a later work, which Hick edited, he looked for a change
from 'exclusive insistence on Jesus as the way for all peoples
and all nations'.[33] There should instead be a recognition that
the life of Jesus is 'one point at which the Logos ... has acted':

[31] *Ibid.*, p. 68.
[32] J. Hick, *God and the Universe of Faiths* (London, 1973), pp. 119, 131, 144.
[33] J. Hick (ed.), *The Myth of God Incarnate* (London, 1977), p. 9.

'we must say ... that all salvation within all religions is the work of the Logos'.[34] In the modern age, he did not believe that there would be a single world religion, for humanity is too 'gloriously various' for that: but the religious traditions would increasingly 'interact with one another' and 'affect one another's future development, enabling each to learn, we may hope, from the other's insights'.[35] He used the experience of British Jewry and its acceptance as a body by the British establishment as an example of the kind of co-existence which was required: acceptance 'as Jews, not merely as not-yet-converted non-Christians'.[36]

Here, and in later writings, Hick has argued against the 'absolute' claim made for Jesus, and especially in the form of treating the incarnation as factual. Rather, it is a piece of 'poetic imagery', 'a way of saying' that Jesus is our 'living contact with the transcendent God'. As such, 'there is something absolute about him, which justifies the absolute language which Christianity has developed', but 'we no longer have to draw the negative conclusion that he is man's one and only effective point of contact with God. We can reverence Christ as the one through whom we have found salvation without having to deny other points of reported saving contact between God and man.'[37] Hick makes an unconvincing comparison between Jesus and the Buddha, unconvincing because, whereas Jesus became the object of worship to Christians within less than a generation, the tradition of Buddhism where Buddha achieved that kind of status (Mahayana, as against Theravada, Buddhism) was slow.[38] While Hick did not anticipate a new world religion, he did anticipate relationships between religions similar to those between Christian denominations in an ecumenical age, with interchange of worship and ministry.[39] Such 'interpenetration of positive values', in Hick's view, has already replaced 'the older missionary policy of the conversion of the world'.[40]

---

[34] *Ibid.*, p. 181. [35] Hick, *God Has Many Names* (London, 1980), pp. 7–8.
[36] *Ibid.*, p. 36.
[37] *Ibid.*, p. 56. [38] *Ibid.*, pp. 60–1. [39] *Ibid.*, p. 58. [40] *Ibid.*, p. 76.

Of those already noted here as theologians of mission, Max
Warren debated Hick's position in an article of March 1974.
His biographer, F. W. Dillistone, himself an eminent theologian, regarded it as the best thing Warren ever wrote.[41] In
it Warren quoted a Cambridge theologian of an earlier time,
J. M. Creed, to the effect that whereas Christian theology did
not need to claim that it contained all truth of religious value,
it was committed to the view that 'in Christ it has found the
deepest truth of God'. Not to do so was for the church to lose
itself.[42] Warren argued for an inclusive uniqueness, whereby
Jesus' relationship to God as 'Abba', father, was distinctive to
himself; but, in it, he was representative of humanity in all of
its relating to God. So, any authentic relationship to God will
bear resemblance to, and be included in, that of Jesus.
Warren pointed to a text like Luke 13:29, where 'many will
come from east and west and sit down in the kingdom' as a
sign that the historical Jesus himself, in his teaching, was inclusive in outlook; and he gave full recognition to the authentic
experience of God outside the Christian tradition. It is, however, still 'Christ who saves', known or unknown. In a correspondence with Hick, the latter conceded that if Christ be seen
as the Universal Logos, Warren's position is tenable with
Hick's proposed theological revolution: but, in so far as
Warren had concentrated on the historical Jesus, 'our Lord as
the most comprehensive model [of God] presented to man's
religious awareness', Hick repudiated his position. Warren
continued to insist to the end on Jesus' distinctiveness, but he
recognised a dynamic movement at work in the universe of
faiths. This was towards convergence and inter-penetration.
Civilisations had always had to be 'mongrelised' to survive.
Indeed, the chief danger of Hick's proposal was its tendency
to solidify the debate into past categories of 'comparative
religion' rather than to recognise that in a world of one
history, 'there is a dynamic at work which makes for conver-

[41] F. W. Dillistone, *Into all the World*, p. 202.
[42] J. M. Creed, *The Divinity of Christ* (Cambridge, 1931), p. 113, quoted in *Modern
Churchman*, 18, nos. 1 and 2 (Winter 1974), p. 59.

gence'. Meanwhile, he wrote to Hick, 'my business is to offer Christ'.[43]

Inclusiveness and exclusiveness as understandings continued to exercise theologians in the 1970s and 1980s. David Brown, an Arabic scholar and missionary in background, but writing as an Anglican bishop in an England, confronted by Muslim and other faith communities in 1976, wrote: 'The uniqueness of God's revelation can be affirmed in two contrasting ways ... in an *exclusive* way i.e. this is a unique event which alone has ultimate significance ... or it may be affirmed in an *inclusive* way i.e. this event is of such unique significance that it is of relevance to everything else in the universe.'[44] Brown preferred the second. In the 1980s, books like those of Alan Race and Paul Knitter raised the same questions about pluralism. Race rehearsed exclusivism and inclusivism at length, but finally jettisoned both in favour of commitment to pluralism, a position which owed much to the German theologian, Ernst Troeltsch, one fairly characterised as 'what you say to be true is true for you, but no more can be claimed'. While Race had warned his readers against Troeltsch and his 'wretched historicism', Knitter held with justice that Race 'seems to end up with the "wretched historicism" and relativism that he warns against in his analysis of Troeltsch'. Knitter gave a masterly survey of the literature, ancient and modern, arising from a wide acquaintance with the whole Christian theological tradition, only to end up by deploying maximum theological weight in an attempt himself to relativise the resurrection of Christ.[45] It is indeed at this point that the proponents of pluralism have difficulty with orthodox Christian faith, for to concede the resurrection is to set Jesus apart from such teachers as Muhammad, Buddha, Confucius and Moses. Associated with this (and, in the Christian tradition, arising directly from it) is the

[43] *Modern Churchman*, 18 (March 1974), pp. 65–6; Dillistone, *Into all the World*, pp. 239–42.

[44] D. Brown, *A New Threshold* (London, 1976), p. 18.

[45] P. Knitter, *No Other Name? A Critical Survey of Christian Attitudes towards the World Religions* (London, 1985), pp. 197–200, 255 note 33; A. Race, *Christianity and Religious Pluralism* (London, 1983), pp. 81–2.

ascription of worship to Jesus as (risen) Lord. This, it would
seem, goes back very early to the Aramaic-speaking communities in the Holy Land, who prayed to Jesus 'Marana tha' (Our
Lord come) (I Cor. 16:22) within a few years of Jesus' death.
Hick's attempts to compare this phenomenon with the reverence accorded to the Buddha must be judged unsuccessful.
Gavin D'Costa, a research student of Hick's, adopted an inclusivist position comparable to David Brown's and Max
Warren's, though in D'Costa's case grounded in the Church
Fathers and classical Roman Catholic sources. Christ is definitive but not exclusively so; and the inclusivist will expect to
find him illuminating any tradition, while also acting as the
judge, a position not dissimilar to that of Oliver Quick, already
examined. D'Costa quoted the English theologian and Bishop,
John Robinson, with approval: 'to believe that God is best
defined by Christ is not to believe that God is confined to
Christ'.[46] D'Costa gave Hick's position extended and critical
treatment on the person of Christ and religious pluralism in a
later book.[47]

Before leaving the important field of religious pluralism for
the equally important field of modern secularism, especially as
addressed by Lesslie Newbigin in the 1980s, it is interesting to
note again how these issues became focussed at the Tambaram
anniversary celebrations of 1988. Here Newbigin, who spoke of
both Hogg and Kraemer as his revered and beloved friends,
made plain his commitment to the truth of the incarnation and
atonement of Christ as God's appointed way of salvation,
uniquely revealed in history, a stance shared by the New
Testament and the creeds of the historic churches. Wilfred
Cantwell Smith, however, went so far as to declare that in the
context of the modern world and its need for unity and peace,
any form of exclusivism in relation to other faiths was a form of
'blasphemy'. In its reports of the various presentations, the
IRM printed a very interesting debate on the issues, recorded

[46] G. D'Costa, *Theology and Religious Pluralism* (Oxford, 1986), p. 135; J. A. T. Robinson, *Truth is Two-Eyed* (London, 1979), p. 129.
[47] G. D'Costa, *John Hick's Theology of Religions: a Critical Evaluation* (New York, 1987).

by Jean Stromberg as it progressed, in which Newbigin, Cantwell Smith, S. J. Samartha, C. F. Hallencreutz, Diana Eck,
M. M. Thomas and others participated. For Cantwell Smith,
Kraemer had been 'intellectually wrong' and had failed to
convince even himself. The present need was to take seriously
God's mission in all religious traditions and it was both intellectually and morally wrong to fail to do so: 'more than simply
wrong theologically one may say that it is blasphemous'.[48]
Those who are 'narrow mission people who reject dialogue ...
are being disloyal to Christ; and, I repeat, blaspheming
God'.[49] He expanded on this in the ensuing debate: 'there is
danger of blasphemy in having ultimate loyalty to empirical
Christianity'.[50] For him, as for John Hick, whom he quoted
here, the recognition of God-given faith in other religions was
the 'crossing of the Rubicon' for modern theologians, a necessary commitment to the future. For Bishop Newbigin, if this
meant commitment to pluralism as a view of reality, he did not
believe it: God is one, the human story one story, not a mixture
of different and contradictory stories; and the 'ultimate
meaning of human history is focussed in those acts which have
their centre in the life, ministry and death of Jesus Christ'. He
added that he did not believe that this indicated a closed mind.
He had, however, 'a clue to follow'.[51]

LESSLIE NEWBIGIN

Lesslie Newbigin (*b.* 1909), whose eightieth birthday was celebrated in the *IRM* in 1990[52] under the appropriate heading of
'Apostolic Faith', has recorded his own history in an auto-
biographical essay *Unfinished Agenda* (1985). The book is well
named: in his eighties, Newbigin has embarked on a whole
fresh missionary project in relation to societies living in the
shadow of the European Enlightenment of the eighteenth
century, as will be discussed. After a Presbyterian upbringing

---

[48] *IRM*, 77, no. 307 (July 1988), p. 367.   [49] *Ibid.*   [50] *Ibid.*, p. 415.
[51] *Ibid.*
[52] *Ibid.*, 79, no. 313 (January 1990), pp. 66–101.

in Northumberland, and attendance at a Quaker school, he went as a student to Queens' College, Cambridge in 1928, where he joined the Student Christian Movement. This led him to Christian commitment by the time he returned for his second university year. He has described his experience of a call to ordination when at a SCM camp gathering at Swanwick, Derbyshire, as he prayed in a Swanwick tent: 'I knew that I had been ordered and that it was settled and that I could not escape.'[53] In 1931 he became a staff worker for the SCM based in Glasgow. At this time he embarked on a study of the Epistle to the Romans. In company with such Christians (not, however, listed by him) as Augustine, Luther and Karl Barth, Paul's letter proved theologically and Christianly decisive: 'I began the study a typical liberal. I ended it with a strong conviction about "the finished work of Christ", about the centrality and objectivity of the atonement accomplished on Calvary.'[54]

It is interesting to note the influence in this shift of perspective of the Scottish theologian and New Testament scholar, James Denney, whose commentary on the Greek text of Romans has remained a classic study. Denney has appeared in these pages as present at the Edinburgh Conference of 1910 and again, with James Orr, as one of the conservative theologians from whom the Laymen's Foreign Mission Inquiry found conservative missionaries and seminary teachers in China drawing their strength. Denney, however, was no fundamentalist but a critical New Testament scholar of authority.

Newbigin studied further at Westminster College, Cambridge, preparing there for Presbyterian ordination (1933-6) before spending periods in India (1936-9; 1939-46). Invited to 'The Moot', an informal gathering of Christian intellectuals, by J. H. Oldham, he had been exposed to a wide variety of Christian stimuli by such minds as T. S. Eliot, Middleton Murray, William Paton, John Baillie and others.[55] Later he

---

[53] Newbigin, *Unfinished Agenda* (London, 1985), pp. 15-16; cf. pp. 5, 10-13.
[54] *Ibid.*, p. 30.
[55] *Ibid.*, pp. 30, 48.

was to meet and admire Hendrik Kraemer, whose criticism of
Rudolf Otto's *India's Religion of Grace*, published in English
translation in 1930 (on *bhakti* forms of Hinduism) he felt to be
justified: 'even this profoundly moving and generous form of
religious devotion had its roots and its only support in the
human need for salvation, not in the divine act of redemption
within the real history of which human life is a part'.[56] He was,
he wrote, captivated by Kraemer's 'strong yet flexible and
open spirit'.[57]

Newbigin became a bishop in the CSI and served from
1947–57 before becoming general secretary of the IMC in the
period leading up to integration and the formation of the new
DWME (Division of World Mission and Evangelism) of the
WCC after the New Delhi meeting of 1961. He also edited the
IRM at this time. He then returned to India as Bishop of
Madras for a second episcopal period in the CSI (1965–74).
Since returning to England, he has worked as an ordained
minister in the United Reformed Church, of which he became
moderator in 1978–9. Throughout this busy pastoral life, as
missionary, bishop and local church minister he has retained
an extraordinary commitment to Christian intellectual
endeavour as theologian and writer. Again and again he has
been among the first to address the contemporary need: one
example of this was his book on the church, *The Household of
God*, in which he was among the first of the ecumenical minds
to point to the importance of the Pentecostal churches for the
future and to the witness of this whole strand of Christian
tradition centring on the Holy Spirit which they bore, needed
by the wider Christian body for its wholeness.

Mission to Western culture

From his base in Birmingham, a religiously pluralist and
modern secular city in England, Newbigin has faced the question which has become a central issue to the modern church
and the missionary movement: how is Christianity to be com-

---

[56] *Ibid.*, pp. 57–8.   [57] *Ibid.*, p. 84.

mended to modern secularised society? In the 1980s a steady
stream of his books have addressed this issue, including *The
Other Side of 1984*, written for the British Council of Churches,
Foolishness to the Greeks and *The Gospel in a Pluralist Society*. He
has discerned the roots of modern disbelief as lying in the
philosophical presuppositions of the Enlightenment. Here fact
and value are separated, fact belonging to the public and
ascertainable world, the public domain, and value which is a
private affair beyond empirical testing. Religion and Christian
faith are put in this latter category and so relegated to the
individual's preference. By such a proposal Christianity has no
social or political relevance and the field is abdicated to other
'scientific' view-points. Science, however, properly understood, as has been demonstrated by Michael Polanyi in, for
example, *Personal Knowledge*, is also based on faith commitments and the scientific community is fiduciary in this sense.
So, Newbigin wrote, there is 'no knowing without believing'.[58]
The Enlightenment search for certainty by way of radical
doubt, initiated by Descartes, is a blind alley. In addition, full
human life and healthy human society is based on commitment
and relationships, in sharp contrast to the Enlightenment ideal
of the autonomous human being governed by reason alone.[59]
Human beings, he wrote, cannot live in the rarefied atmosphere of pure rationality of the Enlightenment. He is one of a
number who believe that a more rounded view of human
beings is required in a post-modern world, one which recognises their need for such aspects as awe, aesthetic experience of
beauty and emotional integration, a view which would lead to
different understandings of education and a 'holism' often
better realised in the (in Western eyes) less advanced societies
of Asia and Africa. Here the atomising and rationalistic tendencies of post-eighteenth-century Europe are less predomi-
nant: 'modernity does not provide enough nourishment for the
human spirit'.[60]

[58] Newbigin, *Gospel*, p. 33.
[59] *Ibid.*, pp. 33, 47–8; *The Other Side of 1984* (Geneva, 1983), p. 56.
[60] Newbigin, *Gospel*, p. 213.

As he reviewed modern European society, Newbigin discerned a loss of hope amounting to despair. He found his view was shared by the German theologian, Jürgen Moltmann, for whom European culture is characterised by 'cold despair, loss of vision, resignation and cynicism'; over it hangs the sign 'No Future'. It is a society of 'technological optimism and literary pessimism' (Carver Yu) and is therefore a culture in crisis.[61] In a striking phrase from Polanyi, Newbigin wrote of the 'incandescence ... of the Christian heritage' burning in the 'oxygen of Greek rationalism' and reaching a position where the 'fuel' is now exhausted.[62] Among other effects of the Enlightenment has been the withdrawal of whole areas of life, such as economics, into autonomy, where moral values are no longer brought to bear on decisions.[63] In such a situation, if the church is to recover its nerve and confidence in its message as one of public truth and significance, it has to escape from the private arena, which some of its own leaders have carved out for it as a form of escape from modernity, a path which even a theologian like Schleiermacher encouraged it to take.[64] The society the church confronts is not so much secular as pagan, as the period 1960–80 has demonstrated, when, far from occupying some neutral position as prophesied by such Christian thinkers as Denys Munby, it has been shown to be 'a pagan society in that it worships gods which are not God'.[65] Newbigin is at pains to underline that he does not believe that there can be a return to the 'Christendom' which followed from Constantine's embrace of Christian faith for the Roman Empire. Nevertheless, then and now, as an 'official religion' Christian faith is public truth and has a bearing on public issues. To evade this by some form of privatised religion is 'in effect to deny the kingship of Christ over all life – public and private', a reality to which Jesus himself bore witness before Pilate when he confronted Pilate with the absolute claim of truth. 'Jesus is

---

[61] *Ibid.*, pp. 91, 111–17, quoting Moltmann and Carver Yu; *Other Side of 1984*, pp. 1–11.
[62] Newbigin, quoting Polyani, *Other Side of 1984*, p. 21.   [63] *Ibid.*, pp. 1–4, 11.
[64] Newbigin, *Foolishness to the Greeks*, pp. 44–5.
[65] Newbigin, *Gospel*, p. 220; cf. *Foolishness to the Greeks*, p. 26.

king in the absolute sense that he bears witness to the truth; the ultimate reality against which all kingship is to be measured is present in him'.[66]

On the issue of truth, scientific or religious, Newbigin has wanted to challenge the prevailing Western consensus, what have been called the 'plausibility structures' by which such societies operate. Plainly, in a pluralist world the question of how truth is apprehended is a crucial one and the technical area of what is called epistemology is highly complex. Newbigin has wanted to maintain that all truth, scientific or religious, fact or value, is arrived at by a common route. This begins with a 'fiduciary act' and leads, through commitment and even passion for discovery, to 'personal knowledge', the title of Polanyi's work to which Newbigin pays tribute. So, a scientist like Einstein bears testimony to an approach to truth of this kind, where his findings were arrived at not by the simple exercise of rationality and the logical working of the intellect, but by a combination of personal imagination, intuition, aesthetic awareness and illumination, which partook of a wholeness of apprehension – quite other than the knowing of Enlightenment thinkers – and based, Einstein wrote, 'upon something like an intellectual love'.[67] Such personal knowing tallies with the Christian understanding of God in Jesus Christ, where a 'fiduciary act', trust issuing in commitment, leads to true knowledge to be pursued with passion and engaging the whole person. The discovery of God in Christ is as much a public and universal truth as the discovery of the scientist and is similarly apprehended. The Christian, like the scientist, should commit himself to a view of reality and its further disclosure 'with universal intent' (Polanyi's phrase), offering testimony to truth rather than 'merely subjective opinion'.[68] If the prevailing plausibility structures stumble at the resurrection of Christ, so central to Christian apprehension of reality, this demonstrates the need for new plausibility structures, which allow for the central reality of the living God. A conver-

---

[66] Newbigin, *Foolishness to the Greeks*, p. 100.   [67] Newbigin, *Gospel*, p. 31.
[68] *Ibid.*, pp. 47–8.

sion of the mind of this magnitude is required in the European consciousness and its preconceptions.[69]

Newbigin advocates neither a return to the old-style Constantinianism of Europe's past nor the kind of theocracy of some modern Islamic states. Rather, he would seek a middle way between pagan secularism and theocracy, one which recognises the place of God revealed in Jesus Christ in public life, including the sphere, for example, of educational curriculum, where such truth should feature alongside the teaching of scientific reality as instanced in the structure of the DNA molecule.[70] Such a Christian society, to be true to its own Christian vision, must make room for tolerance of those who differ and guarantee them the freedom to do so. It has to avoid the 'sacralising of politics' and the 'total identification of a public goal with the will of God': this procedure, he recognises, can become 'demonic', whether as part of the policies of the 'religious Right' in the US or in Islamic Iran.[71] Here there is the ever-present danger of an idolatry which, under the guise of religion, has created false absolutes.[72] An equally prevalent danger, in a pluralist society, is that of polytheism. Plural views of reality and religions are pushed back into the Godhead to make, not a unity-in-diversity, as in Trinitarian understandings, but many different gods. This is the ultimate destination, in his view, of those who embrace pluralism as a religious commitment.[73]

This call for a 'missionary encounter' with Enlightenment culture[74] has given rise to much interest both in Britain and abroad. It has resulted in an on-going programme known as 'The Gospel and Our Culture', which has attracted to it a number of Christian thinkers, writers and leaders. As this is written it is too early to judge how far this movement will have a continuing life. There is, however, no question that by addressing the philosophical, political and social presuppositions of post-Enlightenment society, Lesslie Newbigin has

[69] Newbigin, *Foolishness to the Greeks*, pp. 63-4.   [70] *Ibid.*, p. 67.
[71] *Ibid.*, pp. 116-17.
[72] Newbigin, *Gospel*, p. 162.   [73] *Ibid.*, p. 161.
[74] Newbigin, *Other Side of 1984*, p. 31.

helped the Western church to understand itself as in a missionary situation, holding a minority view of reality in a world of many religions or none, a position not dissimilar to Augustine's in the Mediterranean world of his time, defending a Christian civilisation surrounded by alternative possibilities and threatened by destructive forces.

CHRISTIAN MISSION

How far has this historical and missiological study of eight decades provided an answer to the all-important question: what is Christian mission? Clearly, there is an inner dynamic at work in the Christian religion which causes its adherents to wish to cross frontiers and, in St Paul's terms, 'to preach Christ where he has not been named'. Some compelling motive has been at work, for example, to cause Moravian pioneers to desert the civilised life of eighteenth-century Europe for the hazards of life in Greenland or Tibet; or, in our own period of investigation, to cause Johannes Flierl or Christian Keysser to risk their lives in New Guinea. They would have claimed that it was the same sense of a compelling calling to service that Peter or Andrew experienced when invited to be 'fishers of men', turning from the comparative security of a settled livelihood to the hazards of the financial and personal insecurities of the apostolic band, a dynamic which related ultimately to the divine love and compassion at work in the ministry of Jesus towards human beings in need. For the Moravian missionaries, as for many in the Student Volunteer Movement in the opening years of our century, individual conversions were the aim. Certainly, individual conversion cannot be overlooked. Of the figures in this book, John Mott, converted to Christ by the testimony of J. E. K. Studd at Cornell and to Christ's mission at Northfield, Massachusetts; Kagawa, led to faith in Christ by the two American missionaries in Japan; and C. F. Andrews and Stephen Neill, whose conversions have been described vividly in their writings, are examples in our period that, whatever was at work in Augustine at Thagaste in the fourth century or in John Wesley in Aldersgate Street in the eighteenth, remains a phenomenon which still has far-reaching historical consequences. As the learned ecclesiastical historian, Norman Sykes, wrote in 1960: 'save at the price of making nonsense of his records and thereby conceding the materialist interpretation of the process of history, the ecclesiastical historian may not surrender his conviction of the reality of the influence upon men of the Spirit of God', and 'the record of ecclesiastical history is studded with such religious events as the conversion of Paul, Augustine, Francis of Assisi, Luther, Loyola and Wesley ... whose influence on history is writ in such large letters that he who runs may read and which results in cogent evidence of the importance of the individual'.[75]

Yet, important as the individual may be in Christian understanding, with Jesus laying emphasis in his teaching on the one sheep that is lost and with an individual rite, baptism, as the outward means of joining the church for all, Christian mission is about more than individual conversion, as it is also inclusive of, and larger than, evangelism. From the beginning Christians found themselves shaped into communities, as the apostolic band had been. These communities, even in their earliest Aramaic-speaking days, worshipped Christ as Lord. True, they entered by the individual route of repentance, faith and baptism but this never resulted in *individualism*. From the beginning theirs was essentially a corporate and communal experience. Paul, the early missionary of whom we know most, may have discovered, in Owen Chadwick's words about John Wesley, that the 'unadorned gospel of atonement ... converted on the instant',[76] but much of his effort went into building and maintaining Christian communities. Entered by baptism, these were sustained by what the New Testament calls *koinōnia*, fellowship, a fellowship which centred, apparently, on the corporate act of the eucharist, every repetition of which was understood as a proclamation of 'the death of the Lord until he comes' (I Cor. 11:26). Here was 'the table of the Lord' (I Cor.

---

[75] N. Sykes, *Man as Churchman* (Cambridge, 1960), pp. 28–9.
[76] O. Chadwick, *The Victorian Church*, 2 vols. (London, 1966–70), vol. I, p. 5.

10:21), at which the crucified and risen Christ was understood as present and where his local body was fed and united.

Christians in the twentieth century, as the church became for the first time geographically universal, especially among the so-called 'younger churches', were deeply aware of the intimate connection between the unity of the church and its mission. In the 1920s and 1930s indigenous church leaders were as profoundly convinced of this reality as of their need for greater independence from the 'sending' churches. At the Willingen Conference of 1952 it was the representatives of the younger churches who emphasised that for them such unity was 'imperative'. Ecclesiology, therefore, is not some luxury subject on the missiological agenda. The ecclesial forms in which the gospel is presented will be deeply influential on those who receive the message. The gospel of reconciliation will need to be expressed in reconciled communities, if it is to bring hope to a broken and divided world. For this reason, Christian churches cannot lose sight of the goal of *communio in sacris*, a unity expressed not only by baptism, but in the shared eucharist. This may be maintained in great diversity of cultural, intellectual and liturgical life, of which examples are already to hand in, for example, Orthodox diversity in such varied traditions as those of Greece, Russia and Ethiopia or in the relationship of Uniat bodies to Roman Catholicism, where there is tolerance of considerable divergence and yet mutual communion. To quote the Lima document of 1982 on the place of such eucharistic fellowship in mission: 'insofar as Christians cannot unite in full fellowship around the same table to eat the same loaf and drink from the same cup their missionary witness is weakened at both the individual and corporate levels', for 'the eucharist is precious food for missionaries, bread and wine for pilgrims on their apostolic journey', giving 'everyday form' to the 'proclamation of the gospel, service of the neighbours and faithful presence in the world'.[77] The ideal of one Christian community in each place, indigenous and distinctive but in communion with similar communities throughout the world,

[77] *Baptism, Eucharist and Ministry* (Geneva, 1982), paras. 25, 26.

glimpsed by the Chinese, Japanese and Indian Christians of the earlier years of the century and given partial realisation in the CSI in 1947 cannot be relinquished, however remote its realisation may seem.

Jesus' teaching on the subject of the apostolic community, whereby it was to be salt, light and leaven, points the church always beyond itself to the context in which it is set. Whole societies were to be influenced by these small and apparently insignificant groups of people, the original example being the mighty structure of the Roman Empire of the first three centuries. In their different ways, this understanding of the need to address whole societies was as true of missionaries like Gutmann and Keysser in so-called primitive societies as it was of figures like J. H. Oldham and R. H. Tawney as they confronted the secularisation of the Western world towards the Jerusalem Conference of 1928. The first pair sought the response of a whole people to the Christian message, with an insight into African and Papuan communalism, profoundly at odds with the atomised individualism of the society from which they both came: here was an example of missionary willingness to attend to the context and to learn from other societies. For Oldham and Tawney, the aim of mission was the Christianisation of society. Mission could never stop at the church but often, even usually, through the church must address the great issues of the day, racial discrimination, economic exploitation, industrial relations and political life. The attempt had to be made to extend the influence of Christ's Lordship to create Christian civilisation, one example of which was C. F. Andrews' profound conviction that the plight of Indians experiencing indentured labour in Fiji was a social evil to be challenged by understandings of justice arising from the Christian gospel. This wider social, economic and political thrust to missionary understanding, stressed again so forcefully by Latin American Christians since 1960, looks beyond the church to the kingdom of God: the authority of Christ the King is to penetrate and transform, equally, cannibalistic societies among Papuans and oppressive régimes and governments, those who practise racial discrimination, economic exploitation and injustice. In the pursuit of this aim the church, that realm where Christ is already recognised as supreme, remains the chief agent of his kingdom. In the words of *Evangelii Nuntiandi* in 1975 it is 'the sign and instrument of the reign of God which is to come'.[78]

The temptation here, discerned by Warneck in his criticism of American progressivism, by Hendrik Kraemer in the 1930s, by Walter Freytag in the 1950s and more recently still by Peter Beyerhaus, is utopianism, combined with a human-centred understanding of the kingdom in terms of a reality built by human effort. The kingdom in the New Testament is an eschatological reality, which God himself is to bring in. As Kraemer wrote, it is understood always to be present and latent but it remains at God's disposal. This is, however, no invitation to quietism or lack of intensive effort for justice to be upheld and wrongs set right in human societies. The stress of the German theologians throughout our period on the due recognition of the theological limits to be set on human programmes has been a healthy corrective. Nevertheless, it is also true that a 'fixation on the Parousia' can result in an evasion of present responsibilities and that 'we are to claim this entire world for God as part of God's reign ... [for] submitting to Christ as Saviour is inseparable from submitting to him as Lord not only our personal lives but also political and economic systems in the corporate life of society'.[79] On the basis of the resurrection of Christ, Christian mission looks towards the transformation and reconstitution of the whole created order in God's future, when all that is best in human culture is taken up and perfected (Rev. 21:24–6).

What of the relationship between Christian faith and other faiths, which has featured so prominently and with increasing centrality as the century has progressed? First, there is need for recognition and study, by those to whom the questions appear novel, of minds like those noticed here of the quality of J. N. Farquhar, A. G. Hogg, Hendrik Kraemer, Kenneth Cragg

[78] *Evangelii Nuntiandi* (London, 1975), para. 59.
[79] D. Bosch, *Transforming Mission: Paradigm Shifts in Theology of Mission* (New York, 1991), p. 506.

and others who have reflected deeply on alternative religious traditions and the relationship which Christian faith should adopt. Openness to the truth, wherever it is to be found, is a basic requirement and this will demand sensitive listening and willingness to learn, of the kind practised by E. Stanley Jones in his Round Table conferences in India. Dialogue seems now to be established as a widely approved procedure, whether in Vatican II documents from Roman Catholics, in documents issuing from the Lausanne strand of evangelical tradition or in the programme set up by the WCC. Rigour and integrity in standing for one's own understanding of truth is essential for profound dialogue, and for Christians this will prove especially the case when there is a strong compulsion to jettison those aspects of Christian understanding which embarrass because, in Edwyn Bevan's terms, they are 'intransigent'. Politeness, wrote Stephen Neill in the context of Christian ecumenism, is often the enemy of truth; and clear and unequivocal testimony is fundamental to dialogue.

If there is agreement on dialogue as a method, such can hardly be claimed of the theology of religions. In the period examined, the different approaches of Julius Richter or Heinrich Frick, with their stress on superiority and exclusiveness, through Hendrik Kraemer to the modern writings of Wilfred Cantwell Smith and John Hick there is an indication of wide divergence in the Christian community. So much will hang on the estimate of the person of Christ and so of the gospel. Of the positions reviewed here, that of Oliver Quick, with its double stress on universality and distinctiveness, whereby the light of the gospel both illumines other traditions and, at the same time, draws from them a refraction of light, so that its own truth is better illumined, remains a particularly attractive formulation. If Jesus could teach that 'the children of this world are wiser than the children of light' (Luke 16:8) it must be a presupposition for the Christian that there is truth to be learned from every quarter and that any dialogue may result in discovery. Further, if all truth and goodness are understood to originate in God, affirmations of religious life in terms of 'finding' and not just of 'seeking', in the manner of A. G. Hogg, may be combined with a view of Jesus which makes coherence with his way of life and teaching the criterion of religious truth. Christians who responded warmly to Gandhi, as we have seen, cast this in the form that he had helped them to understand 'our Christ'.

This book began with the issue posed by the relativities of late twentieth-century life, relativities which religious plural- ism has done much to enhance. Absolutes were recognised as having the capacity to oppress and suffocate. In the mid-period of our coverage, Hendrik Kraemer regarded the dissolution of absolutes as the ultimate problem of modern societies: rela- tivism was the mortal, if hidden, wound in the life of 'hosts' of twentieth-century people. The great monotheist religions will continue to regard God as absolute, the one who alone is worthy of supreme loyalty. For Christians, whether before the Roman Emperor (as both Nathan Söderblom and Edwyn Bevan remembered in the 1920s and 1930s) or in the Confess- ing Church in Germany in the Nazi period, it was that supreme allegiance, rooted in Christ as supreme Lord over all temporal and spiritual powers, which enabled resistance to lesser authorities, however overwhelming and threatening their exercise of power. Yet, if the symbol of the Apocalypse is taken seriously, and it is the Lamb, a symbol of vulnerability and sacrifice, which is perceived as on the throne of God, the claim of absolute Lordship for Christ to whom, in St Paul's phrase, 'every knee shall bow' and to whom 'every thought is brought into captivity', can never be made into a threat in an authoritarian and oppressive fashion. Where it has been (as, sadly, all too frequently in Christian history it has), such a stance is precisely to subvert an authority expressed intrinsi- cally in sacrifice and service. To adopt such a position is to stand with Kraemer's example of the missionary who claims superiority, and, in that claim, immediately obscures the message represented. Perhaps the issue for post-Enlightenment human beings is of a deeply valued autonomy, which its possessors are unwilling to surrender to any authority, however gentle the Christ, a new version of the old response 'we will not have this man to reign over us' (Luke 19:14). To this the missionary, the Christian church, the ordinary Christian believer can only reply by quality of life and testimony, to demonstrate that to surrender to an authority expressed in terms of vulnerable love can be the road to discover a service which is perfect freedom.

APPENDIX

Missionary conferences of the twentieth century: a guide

1900   Ecumenical Missionary Conference, New York
1910   World Missionary Conference, Edinburgh
       (Formation of the International Missionary Council, 1921)
1928   International Missionary Council, Jerusalem
1938   International Missionary Council, Tambaram, Madras
1947   International Missionary Council, Whitby, Ontario
       (First Assembly of the World Council of Churches, Amsterdam, 1948)
1952   International Missionary Council, Willingen, Germany
1958   International Missionary Council, Accra, Ghana
       (Integration of IMC and WCC at New Delhi Assembly of WCC, 1961 and formation of the WCC Division of World Mission and Evangelism (later Commission))
1963   Commission on World Mission and Evangelism of WCC, Mexico City
1973   CWME, Bangkok, Thailand 'Salvation Today'
1980   CWME, Melbourne, Australia 'Your Kingdom Come'
1989   CWME, San Antonio, Texas 'Your Will be Done'

LAUSANNE SERIES

1974   Lausanne Congress on World Evangelization
       (Formation of the Lausanne Committee for World Evangelization)
1980   Consultation on World Evangelization, Pattaya, Thailand
1989   LCWE, Manila, Philippines, second International Congress on World Evangelization (Lausanne II)

Select bibliography

Abbott, W. M., ed., *Documents of Vatican II*, London, 1966
Allen, R., *Missionary Methods: St Paul's or Ours?*, London, 1912; new edn, 1960
The Spontaneous Expansion of the Church and the Causes Which Hinder It, London, 1927; new edn, 1960
Jerusalem: a Critical Review of the World Mission of Christianity, London, 1928
Andersen, W., *Towards a Theology of Mission: a Study Encounter between the Missionary Enterprise and the Church and its Theology*, London, 1955
Anderson, G. H., 'The Theology of Missions 1928–58', unpublished Ph.D thesis, Boston University, 1960
Anderson, G. H., and Stransky, T. F., eds., *Mission Trends*, 5 vols., New York, 1974–81
Andrews, C. F., *What I Owe to Christ*, London, 1932
Appleton, G., *On the Eightfold Path: the Christian Presence amid Buddhism*, London, 1961
Assmann, H., *A Practical Theology of Liberation*, London, 1975
Axling, W., *Kagawa*, London, 1932
Baeta, C. G., *Prophetism in Ghana*, London, 1962
Baker, A. G., *Christian Missions and a New World Culture*, Chicago, 1934
Baptism, Eucharist and Ministry (Lima document), Geneva, 1982
Barrett, D. B., *Schism and Renewal in Africa*, Nairobi, 1968
Barrett, D., ed., *World Christian Encyclopaedia*, Nairobi, 1982
Barth, K., 'Die Theologie und die Mission in der Gegenwart', *Zwischen den Zeiten*, 10, no. 3 (1932), pp. 189–215
Theological Existence To-day, Munich, 1933
Bassham, R. C., *Mission Theology 1948–75: Years of Worldwide Creative Tension, Ecumenical, Evangelical and Roman Catholic*, Pasadena, 1979
Bazin, R., *Charles de Foucauld, Hermit and Explorer*, Eng. trans., London, 1923

Beaver, R. P., ed., *American Missions in Bicentennial Perspective*, Pasadena, 1977

Beyerhaus, P., *Die Selbstständigkeit der jungen Kirchen als missionarisches Problem*, Uppsala, 1956

Boff, L., *Ecclesiogenesis: the Base Communities Reinvent the Church*, New York, 1986

Boff, L. and C., *Introducing Liberation Theology*, London, 1987

Bosch, D. J., *Witness to the World: the Christian Mission in Theological Perspective*, London, 1980

    Transforming Mission: Paradigm Shifts in Theology of Mission, New York, 1991

Bria, I., ed., *Go Forth in Peace: Orthodox Perspectives on Mission*, Geneva, 1986

Brown, A. J., *The Foreign Missionary*, New York, 1907

Brown, D., *A New Threshold*, London, 1976

Bullock, A., *Hitler: a Study in Tyranny*, London, 1952

Busch, E., *Karl Barth*, London, 1976

Cantwell Smith, W., *The Meaning and End of Religion*, London, 1978

    Faith and Belief, Princeton, 1979

Chaney, C. L., *The Birth of Missions in America*, Pasadena, 1976

Charley, J. W., *Mission – Some Contemporary Trends*, London, 1973

Common Witness, Geneva, 1982

Cook, G., *The Expectation of the Poor: Latin American Base Ecclesial Communities in Protestant Perspective*, New York, 1985

Cox, J. L., 'The Development of A. G. Hogg's Theology in Relation to non-Christian Faith', unpublished Ph.D. thesis, University of Aberdeen, 1977

Cragg, A. K., *Sandals at the Mosque: Christian Presence amid Islam*, London, 1959

    The Call of the Minaret, 2nd edn, London, 1985

Davey, C. J., *Kagawa of Japan*, London, 1960

D'Costa, G., *Theology and Religious Pluralism*, Oxford, 1986

    John Hick's Theology of Religions: a Critical Evaluation, New York, 1987

    Christian Uniqueness Reconsidered: the Myth of a Pluralistic Theology of Religions, New York, 1990

Dillistone, F. W., *Into all the World: a Biography of Max Warren*, London, 1980

Donovan, V., *Christianity Re-discovered*, Indiana, 1978

Douglas, J. D., ed., *Let the Earth Hear His Voice: International Congress on World Evangelization in Lausanne*, Minneapolis, 1975

    Proclaim Christ until He Comes: International Congress on World Evangelization in Manila, Minneapolis, 1990

Edinburgh World Missionary Conference Report, 9 vols., Edinburgh, 1910
Eilert, H., *Boundlessness: Studies in Karl Reichelt's Missionary Thinking*, Aarhus, 1974
Elliot, E., *Through Gates of Splendour*, London, 1957
Ellul, J., *Violence: Reflections from a Christian Perspective*, London, 1970
Evangelii Nuntiandi, London, 1975
Fairbank, J. K., ed., *The Missionary Enterprise in China and America*, Cambridge, Mass., 1974
Farquhar, J. N., *The Crown of Hinduism*, Oxford, 1913
Fashole-Luke, E., Gray, R., Hastings, A. C., Tasie, G., eds., *Christianity in Independent Africa*, London, 1978
Fiedler, K., *Christentum und afrikanische Kultur: konservative deutsche Missionare in Tanzania 1900–1940*, Gütersloh, 1983
Fleming, D. J., *Contacts with non-Christian Cultures*, New York, 1923
Whither Bound in Missions?, New York, 1925
Attitudes towards Other Faiths, New York, 1928
Ways of Sharing with Other Faiths, New York, 1929
Flierl, J., *Christ in New Guinea*, Tanunda, South Australia, 1932
Fontius, H., *Mission, Gemeinde, Kirche*, Erlangen, 1975
Fremantle, A., *Desert Calling* New York, 1949
Freytag, W., *Reden und Aufsätze*, 2 vols., Munich, 1961
Furey, F. E., 'The Theology of Mission in the Writings of Max Warren', Lic. S.T. thesis, University of Louvain, 1974
Gairdner, W. H. T., *Edinburgh 1910: an Account and Interpretation of the World Missionary Conference*, Edinburgh, 1910
Gensichen, H. W., *Glaube für die Welt*, Gütersloh, 1971
Gill, R., *Beyond Decline*, London, 1988
Godin, H. and Daniel, Y., *France, pays de mission?*, Paris, 1943
Goodall, N., *Second Fiddle*, London, 1979
ed., *Missions under the Cross*, London, 1953
ed., *The Uppsala Report 1968*, Geneva, 1968
Green, M., ed., *The Truth of God Incarnate*, London, 1977
Groves, C. P., *The Planting of Christianity in Africa*, 4 vols., London, 1948–58
Gutierrez, G., *A Theology of Liberation*, London, 1974
Gutmann, B., *Gemeindeaufbau aus dem Evangelium: Grundsatzliches für Mission und Heimatkirche*, Leipzig, 1925
Christusleib und Nachtstenschaft, 1931
Hallencreutz, C. F., *Kraemer towards Tambaram*, Lund, 1966
New Approaches to Men of Other Faiths, Geneva, 1970
Dialogue and Community: Ecumenical Issues in Interreligious Relationships, Geneva, 1977

Hamilton, E., *The Desert My Dwelling: a Study of Charles de Foucauld*, London, 1968

Harr, W., ed., *Factors of the Christian World Mission*, New York, 1962

Hastings, A. C., *A Concise Guide to the Documents of the Second Vatican Council*, 2 vols., London, 1968–9

  A History of African Christianity 1950–1975, London, 1979

  A History of English Christianity 1920–1990, 3rd edn, London, 1991

Hayward, V. E. W., *African Independent Church Movements*, London, 1963

Hefley, M. and J., *Uncle Cam: the Story of William Cameron Townsend, Founder of Wycliffe Bible Translators and the Summer Institute of Linguistics*, London, 1975

Henry, C., *The Uneasy Conscience of Modern Evangelicalism*, New York, 1947

Henry, C., and Mooneyham, W. S., eds., *One Race, One Gospel, One Task: World Congress on Evangelism, Berlin 1966*, 2 vols., Minneapolis, 1967

Hewitt, G. H. G., *The Problems of Success: a History of the Church Missionary Society 1910–1942*, 2 vols., London, 1971, 1977

Hick, J., *God and the Universe of Faiths*, London, 1973

  God Has Many Names, London, 1980

  ed. *The Myth of God Incarnate*, London, 1977

Hocking, W. E., *Living Religions and a World Faith*, London, 1940

  ed. *Rethinking Missions: a Laymen's Inquiry after One Hundred Years*, New York, 1933

Hoekendijk, J. C., *Kirche und Volk in der deutschen Missionswissenschaft*, Munich, 1967

  The Church Inside Out, London, 1967

Hogg, A. G., *Karma and Redemption*, Madras, 1909

  Christ's Message of the Kingdom, Madras, 1911

  The Christian Message to the Hindu, London, 1947

Hogg, W. R., *Ecumenical Foundations*, New York, 1952

Hopkins, C. H., *John Mott: a Biography*, Geneva, 1979

How Shall They Hear? Consultation on World Evangelization, Thailand Reports, Wheaton, Ill., 1980

Hutchison, W. R., *Errand to the World*, Chicago, 1987

Hutchison, W. R., and Christensen, T., *Missionary Ideologies in the Imperial Era* (Aarhus, 1982)

Jackson, E. M., *Red Tape and the Gospel: a Study of the Significance of the Ecumenical Struggle of William Paton (1886–1943)*, Birmingham, 1980

Jaeschke, E., *Bruno Gutmann: His Life, His Thoughts and His Work*, Erlangen, 1985

Jarrett-Kerr, M., *The Secular Promise: the Christian Presence amid Contemporary Humanism*, London, 1964

Jerusalem Meeting of the IMC of 1928: Report and Addresses, 8 vols., London, 1928

Johnson, K., *The Story of the New Tribes Mission*, Sanford, 1985

Jones, E. S., *The Christ of the Indian Road*, New York, 1925
Christ at the Round Table, New York, 1927

Keysser, C., *Anutu im Papuagemeinde*, Nuremberg, 1926
A People Reborn, Eng. edn, Pasadena, 1980

Kirk, J. A., *Liberation Theology: an Evangelical View from the Western World*, London, 1979
Theology Encounters Revolution, Leicester, 1980

Knitter, P. F., *No Other Name? A Critical Survey of Christian Attitudes towards the World Religions*, London, 1985

Kraemer, H., *The Christian Message in a Non-Christian World*, London, 1938

Lamb, C., 'The Call to Retrieval: Kenneth Cragg's Vocation to Islam', unpublished Ph.D. thesis, University of Birmingham, 1987

Latourette, K. S., *A History of the Expansion of Christianity*, 7 vols., New York, 1971

Latourette, K. S., and Hogg, W. R., *Tomorrow is Here*, New York, 1948)
World Community in Action: The Story of World War II and Orphaned Missions (New York, 1949)

Laymen's Foreign Missions Inquiry, Supplementary Series, 7 vols., New York, 1933

Lemopoulos, G., ed., *Your Will Be Done: Orthodoxy in Mission*, Geneva, 1989

Lewis, N., *The Missionaries*, London, 1988

Listowel, J., *The Making of Tanganyika*, London, 1965

Lotz, D., *The Evangelisation of the World in this Generation*, Hamburg, 1970

McGavran, D. A., *The Bridges of God*, London, 1955
How Churches Grow, London, 1959
Understanding Church Growth, New York, 1984; 3rd edn, 1990

Mackay, J. A., *The Other Spanish Christ*, London, 1932

Martin, M.-L., *Prophetic Christianity in the Congo*, Johannesburg, 1968
Kimbangu: an African Prophet and His Church, Oxford, 1975

Matthews, B., *John R. Mott, World Citizen*, London, 1934

Meeking, B. and Stott, J. R. W., *The Evangelical–Roman Catholic Dialogue on Mission*, Exeter, 1986

Metzger, W., *Karl Hartenstein: ein Leben für Kirche und Mission*, Stuttgart, 1954

Miguez Bonino, J., *Revolutionary Theology Comes of Age*, London, 1975
Miller, P., *Errand into the Wilderness*, Cambridge, Mass., 1956
Mission and Evangelism – an Ecumenical Affirmation, Geneva, 1981
Moody, W. R., *D. L. Moody*, New York, 1930
Mott, J. R., *The Evangelisation of the World in this Generation*, New York,
    1900
    The Decisive Hour of Christian Missions, London, 1910
Myklebust, O. G., *The Study of Missions in Theological Education*, 2
    vols., Oslo, 1955–7
Nazir Ali, M., *From Everywhere to Everywhere*, London, 1990
Neill, S. C., *Out of Bondage*, London, 1930
    Creative Tension, London, 1959
    Beliefs, Madras, 1939
    Foundation Beliefs, Madras, 1941
    A History of Christian Missions, London, 1964
    Colonialism and Christian Missions, London, 1966
    Christian Faith and Other Faiths, London, 1968
    The Church and Christian Union, London, 1968
    Bhakti, Hindu and Christian, Mysore, 1974
    Salvation Tomorrow, London, 1976
    Crises of Belief, London, 1984
    A History of Christianity in India, 2 vols., Cambridge, 1984–5
    God's Apprentice, London, 1991
Neill, S. C., Anderson, G. H., and Goodwin, J. F. B., *Concise Diction-
    ary of the Christian World Mission*, London, 1970
Newbigin, J. E. L., *The Open Secret*, Grand Rapids, 1978
    The Other Side of 1984, Geneva, 1983
    Unfinished Agenda, London, 1985
    Foolishness to the Greeks, Geneva, 1986
    The Gospel in a Pluralist Society, Grand Rapids, 1989
New York Ecumenical Missionary Conference 1900, 2 vols., New York, 1900
Niebuhr, H. R., *The Kingdom of God in America*, New York, 1959
O'Connor, D., *Gospel, Raj and Swaraj: the Missionary Years of C. F.
    Andrews 1904–14*, Frankfurt-on-Main, 1990
Oldham, H. W., *Lt.-Col. G. W. Oldham RE: a Memoir*, London, 1926
Orchard, R. K., ed., *The Ghana Assembly of the IMC … 1958*, London,
    1958
    Witness in Six Continents: Records of the CWME … Mexico City 1963,
    London, 1964
Panikkar, R., *The Unknown Christ of Hinduism*, London, 1964
Paton, D., *Christian Missions and the Judgement of God*, London, 1953
    Reform of the Ministry: a Study in the Work of Roland Allen, London,
    1968

Paton, W., *Jerusalem 1928*, London, 1928

Payne, E. A. and Moses, D. G., *Why Integration?*, London, 1957

Peel, J. D. Y., *Aladura: a Religious Movement among the Yoruba*, London, 1968

Pettifer, J., and Bradley, R., *Missionaries*, London, 1990

Pickett, J. W., *Mass Movements in India*, New York, 1933

Polanyi, M., *Personal Knowledge*, London, 1962

Preminger, M. M., *Sands of Tamanrasset*, New York, 1961

Race, A., *Christianity and Religious Pluralism*, London, 1983

Rahner, K., *Theological Investigations*, 23 vols., London, 1963–92

Ranson, C. W., *Renewal and Advance: Christian Witness in a Revolutionary World*, London, 1948

  The Christian Ministry in India, Madras, 1945–6

Religion in Geschichte und Gegenwart, 6 vols., Tübingen, 1957–62

Richardson, A., *History, Sacred and Profane*, London, 1964

Rouse, R., *A History of the World Student Christian Federation*, London, 1948

Ruokanen, M., *The Catholic Doctrine of Non-Christian Religions According to the Second Vatican Council*, Leiden, 1992

Samartha, S. J., *Courage for Dialogue*, Geneva, 1981

San Antonio Report, Geneva, 1990

Schildgren, R., *Toyohiko Kagawa: Apostle of Love and Social Justice*, Berkeley, 1988

Schmidlin, J., *Catholic Mission Theory*, Eng. trans., Techny, 1931

Schneider, P., *Sweeter than Honey: the Christian Presence amid Judaism*, London, 1966

Segundo, J., *The Liberation of Theology*, New York, 1976

Sharpe, E. J., *Not to Destroy but to Fulfil: the Contribution of J. N. Farquhar to Protestant Missionary Thought in India before 1914*, Uppsala, 1965

  The Theology of A. G. Hogg, Bangalore, 1971

Slack, K., *Nairobi Narrative*, London, 1976

Soper, E. D., *The Philosophy of the Christian Mission*, New York, 1943

Speer, R. E., *What Constitutes a Missionary Call?*, New York, 1918

'Re-thinking Missions' Examined, New York, 1933

Stamoolis, J. J., *Eastern Orthodox Mission Theology To-day*, New York, 1986

Stewart, W., *India's Religious Frontier: Christian Presence amid Hinduism*, London, 1964

Stoll, D., *Fishers of Men or Founders of Empire?*, London, 1982

Stott, J. R. W., *Christian Mission in the Modern World*, London, 1975

Stott, J. R. W., and Coote, R., eds., *Down to Earth: Studies in Christianity and Culture*, London, 1980

Sundkler, B. G. M., *Bantu Prophets in South Africa*, London, 1948
  The Christian Ministry in Africa, London, 1960
  Nathan Söderblom: His Life and Work, London, 1968
  Zulu Zion and some Swazi Zionists, London, 1976
Sykes, N., *Man as Churchman*, Cambridge, 1960
Talltorp, A., *Sacrament and Growth: a Study in the Sacramental Dimension of Expansion in the Life of the Local Church as Reflected in the Theology of Roland Allen*, Uppsala, 1989
Tambaram, Madras Papers Series, 7 vols., London, 1939
Tatlow, T., *The Story of the Student Christian Movement of Great Britain and Ireland*, London, 1933
Taylor, J. V., *The Primal Vision: Christian Presence amid African Religion*, London, 1961
Thomas, O. C., ed., *Attitudes to Other Religions*, London, 1969
Tinker, H., *The Ordeal of Love: C. F. Andrews and India*, Oxford, 1979
Turner, H. W., *African Independent Church*, 2 vols., Oxford, 1967
Ustorf, W., *Afrikanische Initiative: das aktive Leiden des propheten Simon Kimbangu*, Frankfurt, 1975
  Mission to Mission? – Rethinking the Agenda, Birmingham, 1991
Ustorf, W., and Weisse, W., eds., *Radiokolleg: Kirchen in Afrika*, Erlangen, 1979
van Leeuwen, A. T., *Christianity in World History: the Meeting of the Faiths of East and West*, London, 1964
Varg, P., *Missionaries, Diplomats and Chinese: the American Protestant Missionary Movement in China 1890–1952*, Princeton, 1958
Verkuyl, J., *Contemporary Missiology: an Introduction*, Grand Rapids, 1978
Vicedom, G., *The Church in New Guinea*, London, 1961
Voillaume, R., *Seeds of the Desert: the Legacy of Charles de Foucauld*, London, 1955
Wagner, C. P., *Our Kind of People*, Atlanta, 1979
Wagner, H., and Reiner, H., eds., *The Lutheran Church in New Guinea: the First 100 Years 1886–1986*, Adelaide, 1986
Wallis, E. E., and Bennett M. A., *Two Thousand Tongues To Go*, New York, 1959
Warneck, G., *An Outline of a History of Protestant Missions from the Reformation to the Present Day*, London, 1906
  Evangelische Missionslehre, 5 vols., Gotha, 1897–1903
Warren, M. A. C., *The Truth of Vision*, London, 1948
  The Christian Mission, London, 1951
  The Missionary Movement from Britain in Modern History, London, 1965
  Social History and Christian Mission, London, 1967

Crowded Canvas, London, 1974
Wilder, R. P., *The Great Commission*, London, 1936
Willingen report of the IMC meeting of 1952 – The Missionary Obligation of the Church, London, 1952
Winter, J. C., *Bruno Gutmann 1876–1966*, Oxford, 1979

Index

Aagaard, J., 210
Absolutes, 5, 109–10, 124, 208, 228, 243, 250
Abyssinia: *see* Ethiopia
Adat, 121
Ad Gentes, 168, 169–73, 174, 190, 197
Adriani, N., 107, 116
Africa, 7, 8, 11, 21, 28–9, 38, 39, 40, 55, 61, 87, 117, 127, 130–2, 133, 136, 139, 149, 166–8, 184, 191, 200, 206, 210, 240
  All-African Conference of Churches, 166, 199
  family in, 41
  increase of Christians in, 130–1
  representatives at Tambaram, 117
  post-colonial leaders in, 133
  view of, at Edinburgh 1910, 28–9
Aggrey, J. E. K., 122
All-African Conference of Churches, 166, 199
Allen, R., 59–63, 65, 67, 70, 74
Alves, R., 185
America, 8–21, 65, 71, 86, 203
American, 8, 11–12, 17–18, 59, 63, 65–6, 79, 86, 89, 92, 94, 109, 111, 116, 121, 135, 164, 184, 205, 210, 244, 248
American Board of Foreign Commissioners, 35, 80
American Presbyterian Board of Foreign Mission, 14
Amsterdam, 118, 128–9, 136, 155–6
Anderson, R., 35, 62, 142
Andrews, C. F., 25, 74–5, 82, 117–18, 122, 134, 139
  against racism, 122
  conversion of, 75, 244
  death of, 134
  example of dialogue, 74–5, 82

  importance in India, 74
  participant at Tambaram, 118, 122
  relationship to Gandhi, 74–5, 148
Anglican, 61, 74, 75, 82, 96, 120, 128, 137, 139, 141, 152, 184, 189, 191, 200, 201, 221, 235
Anglicanism, 137–8, 144
Anglo-Saxon, 7, 18, 20, 33, 35, 58, 107, 111, 115, 140, 153
Animism, 24–5
'Anonymous Christians', 175–7
Anthropologists, 40, 44, 95, 206, 213, 214
Anti-Semitism, 36, 50, 57, 115, 122, 173–4
Anutu, 45, 46
Apartheid, 164
Apostles, 130, 137, 244
Aquinas, St. T., 112
Arabic, 150, 235
Argentina, 177, 202
Arias, Bp. M., 219, 226
Arya Samaj, 73
Ashram, 75–6, 82, 122, 191, 200, 205
Asia, 82, 87, 117, 166, 167, 191, 200, 240
Asians, 6, 133, 136, 176, 227
Assmann, H., 182, 192
Asunción Declaration, 214
Auca, 211–2
Augustine of Hippo, St, 238, 244, 245
Ausschuss, 38
Australia, 48–9, 86, 200–1
Azariah, Bp. V. S., 32, 64, 66, 118, 144

Baillie, J., 22, 33, 135, 238
Baker, A. G., 92, 104, 109
Balfour of Burleigh, Lord 32
Banda, Pres. H., 133
Bangkok, 199, 200, 220

Bantu, 40, 95
Baptism, 46, 51, 61, 171, 176, 246
Baptism, Eucharist and Ministry, 226, 246
Barbados Declaration, 213
Barmen Declaration, 5, 124, 199
Barrington-Ward, Bp. S., 191, 225
Barth, K., 5, 49–53, 90, 99, 105, 107,
    112–13, 114, 115, 118, 123–4, 163,
    199, 238
    attitude to Nazis, 49, 124
    influence on Hartenstein, 105
    influence on Kraemer, 107, 112, 118,
    123–4
    on nature and grace, 50–1
    theology of (at Tambaram), 118
Basel Mission, 37, 105
Bataks, 47, 121
Bea, Cardinal, 167
Bediako, K., 221
Belgian Congo, 131
Belgium, 111, 181
Berlin Congress on Evangelism, 193–4,
    200–1, 208
Berlin Declaration, 200, 205
Bevan, E., 103–4, 148, 249, 250
Beyerhaus, P., 199–200, 204–5, 221, 248
Bhagavadgita, 26, 100
Bhakti, 26, 100, 114, 124, 144, 239
Bible, 54, 59, 83–4, 112, 138, 181, 194,
    211–13, 218
Bible Churchmen's Missionary Society,
    59
Boff, Clodovis, 183–5, 191, 192
Boff, Leonardo, 183–5, 192
Boetzelaer, Baron van, 106, 118
Boetzelaer, Baroness van, 106, 118
Borodin, M., 57
Bosch, D. J., xiii, 208, 222
Boxer Rebellion, 21, 60
Brahmans, 22, 76, 135
Brainerd, D., 10–11
Braun, P., 121
Brazil, 8, 86, 177, 179, 182
Brazilian, 183, 184
Brent, Bp. C. H., 32
Britain, 164, 243
British, 8, 59, 73, 133, 138, 139, 233
Broadcasting, 78
Brown, Bp. D., 235–6
Brunner, E., 50, 54, 90, 105, 113
Buck, P., 72, 90
Buddha, 99, 228, 233, 235–6
Buddhism, 58, 78, 87, 90, 94, 97, 101,
    108, 111, 138, 142, 229, 231, 233

approach of K. L. Reichelt, 83
paper on, 94
renaissance of, 90
Shin-Shu form of, 124
tradition in India, 232
Buddhists, 6, 24, 25, 64, 72, 82, 87, 102,
    104, 113, 120, 158, 162, 173–4, 194,
    205, 209, 227
    and world culture, 227–9
    articles on, 64
    cosmic goals of, 174
    human life in, 113
    impersonal in, 227, 229
    inter-change with (Christian), 72, 82,
    97, 120, 158, 173–4, 228–9
    Nostra Aetate view of, 173–4
Burma, 11, 58–9, 78–9
Butterfield, K., 66

Cairns, D. S., 6, 22, 23–8, 33, 95, 97,
    123–4, 230
Cairo, 25, 27, 65, 116
California, 86, 163
Camara, Abp. H., 183, 190
Cambridge, University of, 139, 143, 144,
    238
Cambridge Mission to Delhi, 25, 74
'Cambridge Seven', 13, 15, 25
Cameron, Bp. D., 221
Canning Town, 56
Canterbury, Abp. of, 32, 34
Cantwell Smith, W., 6, 119, 227, 231,
    236–7, 249
Carey, W., 8, 10–11
Cash, Bp. W., 105, 108, 138
Caste, 76
Castro, Emilio, 219, 225
Ceylon, 25, 58
Chagga, 40–1, 51–2, 56, 132
Chao, J., 200, 206
Chao, T. C., 66, 109, 116, 118,
    136
Chatfield, Sr. J., 221
Chenchiah, P., 66, 100
Cheng, C. Y., 32, 64, 66–8, 80–1
Chiang-Mai, 227
Chile, 177, 182, 190
China, 11, 18, 22, 29, 30, 57, 58–9, 60,
    64, 78, 86–9, 98, 110, 111, 116, 122,
    127, 165, 191, 224, 238
    church leadership of, 80–1
    Communism in, 57–8
    illiteracy in, 80
    Laymen's Inquiry in, 79–86

National Christian Council, 16, 80–1, 83, 85
  practice of foot-binding, 80
  theological tensions in, 79, 82–4
China Inland Mission, 20–21, 59, 83–4, 196, 210
Chinese, 20, 25, 59, 67, 71, 80, 83, 108, 113, 135, 247
Christ, 4, 7, 17, 27, 31, 50, 64, 70, 71, 81, 91, 99, 102, 105, 112, 114–5, 118, 119–20, 121, 123–4, 146–7, 153, 155, 161, 167–8, 170–1, 174, 186, 198, 202–3, 207, 216, 217, 222, 229, 232–3, 235, 236–7, 238, 241–2, 244–5, 249, 250
  conversion to, 34–6, 112–4, 147–8
  encounter with, 145
  Gandhi and, 77, 250
  gentleness of, 250
  group conversion to, 41–9, 106, 206, 215–16
  incarnation of, 154, 170, 236
  inclusive views of, 142, 234, 236
  kingship of, 154, 241–2, 247, 250
  knowledge of, 242
  lordship of, 26, 51, 114, 247–8, 250
  presence of, 141–2
  relation to Hinduism, 98, 149
  relation to Islam, 115, 153–5
  resurrection of, 154, 235, 242, 248
  return of, 9, 199, 248
Christa Seva Sangha, 75
Christianisation, 36, 47, 192, 247
Christianity 28, 87, 99, 103, 107, 114, 121, 130, 224, 228, 229–30, 231
  and civilisation, 69, 244
  communism contends with, 57
  danger of, 237
  empirical view of, 114, 237
  essence of, 232
  Hinduism and, 28, 229
  Islam's meeting with, 152–5
  Japanese respect for, 87
Christianity Today, 94, 195
Church, 41, 60–2, 68, 127–8, 135, 155, 157, 163–4, 169–73, 184–5, 196, 202–3, 221, 241, 246–7, 250
  as form of mission, 121, 127
  base ecclesial communities in, 132, 169, 177, 184–5, 188–9, 191–2
  growth of, 131–2, 215–16
  identity in witness, 109, 172, 186
  kingdom and, 68–70, 120
  local and national (R. Allen), 60–2

Moravian views of, 34–5
  planting of, 35, 170, 173
  relationship to Jews, 169, 173
  social impact of, 241
  tribal forms of, 41–2, 76–7, 131–2, 192
  unity of, 206, 207, 246
  world-wide nature, 157
  see also Ecclesiology
Church growth, 206, 215–19
Church Missionary Society, 19, 29, 35, 38, 59, 135, 138–43, 191, 225
Church of the Cherubim and the Seraphim, 131
Church of South India, 78, 122, 128, 137, 143, 239, 247
Civil Rights Movement, 164, 218
Clark, S., 62
Clement of Alexandria, 95–6, 118
Columbia, 177, 178–9, 183, 187, 190
Commission on World Mission and Evangelism, 165–6, 194, 199, 219, 225–6
Common Witness, 225
Communism, 57, 110, 138, 224
Communists, 58, 79, 124, 130, 135, 165, 196
Confessing Christians, 5, 49, 51, 250
Confucianists, 24, 25, 72, 94, 205, 232
Conservative evangelicals, 83–5, 194–223
Constantine, Emp., 138, 241
Conversion, 34–6, 112–14, 117, 139, 145, 147–8, 160, 162, 171, 186, 194, 216, 233, 242–5
  Gandhi and, 75, 77, 101, 114
  group forms of, 215–6
  of C. F. Andrews, 75, 139, 148
  of S. C. Neill, 147, 244
  Moravian attitudes to, 34–5
  Neill on, 147–8
  Nostra Aetate omits, 174
  stress on, by evangelicals, 55, 194
Coolidge, Pres. C., 66
Coote, R., 209
Costas, O., 200, 221
Cragg, Bp. K., 141–2, 145, 150–5, 158, 162, 248
Creed, J. M., 234
Cuba, 224
Cuban, 164, 178
Culture, 186–7, 205, 207–8, 209, 213, 227, 239, 241, 243, 248
Cyrus, 138, 204
Czechoslovakia, 164, 224

Dagienda, J., 132
Dain, Bp. A. J., 201
Daniel, Y., 136
Datta, S. K., 66
Davidson, Abp. R., 32, 34
Dayuma, 212
D'Costa, G., 228, 236
de las Casas, B., 172
de Nobili, R., 172
de Santa Ana, J., 185
Denney, J., 22, 29, 85, 238
Denominationalism, 38, 206
Descartes, R., 240
Devanandan, P., 176
Dialogue, 108, 141–2, 145–9, 150–5,
    165–6, 169, 171–2, 173, 174, 190,
    207, 209, 221–2, 226–7, 237, 249
    Ad Gentes on, 169
    Christian–Buddhist (K. L. Reichelt),
    82
    Lausanne views on, 207–9, 222
    method of E. Stanley Jones, 222
    Nostra Aetate on, 173–5
    S. C. Neill on, 145
    with Islam (H. Kraemer), 108
Dillistone, F. W., 234
Diment, J., 160
Division of World Mission and
    Evangelism, 157, 239
Donovan, V., 55
Doshisha College, 95
Dresden, 39
Dualism, 182, 202
Dualist, 202
Duff, A., 9, 21–2
Dutch, 59, 65, 66, 106–8, 156, 208
Dutch East Indies, 38, 106
Dyer, Gen. R., 73–4

East Asian Christian Conference, 166
Ecclesiology, 120, 127–30, 137, 168–9,
    194–5, 221, 226, 246
Eck, D., 237
Ecuador, 211
Ecumenical movement, 128–9, 144, 194
Ecumenism, 9, 172, 205, 210, 249
Edinburgh 1910, World Missionary
    Conference, 3, 6, 7, 9, 15, 20,
    31–33, 34, 59, 64–6, 70, 80,, 100,
    106–7, 111, 117, 123, 200, 203, 204,
    225, 230, 238
Eddy, G. S., 14, 25, 29–30, 137, 144
Edwards, D. L., 219
Edwards, J., 10–11

Egypt, 23
Eidem, Abp., 155
Einstein, A., 242
Eisenhower, Pres. D., 164
Elders, tribal, 41–3, 46–8
Eliot, J., 10–11
Eliot, T. S., 238
Ellul, J., 160
El Salvador, 183
England, 139, 201, 235, 239
English, 19, 100, 103, 106, 109, 135,
    137, 157, 198, 227
Enlightenment, 110, 237–44
Epistemology, 180, 242
Eschatology, 4, 9–10, 111, 140
Escobar, S., 200, 203
Ethiopia, 57, 246
Ethiopian, 131
Europe, 8, 86, 96, 110, 117, 124, 163,
    191, 200, 224, 244
European, 42, 47, 66, 115, 143, 163,
    181, 192, 241
Evangelical Alliance Mission, 210
Evangelical Foreign Missions
    Association, 210
Evangelisation, 12, 16, 19, 188–9, 219
Evangelicals, 177, 193–223, 226
    against relativism, 203, 207
    relation to ecumenical movement,
    195, 201
    social emphases, 201–3, 207, 221–3
    syncretism opposed by, 207
    unity of visible church, 207
Evangelii Nuntiandi, 177, 185–191
Evangelism, 78–9, 81, 88–9, 91, 108,
    112, 118, 120–1, 122, 165, 203–5,
    207, 208, 218, 220, 222
    and social concern, 78–9, 203
    as proclamation, 207
    concentration on (Lausanne), 207
    danger of isolation, 208–9
    Kraemer's subject, 108
    para-church agencies and, 205–6
    relation to mission, 245
    Tambaram volume on, 118
Exclusiveness, 29, 96–7, 103, 148, 232,
    235, 236, 249
Exodus, 159, 183, 184

Faith missions, 20–1, 122, 209–14
Farmer, H. H., 118, 123
Farquhar, J. N., 6, 22, 25, 26–7, 31, 97,
    118, 229, 248
Fascism, 110

Fascists, 5, 124
Favelas, 177, 183
Fiji, 74, 247
Finschafen, 44
First World War, 5, 19, 22, 34, 39, 48,
57, 87, 105, 133
Fleming, D. J., 63–5, 67, 97, 102
Flierl, J., 44, 48, 244
Footbinding, 80
Forman Christian College, 63
Forster, E. M., 85
Foucauld, C. de, 136, 158, 160–1
France, 136, 160, 181, 221
Frankfurt Declaration, 199
Fraser, A. G., 23, 25
Fraser, D., 19, 21, 25
Freire, P., 179
French, 59, 106, 160
Frere, Bp. W., 29, 33
Freytag, W., 134–5, 144, 157, 248
Frick, H., 96–7, 249
Frisia, 111
Fulfilment, 26–7, 105, 113
Fuller School of World Mission, 215
Fundamentalism, 5, 89, 116, 156, 201,
225
Fundamentalists, 82–5, 156, 193, 212

Galilee, 103
Gandhi, M. K., 25, 73–5, 76–7, 88, 101,
110, 114, 148, 190, 250
Garbett, C. F., 118
Gagarin, Y., 164
Gatu, J., 199
Gaudium et Spes, 167
Geissen, 97
Geneva, 144, 220
Gentiles, 7, 103
George V, King, 29
German Christians, 49
German Democratic Republic, 224
Germans, 12, 32, 36–7, 59, 65, 66, 109,
121, 133, 248
Germany, 4, 34, 38, 45, 49, 135, 190,
199, 205, 250
Gethsemane, 151, 154
Ghana Assembly 1958 (IMC), 133–4,
149, 157, 165, 193, 196
Gitari, Bp. D., 55, 206, 222
Glasser, A. F., 198
Glover, T. R., 99, 103
Gnostic, 202
Goa, 8
Godin, H., 136

Goodall, N., 155, 193
Gorbachev, M., 224
Gore, Bp. C., 29, 32–3
Gospel, 29, 31, 41, 56, 78, 102, 116, 121,
127–8, 132, 135, 144, 146, 149, 153,
158, 165, 169–70, 186–7, 197–8,
201–2, 206, 217–18, 219, 221–2,
225–6, 227, 229, 249
as proclamation, 78, 170
base communities and, 191
dialogue and, 153, 165–6, 227
Evangelii Nuntiandi on, 186–91
integral nature of, 222
reconciling, 128, 246
social character, 56, 132
syncretism and, 227
Gossner Mission Society, 38
Göttingen, 49
Graham, Billy, 195, 203
Graul, K., 35, 38, 53, 142
Greece, 124, 246
Greek, 143, 145
Green, M., 203
Greenland, 8, 244
Griffith Thomas, W. H., 82–6
Grimshaw, H., 66, 68
Grubb, K., 118, 216
Grubb, W. B., 25
Guatemala, 211
Guevara, Che, 178, 180, 182
Gunning, J. W., 106–7
Gutierrez, G., 180–2, 185, 192
Gutmann, B., 34–44, 48–56, 70, 107,
110, 115–16, 121, 127, 132, 216,
247
against individualism, 42–3
Barth's critique of, 49–53
Kraemer on, 110, 115–16, 121
Lutheranism, 42–3
theory of primal ties, 40–3
view of *Volkskirche*, 40–3
Halle, 19, 23, 52
Hallencreutz, C. F., 228, 237
Hamburg, 144
Harada, T., 95
Harijan, 75
Harris, S., 10
Harris, W. W., 131
Hartenstein, K., 5, 66, 105, 119, 121,
122–3, 134, 196
Harvard, 66
Hastings, A. C., 168, 184, 189
Hastings, J., 83
Hausa, 139

Hayes, Dr W., 84
Heim, K., 65–6, 100, 165
Henry, C., 201, 206
Herberg, W., 148
Herder, J. G., 37
Hick, J., 6, 227, 231–7, 249
Hindu, 5, 24, 25, 26–8, 72, 76, 97–8,
    110, 114, 117, 119, 135, 143–4, 149,
    158, 161–2, 175–6, 227, 230, 232
Hinduism, 25, 26–8, 58, 95, 101, 108,
    111, 114, 138, 142, 173–5, 176, 229,
    239
  finding God in, 95, 173–4, 229–30
  'fulfilment' school, 26–7
  impersonal in, 227
  Jerusalem conference on, 97–8
  karma doctrine, 27–8
  Nostra Aetate on, 173–5
  relativism of, 149
  R. Otto on, 99–100
Hindus, 6, 75, 173, 194, 209, 230
Hirohito, Emp., 86
History, 139–40, 229, 239, 245
Hitler, A., 36, 49, 52, 57, 173
Hocking, W. E., 66, 72–3, 101, 117, 119,
    135, 227–9
Hodgkin, H. T., 29
Hoekendijk, J. C., 53, 54, 56, 106, 163,
    196
Hoffman, G., 203
Hogg, A. G. 22, 25, 27–8, 94, 97, 108,
    118, 119, 135, 227, 229–31, 236,
    248–9
  counters fulfilment, 27–8, 118
  non-christian experience of God, 28,
    119, 229–30
Hogg, W. R., 210
Holland, 4, 53, 107, 156
Hollenweger, W. J., 195
Holocaust, 57
Holism, 92, 208–9, 218–9, 240
Holistic, 219, 221–2
Holy Spirit, 60, 61–2, 92, 150, 217
Hopkins S., 10
Horton, R. F., 31
Horton, W. M., 119–20
Hoste, D. E., 83
House of Lords, 73
Houston, T., 222
Hube, 45
Hudson Taylor, J., 18, 20, 210
Humanae Vitae, 167
Humanisation, 196, 203
Hungary, 164, 224

Huaorani, 211, 213

Illiteracy, 80, 178
Imperialism, 7, 11, 135, 138, 164
India, 8, 9, 21–3, 25–6, 27, 29–30, 40,
    58, 61, 63, 73–9, 82, 85, 87, 110,
    119, 122, 124, 127, 135, 143, 145,
    160, 191, 200, 205, 214–15, 216,
    232, 238–9, 249
  Laymens' Inquiry in, 73–9
  mass movements in, 76–7, 160, 215
  National Christian Council of, 16
  partition of, 135
  see also Bhakti,
Indian, 22, 23, 26, 64, 71, 73, 92, 96, 98,
    100, 114, 135, 143–4, 175, 230, 231,
    247
Indians, 59, 98
Individualism, 42, 47, 56, 240, 245, 247
Indonesia, 106, 133
Integration of IMC/WCC, 132, 155–8,
    165, 193, 199, 239
International Missionary Council
    (IMC) 16, 32, 57, 65–70, 94, 105,
    108–9, 128, 132, 133–4, 138, 141,
    149, 199, 210, 220, 228, 239
  aid to Jews, 57
  Bureau of Social and Economic
    Research, 69
  meeting at Lake Mohonk, 65
  Old Jordans meeting, 108
  relationship to WCC, 122, 132, 141
  succeeded by CWME, 157, 165
  world evangelicalism and, 193–9
International Review of Mission(s)
    (IRM), 6, 48, 62, 95, 96, 102–5,
    123–4, 134, 165, 213, 219, 236–7,
    239
  edited by J. H. Oldham, 58–9, 95–7
  Laymens' Inquiry reviewed, 91–2
  other faiths' articles in (O. C. Quick);
    (E. Bevan); (H. H. Farmer); (D. S.
    Cairns), 102–3, 103–4, 123–4
  title changed, 166
Iona, 141
Iran, 225, 243
Isis, 103
Islam, 28–9, 31, 58, 94, 95, 101, 108,
    111, 114–15, 130, 138, 142, 150–5,
    169, 173, 205, 224–5, 228–9, 231
  Call of the Minaret, 150–55
  fear of, 28–9
  Jerusalem 1928 on, 94, 108
  Kraemer describes, 114–5

Lumen Gentium on, 169
Nostra Aetate on, 173–5
Islamic, 5, 135, 152, 224–5, 243
Israel, 183, 225
Ivory Coast, 131

Jaeschke, E., 50, 51, 56
Jakabanga, 45–6
James, W., 147
Japan, 3, 11, 16, 30, 58–9, 62, 86–90,
  111, 124, 127, 134, 161, 205, 244
  atomic explosions in, 134
  Kingdom of God Movement, 88
  Laymens' Inquiry in, 86–90
  Peasant Gospel Schools, 89
  renaissance of Buddhism, 90
Japanese, 59, 68, 71, 86, 104, 110, 112,
  122, 139, 247
Jarrett-Kerr, M., 142
Java, 106–7, 108
Javanese, 106–7
Jerusalem, 7, 61, 70, 87, 100, 117, 150,
  154, 205
Jerusalem 1928, meeting of the IMC, 16,
  58, 59, 62, 65–70, 71–3, 78, 80–3,
  86, 89, 91, 94, 96, 97–102, 103, 111,
  116, 128, 135, 192, 196, 200
  approach to other faiths, 94, 97–102
  compared to Edinburgh 1910, 65–6
  'comprehensive' approach, 68–71, 78,
    92
  fear of syncretism, 65–6
  kingdom of God theme, 68–70
  Mott as chairman, 65
  report of, 67–70
  younger churches at, 66–7
Jewish, 51, 57, 62, 104, 117, 122, 173–4,
  184, 205, 209
Jewry, 103, 122, 233
Jews, 6, 57, 103, 115, 148–9, 169, 173–4,
  205, 231, 233
Jocists, 136, 180, 192
John Paul II, Pope, 225
Johnson, Pres. L., 164
John the Baptist, 4, 5
John XXIII, Pope, 166–7, 173
Jones, E. Stanley, 76, 79, 101, 114, 118,
  120, 128, 143, 145, 222, 249
Jones, Rufus, 65, 72, 94, 100–2
Judaea, 4, 7, 140
Judaism, 26, 62, 99, 101, 115, 142, 146,
  152, 169
Judson, A., 11, 78
Jungle Aviation and Radio Service, 211

Junod, H., 95–6
Justin Martyr, 95, 172

Kagawa, T., 87–9, 112, 118, 216, 244
Kandy, 25, 226
Kano, 139
Karens, 78
Karma, 27, 229
Kate, 44
Kato, B., 206
Kaunda, K., 133
Kelly, H. H., 29
Kennedy, Pres. J. F., 164, 178
Kenya, 55–6, 63, 133, 191, 206
Kenyatta, Pres. J., 133
Kerala, 218
Keswick Convention, 19, 23
Keysser, C. 34, 37, 44–9, 54–6, 116, 121,
  127, 216, 244, 247
  'christianisation' policy, 44–8, 247
  delay of baptism, 46–7
  McGavran on, 55, 216
  Tambaram citation, 121
Khair Ullah, F. S., 205
Khomeini, Ayatollah, 225
Khrushchev, N., 164
Kibangi, B., 198
Kilimanjaro, Mt., 39, 50, 56
Kimbangu, S., 131–2
King, M. L., 164, 190, 212, 218
Kingdom of God, 9–12, 18–21, 32, 65,
  68–70, 71, 81, 88, 111, 128, 202–4,
  205–6, 222, 247–8
  Americans and, 8–12, 65
  eschatological views of, 248
  Evangelii Nuntiandi and, 248
  Jerusalem 1928, 65–70
  Lausanne I, 202, 205–6
  Laymens' Inquiry, 111
Kingdom of God Movement (Japan),
  88–9
Kingsbury, F., 25
Kirk, J. A., 206
Kirk, K. E., 33
Kivengere, Bp. F., 189, 200, 206
Knak, S., 121
Knitter, P., 228, 235
Kobe, 88
Koinōnia, 245
Kols (of Bengal), 38
Korea, 86
Kraemer, H., 5, 66, 92, 94, 97, 104,
  105–117, 118, 123, 145, 147–8,
  228–9, 230–1, 236–7, 238, 248–9, 250

absolutes, 5, 109–17, 250
conversion and Gandhi, 114
Islam, 114–15
missionary in Java, 106
nature and grace, 112–13
on the kingdom, 111
Tambaram paper, 94
view of Gutmann, 115–16
Kruyt, A. C., 107, 116
Kudo, K., 68
Kuomintang, 79
Kuyper, A., 106

L'Abri, 202
Lahore, 63
Lake Mohonk, 65, 158
Lambeth Conference, 55
Latin America, 11, 17, 117, 132, 134,
    177–85, 200, 202, 211, 213
Latin American, 1, 177, 178, 203, 221,
    222
Latourette, K. S., 91, 118
Lausanne Congress (I), 189, 193, 199,
    200–9, 219, 220, 222–3, 249
Lausanne Covenant, 203, 206, 207
Lausanne Manila Congress (II), 222–3,
    226
Laymens' Foreign Missions Inquiry, 59,
    64, 70–93, 104, 109, 111, 116, 119,
    143, 238
Lazario, Bp. M., 222
League of Nations, 39, 65
Lefroy, Bp. G. A., 96
Legters, L. L., 211
Leiden, 107, 109
Leipzig Missionary Society, 35, 38–9,
    40, 48
Lelean, C. O., 74
Lenin, V. I., 57
Leninism, 224
Lessing, G. E., 112, 140
Leung, S. C., 67
Lewis, N., 214
Liberalism, 83–5, 116
Liberation theology, 179–85, 190, 202,
    204
    background to, 177–8
    base ecclesial communities, 183–5
    Boffs, L. and C., 183–5
    Gutierrez, G., 180–2
    hermeneutical approach, 181–2, 192
    praxis stressed, 179–80
    violence in, 190
Lima, 226, 246

Livingstone, D., 21, 31, 74
Livingstonia Mission, 21
Logan, Dr, 87
Logos, 95–6, 233–4
Löhe, W., 35
London, 9
London Missionary Society (LMS), 12,
    26
Love, 172, 173, 174, 180–2, 203, 208,
    222, 251
Low, S., 12
Loyola, St Ignatius, 245
Luke, St, 3, 4, 5, 7, 8, 45, 179, 217, 234
Lull, R., 172
Lumen Gentium, 168–9, 189
Lusaka, 199
Luther, M., 42, 47, 157, 238, 245
Lutheran, 35, 41, 42, 47, 166, 184, 205
Lutheranism, 53, 127
Lyall, L., 196
Lystra, 60, 113

Maasai, 5, 6
MacArthur, Gen., D., 89
McConnell, Bp. F. J., 67, 69
Macdonald, D. B., 228
McGavran, D. A. 55, 122, 157, 160–2,
    171, 197–8, 204, 206, 209, 214–19,
    221
    and church growth, 215, 217–18
    'homogeneous units', 209, 217
    on Christian presence, 160–1
    'people movements', 55, 215–16
    Uppsala WCC debates, 171, 197
McIntire, C., 195
Mackay, J. A., 91, 101, 104, 134, 194–5
MacKichan, K., 96
Mackie, R. C., 118
MacKinley, Pres., 8
Mackintosh, H. R., 22
Macmillan, H., 164
Macnicol, N., 22, 73, 94, 97–8
Madagascar, 8, 206
Madras, 100, 239
Madras Christian College, 27, 119
Madras Conference (1900), 12
Malawi, 133, 191
Malaysia, 191
Manchu, 79
Manikam, R. B., 176
Manila, 222, 226
Manson, W., 33
Mao Tse-tung, 79, 165, 204
Marcel, G., 160

Marseilles, 136
Marx, K., 179, 180, 192
Marxism, 202, 205
Marxists, 5, 183, 224
Mass Movements, 76, 106, 122, 160, 215
Mbiti, J., 41
Mecca, 154
Medellín, 179–82, 185, 192
Meeking, Mgr. B., 226
Melbourne, 194, 225
Merle Davis, J., 69, 121
Methodist, 128, 166, 219
Methodius, 129
Mexico, 211
Mexico City Conference 1963
    (WCC/CWME), 165–6
Miguez Bonino, J., 178, 185
Millennialism, 10
Miller, Dr W. R. S., 139
Missio Dei, 130, 163, 196
Missiology, 3, 5, 6, 50, 53, 60, 94, 135,
    138, 145
Missiological, 106, 121, 124, 139, 172,
    244, 246
Mission and Evangelism, 226
Missionary Aviation Fellowship, 211
Missionary Conferences
    see appendix,
Missionary Review of the World, 12–13
Mithraism, 103
Molebatsi, C., 222
Moltmann, J., 241
Monism, 98, 124
Montagu-Chelmsford reforms, 73
Montgomery, Bp. H. H., 29
Moody, D. L., 13, 98, 203
Moot, The, 238
Moratorium, 199
Moravians, 8, 34–5, 37, 121, 244
Moses, 146, 235
Moses, D. G., 136
Moshi, 56
Mott, J. R., 8, 13–14, 24, 26, 28–32,
    58–9, 75, 83, 94, 98, 106–8, 133–4,
    137, 144, 244
    background, 13–17
    chairman at Edinburgh 1910, 22,
    28–32
    chairman of Jerusalem 1928, 65–70
    conversion and Gandhi, 75
    debate with G. Warneck, 18–20
Moule, A. E., 25
Muhammad, 99, 115, 151, 154, 228, 235
Müller, Reichsbischof L., 49

Multi-nationals, 179
Muslims, 6, 23, 24, 75–6, 102, 106–8,
    117, 135, 139, 150–5, 158, 162, 169,
    173–4, 194, 227, 230
    Dutch missions to, 106–8
    experience of God, 152, 230
    understanding of (K. Cragg), 151–5
    Vatican II documents, 169, 173–5
    witness to, 153–5, 160
    see also Islam,
Mussolini, B., 57
Myers, Dr, 87
Mysticism, 107, 115, 173–4

Nairobi Assembly 1975 (WCC), 204,
    219–23, 226
National Christian Councils, 16, 58, 59,
    64, 79, 80
National Socialism, 36, 54, 110, 115,
    124
Nazis, 37, 49, 50, 52, 53, 103, 250
Neesima, Dr. 87
Nehru, J., 110
Neill, Bp. S. C. 4, 118, 127, 135–6,
    143–50, 156–7, 161, 162, 166, 199,
    244, 249
    on conversion, 147–8
    on dialogue, 145
    on relativism, 148–9
    on the church, 127
Netherlands Bible Society, 107
Netherlands Missionary Society, 106
Neuendettelsau Missionary Society, 44,
    48
Newbigin, Bp. L., 63, 157, 163, 165,
    196, 218, 230–1, 236–7
New Delhi Assembly 1961 (WCC), 129,
    157, 165, 220, 239
New England, 9, 10
New Guinea, 34, 44, 48, 54, 144, 244
New Testament, 3, 11, 27, 62, 69, 99,
    102, 111, 144, 161, 176, 179, 204,
    208, 212, 216, 218, 238, 248
    eschatology of, 111, 248
    'holism', 208
    names in, 176
    salvation, 231
    translation of, 212
New Tribes Mission, 210, 213–14
New York, Ecumenical Missionary
    Conference (1900), 8, 11, 12–21,
    37, 65
New Zealand, 8, 61
Nida, E., 211

Niebuhr, Reinhold, 148, 206
Nielsen, E., 156
Nigeria, 131
Nikolai, Abp., 3
Niles, D. T., 163, 176, 198
Nitobe, Dr., 87
Nkrumah, K., 133
Nock, A. D., 112
Nommensen, L., 47
Northfield, Mass., 13, 15, 16, 17, 98, 244
North America, 4, 9, 10, 86, 117, 163,
    191, 193, 195, 200–1, 212
North American, 8, 9, 13, 17, 38, 39, 63,
    117, 128, 163, 201, 210–11
North German Missionary Society, 38
Norwegian Missionary Society, 82
Nostra Aetate, 168, 173–5, 190
Nyerere, Pres. J., 133

Oceania, 6, 167
Oldham, J. H., 16, 22, 29–33, 34, 58,
    65, 94, 96, 107–8, 247
    background, 22–4
    choice of Kraemer, 108
    Christianisation ideas, 247
    deafness of, 23
    Edinburgh 1910, 29–33
    editor of IRM, 58–9, 95–6
    influence on Jerusalem 1928, 94
    Laymens' Inquiry reaction, 92
Old Jordans, 108
Old Testament, 105, 138, 159, 176, 183,
    204
Orient, 57, 59, 71
Orientals, 109
Orr, J., 22, 85, 238
Orthodox Church 3, 129–30, 131, 137,
    165, 167, 171, 194, 222–3, 227, 246
    Anglicanism and, 137
    eucharist in mission, 129–30, 171
    Mott's relations with, 16
    national identification of, 130
    view of unity, 129
Orthopraxis, 179–80, 185, 202
Osei-Menseh, G., 221
Ostathios, Mar, 208
Otto, R., 100, 239
Overseas Missionary Fellowship (CIM),
    196
Oxford, 23, 26, 127, 144
Oxford Groups, 122

Padilla, R., 200, 202
Pakenham Walsh, Bp., 122

Pakistan, 6, 135, 162
Palestinians, 225
Pannikkar, R., 176
Papua, 45, 61
Papuans, 44, 121, 247
Paraguay, 25, 177, 182, 190
Parousia, 159, 248
Partnership, 165
Pascal, B., 115
Pathans, 162
Paton, W. 33, 66, 68, 108–9, 118, 122–3,
    134, 135, 238
    early death, 134
    editor of IRM, 58
    Jerusalem 1928, 68–70
    Laymens' Inquiry, 92
Pattaya, Thailand, 194, 209, 225
Paul, K. T., 66, 74
Paul, St, 3, 5, 7, 60–2, 81, 112–3, 174,
    216, 238, 245
Paul VI, Pope, 186, 187
Peking (Beijing), 60
Pentecost, 170
Pentecostal Churches, 136, 239
Pentecostalism, 177
Peru, 177, 180, 211
Peruvian, 180
Peters, K., 38
Petty, O. A., 92
Philip, P. O., 66
Philippines, 11, 191
Pickett, J. W., 76, 122, 160, 160, 215,
    216
Pierson, A. T., 12–13, 18
Pietism, 35
Pike, K., 211
Pilate, 4, 241
Pitt, W. (1st Earl of Chatham), 137
Pius IX, Pope, 167
Plato, 124, 202
Plessis, D. du, 136
Pluralism, 148, 161, 227, 235, 236–7,
    242, 243, 250
Pluralist, 226, 239, 243
Polanyi, M., 240–1, 242
Poor, 88, 180, 184, 191, 192, 200, 218,
    221–2
Portugal, 8
Potter, P., 159–60
Prague, 122, 164
Praxis, 50, 180, 184, 192
Preaching, 78–9, 85, 124, 170
Presence, 136–43, 150–5, 158–62,
    169–71, 207, 218

Pretoria, 164
Primal ties, 41–4
Princeton Theological Seminary, 91,
    134
Princeton, University of, 13, 14
Proclamation 92, 112, 161, 169–70, 173,
    190, 198, 200, 207, 208, 219, 221–2,
    245–6
  eucharist as, 245–6
  evangelicals and, 207
  Evangelii Nuntiandi and, 186–90
  Lausanne I on, 207, 209
  Vatican II emphasis on, 170, 172–3,
    189–90
Programme to Combat Racism, 199
Prophetism, 131
Protestants, 8, 12, 59, 79–80, 83, 86–7,
    127, 137, 167
Protestantism, 11, 92, 128, 166, 192
Punjab, 77
Puritanism, 9–10

Quaker, 29, 65, 94, 238
Quichua, 212
Quick, O. C., 110, 102–3, 172, 236, 249
Qu'ran, 150–1

Race, A., 228, 235
Race relations, 70
Radhakrishnan, S., 114, 231
Rahner, K., 175
Ramabai, Pandita, 25, 100, 114
Ranson, C. W., 149
Raum, J., 48
Raum, O., 48
Recife, 183
Reconception, 228–9
Reformation, 124
Regions Beyond Missionary Union, 210
Reichelt, K. L., 82, 108, 118
Reischauer, A. K., 87, 94, 97, 108
Relativism, 66, 102, 103, 104, 110, 114,
    148, 203, 235, 250
Resurrection, 235, 242–3
Retrieval, 153
Rhenish Missionary Society, 37
Rhodes, C., 38
Richard, T., 25
Richardson, A., 139
Richter, J., 32, 96, 100, 249
Riehl, W. H., 40
Robinson, Bp. J., 236
Rockefeller, J. D., 71, 149
Roehm, E., 52

Roman Catholic Church, 8, 29, 42, 129,
    131–2, 137, 166–7, 176–7, 184, 189,
    192, 194, 198, 219, 222–3, 225
  and dialogue, 171–2, 173–5
  ecclesiology of, 132, 168–9
  eucharist as missionary, 171, 188
  in France, 136–7, 160
  Medellín bishops' meeting, 179–82
  Pope John XXIII, 166–7, 173
  proclamation and, 170–3, 198
  relation to Jews, 173–4
  size of, 166–7, 177
  Vatican II documents of, 166–77
  violence, 187–8, 190
Roman Catholics, 12, 80, 127, 166, 177,
    212–13
Roman Empire, 99, 241, 247
Romans, Epistle to, 7, 49, 105, 161, 176,
    238
Rome, 7, 124, 129, 141, 220
Romero, Abp. O., 183, 190
Roosevelt, Pres. T., 9, 12, 29
Rosenberg, A., 37
Rossano, Mgr. P., 221
Ruanda, 191
Rudra, S. K., 74
Rumania, 130, 224
Rural development, 70, 71, 88–9
Russell, B., 98
Russia, 16, 30, 79, 224, 246
Russian, 57, 130, 164, 224

Safenwil, 49
Saint, N., 211
Saint, R., 212
Salvation, 148, 151, 169, 170–1, 186,
    202, 204, 207, 208, 220, 232–3, 236,
    239
Salvific, 169, 207
Samartha, S., 226–7, 237
San Antonio Conference 1990
    (WCC/CWME), 226
Satineketam, 74
Sato, Baron, 87
Sattelberg, 44, 46, 56
Scandinavia, 4, 205
Scandinavians, 59, 65
Schleiermacher, F. D. E., 100, 241
Schmidlin, J., 4
Schreiber, Dr, 37
Schweitzer, A., 39
Scotland, 21–3
Scottish, 9, 21, 31, 134, 238
Scriptures, 161, 194, 198

Second World War, 39, 53, 89, 94, 123, 133
Secretariat for Christian Unity, 167
Secular, 94, 101, 142, 239
Secularism, 101–2, 110, 243
Segundo, J. L., 181–2, 185
Shaeffer, F., 202
Shaftesbury, Lord (7th Earl), 201
Shalom, 197
Shanghai, 19, 86
Sharpeville, 164, 190
Shedd, W. A., 25
Sheppard, Bp. D. S., 55
Shinto, 90, 139
Shirk, 151
Singh, L., 20
Singh, N., 25
Singh, Sundar, 76, 216
Slack, K., 220
Slater, T. E., 25
Sloan, G., 122
Smith, A. H., 85
Smith, Edwin, 54
Smith, Eugene, 195
Social Gospel, 10, 65, 201, 203, 223
Social Justice, 69, 200, 205, 207, 218, 221–2, 247
Society for the Propagation of the Gospel (SPG), 29, 38, 60
Söderblom, Abp. N., 14, 91, 98–9, 103, 124, 250
Soper, E. D., 135
South Africa, 4, 164, 190
South America, 91, 136, 178
see Latin America,
South India United Church, 30
Spain, 7, 8, 86
Speer, R. E., 14–15, 16, 19, 66, 72, 84, 90, 101, 102, 137, 144
    at Edinburgh 1910, 32
    drafts Jerusalem 1928 message, 66
    reacts to Laymens' Inquiry, 72, 90
Sri Lanka, 25
Stalin, J., 57
Stock, E., 19, 29
Stott, J. R. W., 198, 200, 207–9, 220–1, 223, 226
Stransky, T., 221, 225
Studd, C. T., 13
Studd, J. E. K., 15, 75, 244
Student Christian Movement (SCM), 22, 23, 33, 58, 107, 238
Student Volunteer Movement (SVM), 11, 12, 13, 14, 15, 17–20, 214, 244

Student World, 159
Stuttgart, 105
Subamma, B. V., 200, 205
Sudan Interior Mission, 210
Sudan United Mission, 210
Sufism, 152
Sugden, C., 194
Sukarno, Pres., 133
Summer Institute of Linguistics (SIL), 211–3
Sundkler, Bp. B., 149
Sun Yat Sen, 79, 110, 216
Switzerland, 37, 49, 202
Sykes, N., 245
Syncretism, 65, 206–7, 227, 228
Syrian Orthodox, 122, 208

Tabu, 124
Tagore, R., 74, 77, 114
Talbot, N., 29, 33
Tamanrasset, 136
Tambaram, Madras Assembly 1938 (IMC) 16, 94, 106, 108, 117–24, 127, 133–4, 135, 146, 200, 228, 230, 236
    approach to other religions, 118–20, 230–1
    choice of H. Kraemer for, 108
    jubilee of, 230, 236–7
Tamil, 143
Tanganyika (Tanzania), 38–9, 56, 133, 191
Taoist, 232
Tawney, R. H., 66–70, 99, 192, 247
Taylor, J. V., 41, 54, 142–3, 191, 197–8
Temple Abp. W., 66–8, 91, 101, 102, 117, 119, 134
Temple Gairdner, W. H., 23, 24, 25, 94, 108, 152
Tertullian, 96, 205
Theological Education Fund, 149
Third World, 180, 225
Thomas, M. M., 176, 220, 237
Tibet, 8, 244
Tilak, T. N., 100
Tippett, A. R., 206
Tirunelveli, 143
Tokyo, 90
Toradjan people, 107
Torrance, J. B., 22
Torrance, T. F., 22
Torres, C., 178, 181–2, 187, 190
Totalitarianism, 201
Touareg, 136

Townsend, W. C., 211–3
Toynbee, A., 148
Tribe, 110, 130, 211, 212
Troeltsch, E., 235
Tübingen, 105
Tucker, Bp. A. R., 30
Tukaram, 95
Uganda, 139
Ugandan, 189, 200
Uniat churches, 246
Union Theological Seminary, 63
Uniqueness, 99, 100–1, 103, 115, 207, 234–5
United Free Church of Scotland, 21, 22, 23, 27
United Reformed Church, 239
Unity, 29, 128–9, 137, 206, 207, 226, 246
Universality, 100–1, 207, 249
Universities' Mission to Central Africa (UMCA), 38
Uppsala, 98, 164, 196, 197–8, 200, 219, 223
Uruguay, 177, 181, 219
US, 11, 16, 63, 86, 128, 139, 164, 180, 195, 205, 210, 224, 243
USSR, 57, 130, 164, 224
Utrecht, 128
Uzaki, Bp. K., 66

Vancouver Assembly 1983 (WCC), 226
Van Dusen, H. P., 120, 135
Van Randwijck, S. C., 156
Vatican II 132, 162, 166–7, 168–75, 179
  see also Roman Catholic Church
Venice, 221
Venn, H., 35, 61, 142
Vergil, 121
Versailles, Treaty of, 34, 39, 49, 134
Vicedom, G., 144
Vietnam, 163–4, 224
Violence, 181, 183, 187–8, 206
Visser't Hooft, W., 106, 118, 163
Volk, 36–7, 40, 42, 46, 50
Volkskirche, 34–5, 37–43, 46–8, 53, 121, 192
Von Lettow, Gen., 39

Wagner, C. P., 206, 217
Wall Street, crash of 1929, 57
Warneck, G. 4, 18, 21, 22, 23, 28–9, 31, 35–6, 62, 205, 248
  place of individual conversion, 35–6
  protests at Anglo-Saxons, 18–20

stress on national culture, 35–6
view of mission, 18–19, 21
Warneck, J., 47
Warren, M. A. C., 138–143, 150, 155–7, 160–2, 182, 191, 193, 234–5, 236
  debates with Hick, 234–5
  editor of 'Christian Presence' series, 141–2
  on integration of IMC/WCC, 141, 155–7, 193
  missionary service of, 139
  view of history, 139–40, 234
Washington Missionary Conference (1925), 65–6
Watchword, 17–21
Weber, M., 114
Wesley, J., 244–5
Westmann, K. B., 155
Wheaton Congress, 193, 195
Whitby, Ontario Conference 1947 (IMC), 128, 134–5, 165, 199
Wilberforce, W., 201
Wilder, R., 13
Wilder, R. P., 13, 18, 19
Wilhelm II, Kaiser, 105
Williams, Bp. R., 135
Willingen Conference 1952 (IMC), 128, 134, 135, 165, 196, 199, 246
Willowbank Consultation, Bermuda, 209
Wilson College, Bombay, 96
Winslow, J. C., 75
Winter, R., 193
World Christian Books, 144, 147
World Council of Churches 17, 105, 118, 128–9, 131–2, 134, 136, 141, 144, 155–8, 164–6, 171, 193–4, 196, 198, 199, 203, 210, 214, 219, 220, 222, 225–6, 228, 239, 249
  Asunción Declaration, 214
  basis of, 194
  Commission on World Mission and Evangelism, 165–6, 194, 199, 219, 225
  dialogue and, 226–7
  documents of, 225–7
  IMC relationship to, 122, 132, 141, 155–8
  Kimbanguist church and, 131
  Nairobi meeting of, 219–23, 226
  Orthodox membership of, 129–30
  relationship to evangelicals, 193–205
  Uppsala meeting of, 164, 171, 196–7, 199–200, 201, 219, 223

World Sunday School Association, 84
World Student Christian Federation
    (WSCF), 11, 15, 107, 118, 159–60,
    163, 165
Worship, 223
Wundt, W., 40
Wycliffe Bible Translators (WBT),
    210–13
Wycliffe College, Toronto, 82

Xavier, St Francis, 172

Yale, University of, 14, 24
Yen, Dr Y. C. J. ('Jimmie'), 80
Young Men's Christian Association
    (YMCA), 11, 14, 15, 23, 26, 29, 39,
    58, 214

Yu-Chen, K., 85–6
Yui, D., 66–7
Yuqu people, 213

Zaire, 131, 191
Zake, 45
Zambia, 133
Zanzibar, 38
Zaria, 139
Zeisberger, D., 121
Zinzendorf, N., 8, 34–5
Zionism, 131
Zoroaster, 124
Zoroastrianism, 124
Zwemer, S. M., 101, 108